中国文化概况

（英汉对照版）

主　编　符　存　王　倩　张　玲
副主编　张梅琳　胡竞宇　汤　璐　商秀春
　　　　王钰灵　牟　莉　潘英典　罗小虎
审　校　[美] Vanessa

中国人民大学出版社
·北京·

图书在版编目（CIP）数据

中国文化概况：英汉对照 / 符存，王倩，张玲主编. —北京：中国人民大学出版社，2020.9

ISBN 978-7-300-28530-6

Ⅰ. ①中…　Ⅱ. ①符…　②王…　③张…　Ⅲ. ①中华文化—介绍—汉、英　Ⅳ. ①K203

中国版本图书馆 CIP 数据核字（2020）第 169436 号

中国文化概况（英汉对照版）

主　编　符　存　王　倩　张　玲
副主编　张梅琳　胡竞宇　汤　璐　商秀春
　　　　王钰灵　牟　莉　潘英典　罗小虎
审　校　[美] Vanessa

Zhongguo Wenhua Gaikuang (Yinghan Duizhao Ban)

出版发行	中国人民大学出版社		
社　　址	北京中关村大街 31 号	**邮政编码**	100080
电　　话	010-62511242（总编室）		010-62511770（质管部）
	010-82501766（邮购部）		010-62514148（门市部）
	010-62515195（发行公司）		010-62515275（盗版举报）
网　　址	http:// www. crup. com. cn		
经　　销	新华书店		
印　　刷	唐山玺诚印务有限公司		
开　　本	720 mm × 1000 mm　1/16	**版　　次**	2020 年 9 月第 1 版
印　　张	19.5	**印　　次**	2025 年 10 月第 14 次印刷
字　　数	363 000	**定　　价**	52.80 元

前言

为什么要编写这么一本《中国文化概况（英汉对照版）》呢？首先，出于解决文化教学困境的需要。中国文化是一个具有人文意蕴的概念，简单来说，就是中国人的生活要素形态的统称，即衣、食、住、行、文、物等。要讲好“中国故事”，传播中国文化，适合的教材必不可少。我们的初心很简单，就是要编写一本既能精要介绍中国文化的精髓，又兼具生活实用性的教材。因此，在内容选择上，我们选取了代表中国文化的哲学、艺术、戏剧等传统内容，还安排了家庭、饮食、服装、旅游等生活日常。我们想通过这样的努力，使文化教学扎根于中国人日常的思维方式，来源于中国人真实的日常生活，解决文化教学乏味、艰涩、无趣的困境。其次，出于提升学生文化交流能力的需要。在跨文化交流中，无论是外国学生还是中国学生，似乎都可以聊聊中国文化，但大都是浅尝辄止、泛泛而谈，无法深入谈论其本质。究其原因是缺乏合适的中国文化双语教材，这使中国学生不知道如何用英文表达中国文化，外国学生无法用中文恰当地表达中国文化，两者之间存在“语言沟”。这本教材采用中英双语对照的形式编写，前面是中文后面是英文，能较好地填平文化交流中存在的“语言沟”问题。

那么，这本教材有什么特色呢？按照汉语字典的解释，“特色”是一个事物或一种事物显著区别于其他事物的风格和形式，是其所独有的。这本教材有三大特色：

其一，这是一本英汉双语对照的中国文化概况教材。目前，国内的中国文化概况教材要么是中文版的，要么是英文版的，中英对照的教材凤毛麟角。单语教材不仅给教师教学带来极大的不便，也给学生的跨文化交流造成不小的语言障碍。这本教材按照中文在前英文在后，一段一段双语对照的格式编排，能帮助学生掌握相应的中英文表达法，有效解决教师教学和学生交流方面的困难。实现教材内容英汉对照，我们付出了艰辛的努力，邀请了外籍教师和我们一起逐句核定英语句式表达，确保了内容一致，表达通俗易懂。

其二，这是一本“接地气”的教材，内容来源于中国人真实的日常生活。全书共十一章，涵盖地理、对外交流、家庭、教育、哲学、政治、节日等内容。每章都由课前思考问题引入主要内容，还设有“你知道吗”生活小知识和“地方频道”介绍中国有特色的城市，最后以形式多样的练习题结束。如第一章中国地理概况，教材在介绍了中国的地理位置、地形地貌、名山大川后，安排了一节内容“游在中国”，提供了实用的旅游知识和攻略。第三章介绍了中国的婚礼习俗、餐桌礼仪、“二孩”政策、5G 技术、微信、支付宝、广场舞、麻将等与中国人生活密切相关的知识。对外国留学生而言，这是一本在中国学习和生活的指南书；对中国学生而言，这是一本介绍中国文化和中国人日常生活的跨文化交流手册。教材中使用的语言和表达，我们都尽力做到简单、直接、明了，没有高深的英语词汇，也没有艰涩的汉语表达，让所有具备一定中英文基础的学生都能读得懂，都能用得上。

其三，这是一本师生合作完成的教材。这本教材是集体教学经验总结的成果，教材主编为符存、王倩、张玲老师，负责全书的设计、定位和组织工作，并承担全书统稿。全书共有 11 名教师参与，全都是具有丰富教学经验的中国文化概况教学一线教师。本书的具体编写分工为：第一章由张梅琳老师编写，第二章由王钰灵老师编写，第三章和第九章由胡竞宇老师编写，第四章由汤璐老师编写，第五章由王倩和商秀春老师编写，第六章由牟莉老师编写，第七章由王倩老师编写，第八章由张玲老师编写，第十章由潘英典老师编写，第十一章由罗小虎老师编写。在成书之前，老师们已经将大部分内容运用于教学实践；成书之后，我们邀请大量外国留学生和中国学生阅读了全书，广泛吸收了这些学生的反馈和建议，使教材结构更加合理，语言表达更加通俗易懂。这本教材立足于学生实际，回归于学生需求，是我们师生广泛互动和深入交流的成果。

在教材编写过程中，我们参考了相关的书籍和许多网站，得到了中国人民大学出版社外语分社的鼎力支持，得到了美籍教师 Vanessa 的大力协助，在此一并表示诚挚的感谢。由于时间仓促，水平有限，书中难免有不尽如人意的地方，恳请老师和同学们在使用过程中给予反馈，以便我们后续日臻完善。

本书的课后练习题均配有参考答案，请登录中国人民大学出版社官方网站 http:www.crup.com.cn，搜索本书后下载使用，或联系出版社免费索取：010-62515580，010-62512737，wangxw@crup.com.cn，huangt@crup.com.cn。

编者

2020 年 5 月

目　录
Contents

Contents

第一章

中国的地理

Chinese Geography

课前思考
Lead-in Questions

1. “五岳”指哪五座山？
Which five mountains do the “Five Great Mountains” refer to?
2. 中华民族的“母亲河”是什么河？你们国家有“母亲河”吗？
Which river is called “Mother River” by Chinese people? Is there a “Mother River” in your country?

一、行政区域
Administrative Area

（一）行政区划分
Administrative Division

中国是一个幅员辽阔的国家，国土面积960多万平方千米，位居世界第三位。第一位和第二位分别是俄罗斯与加拿大，美国、巴西、澳大利亚的国土面积紧随中国之后。这些国家的面积都在500万平方千米以上，属于“巨型国家”。

China is a vast country with an area of more than 9.6 million square kilometers, ranking third in the world. The first and second places are Russia and Canada, respectively. The territories of the United States, Brazil and Australia are close behind China. These countries, with an area of more than 5 million square kilometers, are “mega-countries”.

打开世界地图，我们不难找到中国的位置。中国位于亚洲东部，太平洋西岸。从地图上看，中国就像一只雄鸡屹立在世界的东方。

As we take a closer look at the map of the world, it is not difficult for us to find the location of China. China is located in the east of Asia and the west coast of the Pacific Ocean. On the map, China stands like a rooster in the east of the world.

为了方便治理国家和分级管理，国家一般会进行行政区域划分，简称“行政区划”。那么中国是怎么划分行政区域的呢？

In order to facilitate the governance of the nation and hierarchical management, generally the state divides administrative areas which are referred to as “administrative divisions”. So how does China divide administrative areas?

首先，比国家小一个单位的，我们称之为“省级行政区”，类似于美国的“州”。目前，全国有34个省级行政区，包括23个省、5个自治区、4个直辖市和2个特别行政区。

First of all, a unit smaller than a nation, is referred to as a “provincial administrative region”, similar to the “state” of the United States. At present, there are 34 provincial administrative regions in China, including 23 provinces, 5 autonomous regions, 4 municipalities directly under the Central Government and 2 special administrative regions.

其中，5个自治区是以少数民族聚居区为基础发展而来的。它们分别是：内蒙古自治区（以下简称“内蒙古”）、新疆维吾尔自治区（以下简称“新疆”）、西藏自治区（以下简称“西藏”）、广西壮族自治区（以下简称“广西”）和宁夏回族自治区（以下简称“宁夏”）。内蒙古是蒙古族的聚居地，新疆是维吾尔族的聚居地，西藏是藏族的聚居地，广西是壮族的聚居地，宁夏是回族的聚居地。在少数民族自治区，不仅可以欣赏美丽怡人的自然风光，还可以感受别具一格的民族风情。

Among them, five autonomous regions have developed on the basis of ethnic minority inhabited areas. They are: Inner Mongolia Autonomous Region (hereinafter referred to as "Inner Mongolia"), Xinjiang Uygur Autonomous Region (hereinafter referred to as "Xinjiang"), Xizang Autonomous Region (hereinafter referred to as "Xizang"), Guangxi Zhuang Autonomous Region (hereinafter referred to as "Guangxi") and Ningxia Hui Autonomous Region (hereinafter referred to as "Ningxia"). Inner Mongolia is chiefly inhabited by Mongolians, Xinjiang is chiefly inhabited by Uygurs, Xizang is chiefly inhabited by Tibetans, Guangxi is chiefly inhabited by Zhuang people, and Ningxia is chiefly inhabited by Hui people. In ethnic minority autonomous regions, you can not only enjoy the beautiful and pleasant natural scenery, but also experience the unique ethnic customs.

中国有4个直辖市，它们分别是北京市、天津市、上海市和重庆市。直辖市，顾名思义，就是直接由中央政府管辖的城市。虽然它们被称作“市”，但是实际上跟“省”是同一级别的行政单位。成为直辖市要满足一定的条件，往往需要较多的居住人口（不少于600万人），并且在全国的政治、经济和文化等各方面具有重要的地位。

There are four municipalities directly under the Central Government in China. They are Beijing, Tianjin, Shanghai and Chongqing. The municipality directly under the Central Government, as its name implies, is a city directly under the jurisdiction of the Central Government. Although they are called "municipalities", they are actually administrative units of the same level as "provinces". To qualify itself as a municipality directly under the Central Government, a city needs a larger population (not less than 6 million people) and has an important position in the politics, economics and culture of the country.

香港特别行政区和澳门特别行政区是中国的两个特别行政区。历史上，香港曾被英国殖民统治，澳门曾被葡萄牙殖民统治。经过中国政府的不断努力和谈判磋商，1997 年 7 月 1 日，香港回归中国；1999 年 12 月 20 日，澳门回归中国。中国分别成立香港特别行政区和澳门特别行政区，对香港和澳门恢复行使主权。

The Hong Kong Special Administrative Region and the Macao Special Administrative Region are two special administrative regions of China. Historically, Hong Kong was colonized by British and Macao by Portuguese. After continuous efforts and negotiations by the Chinese Government, Hong Kong returned to China on July 1, 1997 and Macao returned to China on December 20, 1999. China has established the Hong Kong Special Administrative Region and the Macao Special Administrative Region, respectively, to restore sovereignty over Hong Kong and Macao.

中国的国土面积广阔，相应的，大多数省级行政区的面积也比较大。其中，

最大的是新疆，面积约为 166 万平方千米。

China's territory is vast, and correspondingly, most provincial administrative regions are relatively large. Among them, the largest is Xinjiang, with an area of about 1.66 million square kilometers.

省级行政区可以继续往下分，一般来说，比省、自治区小一个单位的是市或自治州，比如山东省的济南市、西藏自治区的拉萨市、湖南省的湘西土家族苗族自治州、新疆维吾尔自治区的伊犁哈萨克自治州；直辖市的下一级单位为区、县，比如天津市的南开区、重庆市的丰都县。香港特别行政区下辖 18 个区，澳门以"堂区"作为行政区划单位，共有 7 个堂区，外加路氹（dàng）城。

Provincial administrative regions can continue to be divided into the following parts. Generally speaking, smaller units of provinces and autonomous regions are cities or autonomous prefectures, such as Jinan City in Shandong Province, Lhasa City in Xizang Autonomous Region, Xiangxi Tujia and Miao Autonomous Prefecture in Hunan Province, and Yili Kazakh Autonomous Prefecture in Xinjiang Uygur Autonomous Region. The subordinate units of municipalities directly under the Central Government are districts and counties, such as Nankai District of Tianjin and Fengdu County of Chongqing. There are 18 districts under the jurisdiction of the Hong Kong Special Administrative Region. Macao takes "parish" as its administrative divisional unit. Macao consists of seven parishes and "Cotai".

（二）首都概况
Introduction of the Capital

中国历史上，有很多城市都成为过首都，比如：西安曾经是唐朝的首都，开封曾经是北宋的首都。1927 年国民政府定都南京，将南京称为"首都"。至此，中国第一次有了"首都"的称呼，并将该词沿用至今。

In Chinese history, many cities turned to be capitals. For example, Xi'an was the capital of the Tang Dynasty and Kaifeng was the capital of the Northern Song Dynasty. In 1927, the national government designated Nanjing as the "capital." Since then, for the first time, China has the title of "shoudu" and has used the term to this day.

1949 年 10 月 1 日，毛泽东主席在北京天安门城楼上向世界庄严宣告："中华人民共和国中央人民政府今天成立了！"北京成为新中国的首都。

On October 1, 1949, Chairman Mao Zedong solemnly declared to the world on the Tiananmen Rostrum in Beijing that the Central People's Government of the People's

Republic of China is established. Since then, Beijing has become the capital of New China.

为了使北京以及周边地区都能得到健康发展，2017 年 4 月 1 日，中国政府决定设立雄安新区，来承接北京的部分非首都职能，为北京实现“瘦身健体”。目前聚集在北京的非首都职能有：一般的制造业、区域性的物流基地和批发市场、过于密集的教育医疗资源，以及部分行政、事业单位等。

In order to ensure the healthy development of Beijing and its surrounding areas, on April 1, 2017, the Chinese Government decided to establish Xiongan New Area to undertake some non-capital functions of Beijing and to achieve “lean and healthy structure” for Beijing. At present, the non-capital functions gathered in Beijing include: general manufacturing industry, regional logistics base and wholesale market, over-intensive educational and medical resources, and some administrative, public institutions.

雄安新区位于河北省保定市境内，规划范围涵盖河北省雄县、容城县、安新县及周边部分区域。其位于距离北京 100 多千米的地方，地理位置优越。并且，雄安交通便捷，生态资源环境优良，开发潜力无限，为北京提供了优良的条件。

Xiongan New Area is located in Baoding City, Hebei Province. The planning area covers three counties, including Xiongxian, Rongcheng, Anxin, and some surrounding areas in Hebei Province. Located more than 100 kilometers away from Beijing, it has an advantageous geographical position. Moreover, Xiongan New Area has convenient transportation, excellent ecological resources and environment, and unlimited development potential, which provide excellent conditions for Beijing.

你知道吗？
Do you know?

省级行政区简称（别称）
Abbreviations (Aliases) of Provincial Administrative Regions

省级行政区简称（别称）表

Provincial Administrative Region Abbreviation (Alias) Table

序号	名称	简称	行政中心	序号	名称	简称	行政中心
1	北京市	京	北京	18	湖南省	湘	长沙
2	天津市	津	天津	19	广东省	粤	广州
3	河北省	冀	石家庄	20	广西壮族自治区	桂	南宁
4	山西省	晋	太原	21	海南省	琼	海口
5	内蒙古自治区	内蒙古	呼和浩特	22	四川省	川或蜀	成都
6	辽宁省	辽	沈阳	23	贵州省	贵或黔	贵阳
7	吉林省	吉	长春	24	云南省	云或滇	昆明
8	黑龙江省	黑	哈尔滨	25	重庆市	渝	重庆
9	上海市	沪或申	上海	26	西藏自治区	藏	拉萨
10	江苏省	苏	南京	27	陕西省	陕或秦	西安
11	浙江省	浙	杭州	28	甘肃省	甘或陇	兰州
12	安徽省	皖	合肥	29	青海省	青	西宁
13	福建省	闽	福州	30	宁夏回族自治区	宁	银川
14	江西省	赣	南昌	31	新疆维吾尔自治区	新	乌鲁木齐
15	山东省	鲁	济南	32	香港特别行政区	港	香港
16	河南省	豫	郑州	33	澳门特别行政区	澳	澳门
17	湖北省	鄂	武汉	34	台湾省	台	台北

二、地形与气候
Topography and Climate

（一）地势地形
Topography

如果你有机会从中国东部沿海的上海坐火车到中国西部内陆的拉萨，那么，除了感受到不断向西的横向坐标移动以外，还能感受到不断向上的纵向坐标移动。因为，上海的平均海拔不到 5 米，而拉萨的平均海拔达到了 3 650 米。

If you have the opportunity to travel by train from Shanghai on the east coast of China to Lhasa in the interior of western China, you will not only feel the horizontal movement to the west but also the vertical and upward movement in addition. The average altitude in Shanghai is less than 5 meters above sea level, while the average altitude in Lhasa is 3,650 meters above sea level.

中国的地表高低起伏，地势西高东低，向海洋倾斜，大致呈阶梯状分布。一般分为三级阶梯：第一级阶梯是青藏高原，平均海拔在 4 000 米以上，其北部与东部边缘以昆仑山脉、祁连山脉、横断山脉与第二级阶梯分界；第二级阶梯平均海拔在 1 000~2 000 米，其间分布着大型的盆地和高原，东面以大兴安岭、太行山脉、巫山、雪峰山与第三级阶梯分界；第三级阶梯上分布着广阔的平原，间有丘陵和低山，海拔多在 500 米以下。因此，如果从上海坐火车到拉萨，将会由东向西，从第三级阶梯到第二级阶梯，再从第二级阶梯到第一级阶梯，沿途可以感受到各种地形的特点，欣赏截然不同的美景，不过得小心高原反应。

China's land surface is undulating. The terrain is high in the west and low in the east, inclined to the ocean. It is generally distributed in a ladder shape and divided into three steps. The first step is the Qinghai-Xizang Plateau, with an average altitude of more than 4,000 meters. The Kunlun Mountains, Qilian Mountains and Hengduan Mountains on the northern and eastern edge of the first step are the boundaries of the first step and the second step. The average altitude of the second step is between 1,000 and 2,000 meters, on which large basins and plateaus are distributed. The Greater Khingan Range, Tai-hang Mountains, Wushan Mountains, Xuefeng Mountains in the east of the second step separate the third step from the second step. The third step is a vast plain with hills and low mountains, most of which are less than 500 meters above sea level. Therefore, if you take the train from Shanghai to Lhasa, you will go from east to west, from the third step to the second step, and then to the first step. Along the way, you can feel the characteristics of all kinds of terrain and appreciate the different scenery, but you should be careful of the high altitude reaction.

（二）气候天气
Climate and Weather

中国地处北半球，和其他北半球国家一样，3 月至 5 月为春季，6 月至 8 月为夏季，9 月至 11 月为秋季，12 月至次年 2 月为冬季。而地处南半球的国家，如：澳大利亚、新西兰、巴西、阿根廷、南非等，季节则与中国刚好相反。

China is located in the northern hemisphere. Like other countries in the northern hemisphere, spring is from March to May, summer is from June to August, autumn is from September to November, and winter is from December to February. Countries in the southern hemisphere, such as Australia, New Zealand, Brazil, Argentina and South Africa, have the opposite seasons with China.

中国南北跨纬度广，各地接受太阳辐射的热量不均衡。自南向北，由低纬度向高纬度，按照接受的太阳辐射热量的逐渐减少，划分出热带、亚热带、暖温带、中温带和寒温带，除此之外，还有特殊的青藏高寒区（青藏高寒区海拔较高，本区高原地势作用超过了纬度的影响，表现为中、低纬度内独特的大面积高寒环境）。在各温度带中，寒温带只占国土总面积的 1.2%，青藏高寒区占国土总面积的26.7%，其余占国土总面积72.1%的地区属于热带、亚热带、暖温带和中温带。因此，中国以温暖气候为主。

China has a wide latitude scope from north to south, and the amount of heat received by the sun varies from place to place. From south to north, from low latitude to high latitude, the receiving solar heat gradually reduces, so Tropical, Subtropical, Warm Temperate, Medium Temperate and Cold Temperate zones are classified. In addition, there are special Qinghai-Xizang Plateau Cold Area (with the relatively high elevation, the effect of plateau topography exceeds that of latitude in Qinghai-Xizang Plateau, which is characterized by a large area of alpine environment in middle and low latitudes). Among the temperature zones, the Cold Temperate zone accounts for only 1.2% of the total land area, the Qinghai-Xizang Plateau takes up 26.7%, and the remaining 72.1% belongs to the Tropical, Subtropical, Warm Temperate and Medium Temperate zones. Therefore, it can be said that China mainly has a warm climate.

中国幅员辽阔，跨纬度较广，距海远近差距较大，加之地势高低不同，地形类型及山脉走向多样，因而气温和降水的组合多种多样，形成了多种多样的气候。从气候类型上看，东部属季风气候（又可分为热带季风气候、亚热带季风气候和温带季风气候）；西北部属温带大陆性气候；青藏高原属高原山地气候（高寒气候）。

China has a vast territory, a wide range of latitudes, distances from the sea, altitudes, terrain types and mountain ranges. As a result, the combination of temperature and precipitation is diverse, forming a variety of climates. In terms of climate type, the east belongs to Monsoon Climate (which can be divided into Tropical Monsoon Climate, Subtropical Monsoon Climate and Temperate Monsoon Climate), the northwest belongs to Temperate Continental Climate, and the Qinghai-Xizang Plateau belongs to Alpine Climate.

总体来说，中国的气候具有夏季高温多雨、冬季寒冷少雨、高温期与多雨期一致的季风气候特征。中国夏季普遍高温，除青藏高原等地势高的地区外，大部分地区在20℃以上，南方（热带季风气候带、亚热带季风气候带）许多地方在28℃以上，南北气温差别不大是中国夏季的特征。相反，南北气温差别大是中国冬季的特征。冬天南方比较温暖，其中，最南部的海南省三亚市气温可达到20℃以上；而北方（温带季风气候带、温带大陆性气候带）比较寒冷，最北部的黑龙江省漠河市的气温可低至-30℃以下。

Generally speaking, China's climate shows the features of Monsoon Climate which is characterized by hot and rainy summer, cold and dry winter and the consistency of high temperature periods and rainy periods. High temperatures are common in summer in China. Except for the Qinghai-Xizang Plateau and other high-altitude areas, most areas are above 20 ℃ , and many places in the south (Tropical Monsoon Climate zone and Subtropical Monsoon Climate zone) are above 28℃ . In summer, there is little difference in temperature between north and south. On the contrary, there is great difference in temperature between north and south. In winter, the south is relatively warm. The temperature in Sanya, the city in Hainan, the southernmost province, can reach more than 20℃ . However, the north (Temperate Monsoon Climate zone, Temperate Continental Climate zone) is relatively cold, and the temperature in Mohe city, Heilongjiang province, the northernmost part of China, can be lower than –30℃ .

由于北方地区冬季比较寒冷，因此，北方每年冬季都会集中供暖，即由供热单位把集中的热源通过管路将热量传递给用户。集中供暖十分安全，不易发生火灾和一氧化碳中毒。

Since it is cold in winter in northern China, central heating is provided every winter in the north. That is to say, the heating sector transfers the heat from the centralized heat source to the user through pipelines. Central heating is very safe, not prone to fire and carbon monoxide poisoning.

那么，一般北方冬天的供暖时长是多久呢？因为我国北方各城市变冷的时间各不相同，所以供暖时间也有所差异。一般情况下，大部分北方地区每年的供暖时间是从 11 月中旬开始，一直到次年的 3 月中旬，供暖时长约为 4 个月。例如北京，每年都是 11 月 15 日左右开始供暖，次年 3 月 15 日左右结束。

So how long does the heating supply last on average during winter in the north? Because the period of extremely cold weather varies from city to city in northern China, the heating time is also different. Generally speaking, the heating time in most northern areas starts from Mid-November to Mid-March of the next year, which lasts for about 4 months. For example, in Beijing, heating supply starts around November 15 and ends around March 15 every year.

在北方居住的人，冬天离不开暖气，有了暖气，室内温度可达20℃以上，进屋还得脱外套。而本来较温暖的部分南方地区，冬季室内温度有可能还不到10℃，屋里屋外一样冷，进屋也得把自己裹得严严实实的，还冻得直哆嗦。特别是早上起床，对南方居民来说，也会成为巨大的挑战，因为他们根本不愿意离开温暖的被窝。可见，北方的冬天可能比南方的冬天好过一些。不过，虽然南方没有集中供暖，但是南方居民可以通过其他方式取暖，比如：空调、地暖、“小太阳”取暖器、电热毯、热水袋等。

People living in the north cannot live without heating in winter. With heating, the indoor temperature can reach 20℃ and above. When people enter the room, they have to take off their coats. However, in some warm southern regions, the indoor temperature may be less than 10℃ in winter. The indoor temperature is just as cold as that of outside. Even in the house, people have to wrap themselves in warm coats but still shiver with cold. In particular, getting up in the morning can be a huge challenge for southern residents, who are reluctant to leave their warm beds. Therefore, the northern winter is likely to be better than the southern winter. However, although there is no central heating in the south, residents can get warm in other ways, such as air conditioning, floor heating, “little sun” heater, electric blankets, and hot water bags.

你知道吗？
Do you know?

（1）上海—拉萨列车
The Train from Shanghai to Lhasa

班次：Z164，历时：47 小时 27 分钟

Train schedule: Z164, duration: 47 hours and 27 minutes

（2）高原反应
High Altitude Reaction

高原反应，是人体急速进入海拔 3 000 米以上的高原，暴露于低压低氧环境后产生的各种不适，是高原地区独有的常见病。常见的症状有头痛、失眠、食欲减退、疲倦、呼吸困难等。

High altitude reaction is a kind of discomfort caused by the exposure to low-pressure and low-oxygen environment after the human body rapidly enters the plateau over 3,000 meters above sea level. It is a common disease, but it only happens in the plateau area. Common symptoms are headache, insomnia, loss of appetite, fatigue, dyspnea, etc.

（3）青藏高寒区
Qinghai-Xizang Plateau Cold Area

青藏高寒区空气稀薄，大气干燥，风力强劲，降水稀少，太阳辐射强烈，气温低而且年差较小，日差较大。青藏高寒区由于自然条件限制，居民稀少，经济尚不发达，所以保留了比较完整的原始自然状态，是人类探索自然奥秘的宝贵场所。

Qinghai-Xizang Plateau Cold Area shows the feature of thin air, dry atmosphere, strong wind, rare precipitation, strong solar radiation, low temperature with the small annual range and the large daily range. Due to the limitations of natural conditions, the Qinghai-Xizang Plateau Cold Area has few residents and underdeveloped economy, so it has retained a relatively complete original natural state and is a valuable place for human beings to explore the mysteries of nature.

（4）炎热中心
Hot Center

新疆吐鲁番盆地（海拔 –154 米）7 月份的平均气温在 35℃左右，是中国夏季的炎热中心。

Xinjiang Turpan Basin (–154 m above sea level) is a summer hot center in China with an average temperature of 35℃ in July.

（5）漠河北极村
Mohe Arctic Village

北极村位于黑龙江省漠河市漠河乡，地处北纬53°33′30″，是中国最北的城镇。

Located in Mohe township, Mohe city, Heilongjiang Province, Arctic Village is the northernmost town in China, located at 53°33′30″ north latitude.

三、名山大川
Famous Mountains and Large Rivers

（一）名山
Famous Mountains

中国有成千上万的山脉，说到中国的名山，最有名的就是“五岳”了。“岳”的意思是“高大的山”，“五岳”具体指泰山、华山、衡山、恒山和嵩山。从遥远的古代开始，人们就把这五座山尊称为“五岳”。“五岳”是古代民间山神崇拜、五行观念和帝王封禅相结合的产物。

There are thousands of mountains in China. When it comes to China's famous mountains, the most famous ones are the “Five Great Mountains”. “岳 (Yue)” means “Great Mountain” and “Five Great Mountains” specifically refer to Mount Tai, Mount Hua, Mount Heng, Hengshan Mountain and Mount Song. From the remote ancient times, people honored the five mountains as “Five Great Mountains”. The “Five Great Mountains” are combinations of ancient folk worship of mountain gods, the concept of Five Elements and imperial mountain-top worship of Heaven and Earth.

从地理位置来看，泰山在山东省，称“东岳”;华山在陕西省，称“西岳”;衡山在湖南省，称“南岳”；嵩山在河南省，称“中岳”；恒山在山西省，称为“北岳”。

Geographically, Mount Tai is called “Dongyue (East Great Mountain)” in Shandong Province; Mount Hua is called “Xiyue (West Great Mountain)” in Shaanxi Province; Mount Heng is called “Nanyue (South Great Mountain)” in Hunan Province; Mount Song is called “Zhongyue (Central Great Mountain)” in Henan Province; and Hengshan Mountain is called “Beiyue (North Great Mountain)” in Shanxi Province.

其中，东岳泰山是“五岳”之首，有“天下第一山”的美誉。泰山巍峨陡峻，气势磅礴，主峰玉皇顶海拔 1 532 米，与周围的平原、丘陵相对高差 1 000 余米，形成强烈的对比，因而在视觉上显得格外高大。孔子曾有“登泰山而小天下”之叹，唐代诗人杜甫则写下了“会当凌绝顶，一览众山小”的豪言壮语。

Among them, “Dongyue” Mount Tai is the head of the “Five Great Mountains” and has the reputation of the No.1 mountain in the world. Mount Tai is lofty, magnificent, and its main peak, Jade Emperor Peak, is 1,532 meters above sea level, with a relative height difference of more than 1,000 meters from the surrounding plains and hills, forming a strong contrast, which makes it particularly high in vision. Confucius once praised that “the world seems so small on top of the Mount Tai”, while Du Fu, a poet of the Tang Dynasty, wrote the bold words like “The time will come when I climb to its very summit and see how tiny the other mountains are”.

泰山被古人视为“直通帝座”的宝地，成为百姓崇拜、帝王告祭的神山，有“泰山安，四海皆安”的说法。自秦始皇开始到清代，至少有 13 代帝王亲登泰山

封禅或祭祀。

Mount Tai is regarded as the magic land of "the direct path to Heaven" by the ancients, and it has become the holy mountain worshipped by the people and sacrificed to by the emperor. There is a saying that Mount Tai is peaceful and the world is peaceful. From the First Emperor of Qin to Qing Dynasty, there were at least 13 emperors who went to Mount Tai to worship Heaven and Earth or sacrifice.

西岳华山，险居五岳之首，自古以来就有"奇险天下第一山"的说法。位于华山南峰东侧山腰的长空栈道，是华山险道的险中之险，被誉为"华山第一天险"。长空栈道有700余年的历史，是元代道士贺志真为远离尘世、静修成仙，在万仞绝壁上镶嵌石钉、搭木椽而筑。栈道上下皆是悬崖绝壁，古往今来，历险探胜者络绎不绝。

"Xiyue" Mount Hua is the most dangerous mountain in the "Five Great Mountains". Since ancient times, there has been a saying that it is the most dangerous mountain in the world. Located on the eastern mountainside of the south peak, the Changkong Trestle is the most dangerous part and is known as "the first natural barrier of Mount Hua". The Changkong Trestle has a history of more than 700 years. It was built by Taoist priest He Zhizhen in Yuan Dynasty to stay away from the world and became immortal in retreat. It was built with stone nails and wooden rafters on the bold cliff. Up and down the trestle are precipices. Through the ages, there has been an endless stream of adventurers and tourists.

南岳衡山地临湘水之滨，林木苍郁，景色秀丽，享有"五岳独秀"的美名。衡山是中国著名的道教、佛教圣地，有寺、庙、庵、观200多处。其主要山峰有回雁峰、祝融峰、紫盖峰、岳麓山等，最高峰祝融峰海拔1 300.2米。

"Nanyue" Mount Heng is near the shore of Xiangjiang River. It has lush forests and beautiful scenery. It enjoys the reputation of "the most graceful of the Five Great Mountains". Mount Heng is a famous Taoist and Buddhist holy place in China, with more than 200 Buddhist temples, nunneries and Taoist temples. The main peaks are Huiyan Peak, Zhurong Peak, Zigai Peak and Yuelu Mountain. The highest peak is Zhurong Peak at 1,300.2 meters above sea level.

中岳嵩山的特点突出在一个“奥”字上。嵩山是古都洛阳东边的重要屏障，素为京畿之地，具有深厚的文化底蕴，是中国佛教禅宗的发源地和道教圣地。嵩山由太室山与少室山组成，共 72 峰。主峰峻极峰位于太室山，高 1 491.7 米；最高峰连天峰位于少室山，高 1 512 米。

"Zhongyue" Mount Song is characterized by the word "profound". Mount Song is an important barrier to the east of Luoyang, the ancient capital city. It has a profound cultural background and is the birthplace of the Chan Sector of Chinese Buddhism and the holy place of Taoism. Mount Song is composed of Taishi Mountain and Shaoshi Mountain, with 72 peaks in total. The main peak is Junji Peak with 1,491.7 meters high, and the highest peak is Liantian Peak with 1,512 meters high.

坐落于少室山的少林寺，是世界著名的佛教寺院，被誉为“天下第一名刹”。同时，它也是中国功夫的发源地，因其历代少林武僧潜心研创和不断发展的少林功夫而名扬天下，素有“天下功夫出少林，少林功夫甲天下”之说。不少外国人也慕名前去学习功夫，感受中国功夫的魅力。

Located in Shaoshi Mountain, Shaolin Temple is a world-famous Buddhist temple, known as the No.1 temple in the world. At the same time, it is also the birthplace of Chinese Kung Fu. It is well-known for its devoted research and continuous development of Shaolin Kung Fu, known as "all Kung Fu comes from Shaolin, and Shaolin Kung Fu is the best of the world". Many foreigners also come to learn and feel the charm of Chinese Kung Fu.

北岳恒山因其险峻的山势和地理位置，成为兵家必争之地。许多帝王、名将都在此打过仗，古代的关隘、城堡、烽火台等众多古代战场遗迹被保存了下来。虽然交通不便，山势陡峭，却是深山藏宝，著名的悬空寺便隐匿其中。恒山悬空寺建于公元 491 年，是佛、道、儒三教合一的独特寺庙。2010 年悬空寺入选美国《时代周刊》世界岌岌可危十大建筑。

"Beiyue" Hengshan Mountain has become a place for military strategists to contend for because of its precipitous terrain and geographical location. Many emperors and famous generals have fought here. And many ancient battlefield relics, such as ancient passes, castles, beacon towers, have been preserved. Although the traffic is inconvenient and the mountain is steep, there is a treasure in the deep mountains. The famous Hanging Temple is hidden in it. The Hanging Temple in Hengshan Mountain was built in A.D. 491 and is a unique temple that combines Buddhism, Taoism and Confucianism. In 2010, Hanging Temple was selected as one of the ten most endangered buildings in the world by *Time* Magazine.

俗话说："五岳归来不看山，黄山归来不看岳"，意思是说：去过五岳之后，便会发现其他的山也不过如此，无须再看；而看过黄山之后，便觉五岳也不过如此了。这句话生动展现了"天下第一奇山——黄山"的魅力。

As the saying goes, "No more mountains after visiting the Five Great Mountains, and no more Great Mountains after visiting Mount Huangshan". This means that after visiting the Five Great Mountains, you do not need to go to any other mountains because you will find them less fascinating. But after seeing Mount Huangshan, you will feel that the Five Great Mountains are just ordinary. This sentence vividly demonstrates the charm of Mount Huangshan, the No.1 miracle mountain in the world.

黄山位于安徽省黄山市，是安徽旅游业的标志，代表景观有"四绝三瀑"。四绝：奇松、怪石、云海、温泉，三瀑：人字瀑、百丈泉、九龙瀑。黄山迎客松是安徽人民热情友好的象征，承载着拥抱世界的东方礼仪文化。

Mount Huangshan, located in the Huangshan city, Anhui Province, is the symbol of Anhui tourism. Its representative landscapes are "Four Wonders and Three Falls". Four Wonders include strangely-shaped pines, grotesque rocks, the sea of clouds and hot springs, and Three Falls include the Herringbone Waterfall, Hundred-zhang Spring and Nine-dragon Waterfall. The Pine Greeting Guests in Mount Huangshan is a symbol of the hospitality and friendliness of Anhui people, carrying the Oriental etiquette culture embracing the world.

在青藏高原南部边缘，还耸立着世界上最高大、最雄伟的喜马拉雅山，藏语意为“雪的故乡”。它的主峰珠穆朗玛峰终年积雪，是世界最高峰，因此成了登山者的圣地。2020 年 12 月 9 日，中国和尼泊尔共同宣布，珠穆朗玛峰的新高度是 8848.86 米。

Further west, on the southern edge of the Qinghai-Xizang Plateau, there stands the world's tallest and most magnificent Himalayas, which means "home of snow" in Tibetan. Its main peak, Mount Qomolangma, is covered with snow all the year round. It is the highest mountain in the world, so it has become a holy place for climbers. The new height of Mount Qomolangma is 8848.86 meters, China and Nepal jointly announced on December 9, 2020.

（二）大川
Large Rivers

《全球通史》中提及：“中东、印度、中国和欧洲这四块地区的肥沃的大河流域和平原，孕育了历史上最伟大的文明。这些文明使欧亚大陆成为起重大作用的世界历史中心地区。”

The book called *A Global History* mentions that the fertile large river basins and plains of the four regions of the Middle East, India, China and Europe have nurtured the greatest civilization in history, and these civilizations have made the Eurasian Continent the center of world history that plays an important role.

古中国的文明中心是黄河流域和长江流域。黄河和长江世世代代滋润着大地、哺育着中华儿女，成为中华文明发展的摇篮。黄河还被中国人称为“母亲河”。

The center of civilization in ancient China was the Yellow River Basin and the Yangtze River Basin. The Yellow River and Yangtze River have moistened the earth and nurtured Chinese nation for generations. They have become the cradle of the development of Chinese civilization. And the Yellow River is called "Mother River" by Chinese people.

而在文明初生的石器时代，黄河流域松软的土壤显然比长江流域密致的土壤更容易用木石工具来耕种，于是华夏文明最早在黄河两岸蓬勃生长。黄河位于中国北方，呈“几”字形，全长约 5 464 千米，是中国的第二长河。黄河发源于青藏高原巴颜喀拉山北麓，蜿蜒东流，自西向东分别流经青海、四川、甘肃、宁夏、内蒙古、陕西、山西、河南、山东 9 个省、自治区，最后注入渤海。

In the early Stone Age, the soft soil in the Yellow River Basin was obviously easier to cultivate with wood and stone tools than the dense soil in the Yangtze River Basin, so Chinese civilization flourished on both sides of the Yellow River at the earliest time. The Yellow River is situated in the north of China and has the shape of " 几 (ji)". It is the second longest river in China with about 5,464 kilometers. The Yellow River originated at the northern foot of the Bayankala Mountains on the Qinghai-Xizang Plateau and flows eastward. It flows through Qinghai, Sichuan, Gansu, Ningxia, Inner Mongolia, Shaanxi, Shanxi, Henan and Shandong provinces and autonomous regions from west to east, and finally into the Bohai Sea.

黄河中上游以山地为主，中下游以平原、丘陵为主。由于河流中段流经中国黄土高原地区，因此夹带了大量的泥沙，所以它也被称为世界上含沙量最多的河流。大量泥沙常年留在黄河下游，形成冲积平原，有利于种植。

The middle and upper reaches of the Yellow River are dominated by mountains, while the middle and lower reaches are dominated by plains and hills. Because the middle part of the river flows through the Loess Plateau of China, it carries a large amount of sediment, so it is also known as the most sediment-laden river in the world.

A large amount of sediment remains in the lower reaches of the Yellow River for a long time, forming an alluvial plain, which is conducive to planting.

中国人对长江的认知比黄河迟滞了上千年，直到 1976 年，人们对长江源头才有了相对准确的认知。长江发源于青藏高原唐古拉山的主峰各拉丹冬雪山，全长 6 387 千米，比黄河长 900 多千米。它是亚洲第一长河、世界第三长河，仅次于非洲的尼罗河与南美洲的亚马孙河。

The Chinese people's knowledge of the Yangtze River lagged behind that of the Yellow River for thousands of years. Until 1976, people finally had a relatively accurate knowledge of the headstream of the Yangtze River. The Yangtze River originates from the main peak of Tanggula Mountains in the Qinghai-Xizang Plateau, the Geladandong Peak. With a total length of 6,387 kilometers, Yangtze River is more than 900 kilometers longer than the Yellow River. It is the first longest river in Asia and the third in the world, just shorter than the Nile River in Africa and the Amazon River in South America.

长江干流自西而东横贯中国中部。干流先后流经青海、四川、西藏、云南、重庆、湖北、湖南、江西、安徽、江苏、上海共 11 个省、自治区和直辖市，最后注入东海。

The main stream of the Yangtze River runs through central China from west to east. It flows successively through Qinghai, Sichuan, Xizang, Yunnan, Chongqing, Hubei, Hunan, Jiangxi, Anhui, Jiangsu and Shanghai, 11 provinces, autonomous regions and municipalities in total, and finally into the East Sea.

长江是中国第一大河，是横贯我国东西的水运大动脉，货运量位居全球内河第一，素有“黄金水道”之称。长江干线航道上起云南水富港，下至长江入海口，全长 2 838 千米。利用长江黄金水道优势降低物流成本，是在内陆地区发展钢铁、汽车等产业的重要条件。

The Yangtze River is the largest river in China. It is the main water transport artery across China’s east and west. The volume of freight transportation ranks first in the world’s inland rivers, known as the “Golden Waterway”. The Yangtze River main channel rises from Shuifu Port in Yunnan to the estuary of the Yangtze River, with a total length of 2,838 kilometers. Taking advantage of the superiority of the Yangtze River Golden Waterway to reduce logistics costs is an important condition for the development of iron and steel, automobile and other industries in inland areas.

中国是世界上河流最多的国家之一，有许多源远流长的大江大河，其中流域面积超过 1 000 平方千米的河流就有 1 500 多条。出名的除了黄河和长江以外，还有珠江、黑龙江、松花江、辽河、雅鲁藏布江、澜沧江、怒江和汉江等。

China is one of the countries with the most rivers in the world. There are many long-standing large rivers. There are more than 1,500 rivers with a basin area of more than 1,000 square kilometers. Except the Yellow River and Yangtze River, the Pearl River, Heilong River, Songhua River, Liao River, Yarlung Zangbo River, Lancang River, Nujiang River and Han River are the most famous ones.

中国除天然河流外，还有许多人工开凿的运河，其中世界上开凿最早、最长的京杭大运河，是中国历史上与万里长城齐名的伟大工程。京杭大运河南起杭州、北到北京，途经浙江、江苏、山东、河北四省及天津、北京两市，贯通钱塘江、长江、淮河、黄河、海河五大水系，全长约 1 800 千米。

In addition to natural rivers, there are many artificially excavated canals in China, including the earliest and longest canal in the world, the Beijing-Hangzhou Grand Canal. It is a great project and enjoys equal popularity with the Great Wall in Chinese history. From Hangzhou in the south to Beijing in the north, the Grand Canal runs through Zhejiang, Jiangsu, Shandong, Hebei, Tianjin and Beijing. It links up the five major river systems of Qiantang River, Yangtze River, Huai River, Yellow River and Haihe River with a total length of about 1,800 km.

大运河从开凿至今已有 2 000 多年的历史，对沟通中国南北交通曾起过重大的作用，促进了中国南北地区之间的经济、文化发展与交流，特别是对沿线地区工农业经济的发展起了巨大的推动作用。

The Grand Canal has a history of more than 2,000 years since its excavation. It has played an important role in the communication between north and south China. It has promoted the economic and cultural development and exchanges between the two regions, especially the development of industry and agriculture along the canal.

你知道吗？
Do you know?

封禅
Imperial Mountain-top Worship of Heaven and Earth

封禅，封为“祭天”，禅为“祭地”，是指中国古代帝王在太平盛世或天降祥瑞之时祭祀天地的大型典礼。封禅仪式在嵩山和泰山都曾举行过，但以泰山的次数多且影响大而出名。

Imperial mountain-top worship of Heaven and Earth is called “Fengshan” in Chinese. “Feng” means “sacrifice to Heaven” and “shan” means “sacrifice to Earth”. It refers to the large-scale ceremonies of ancient Chinese emperors sacrificing Heaven and Earth in the time of peace and prosperity or when Heaven descends auspicious sign. The Fengshan ceremony has been held in both Mount Song and Mount Tai, but Mount Tai is famous for its great influence.

四、游在中国
Travel in China

（一）旅游发展
Tourism Development

改革开放以来，中国旅游业接待规模持续扩大，接待能力和水平不断提高，现已成为全球国际游客到访量最大的国家之一。1978 年，中国改革开放的第一年，中国共接待的入境过夜游客仅为 71 万人次，旅游收入不到 3 亿美元，两项指标在世界的排名分别是第 41 位和第 48 位；而到 2015 年，中国共接待入境过夜游客 5 689 万人次，比 1978 年增长了 79 倍，旅游收入 1 137 亿美元，较 1978 年增长了 431 倍，两项数据分别攀升至世界第 4 位和第 2 位。

Since the Economic Reform and Opening-up, China's tourism has continuously expanded its reception scale and improved its reception capacity and level. It has become one of the countries with the largest number of international tourists in the world. In 1978, the first year of China's Economic Reform and Opening-up, only 710,000 overnight tourists were received in China, with tourism income less than 300 million USD, ranking 41st and 48th in the world respectively. By 2015, 56.89 million overnight tourists were received in China, an increase of 79 times over 1978. The tourism income was 113.7 billion USD, 431 times higher than in 1978. The two figures climbed to the fourth and second place in the world, respectively.

中国在世界入境旅游市场中的业绩表现及排名变化示意表

Performance and Ranking Change of China in the World Inbound Tourism Market

年份	入境过夜游客人数 / 百万人次	世界排名	入境旅游收入 / 亿美元	世界排名
1978	0.71	41	2.63	48
1980	3.50	18	6.17	34
1982	3.92	16	8.43	29
1984	5.14	14	11.31	21
1986	9.0	12	15.31	22
1988	12.36	10	22.47	26
1990	10.48	11	22.18	25
1992	16.51	9	39.47	17
1994	21.07	6	73.23	10
1996	22.77	6	102.0	9
1998	25.07	6	126.02	7
2000	31.23	5	162.24	7
2002	36.80	5	203.85	5
2004	41.76	4	257.39	7
2006	49.91	4	339.49	5
2008	53.05	4	408.43	5
2010	55.67	3	458.14	5
2012	57.72	3	500.28	4
2014	55.62	4	1053.8	3
2015	56.89	4	1137	2

中国作为旅游目的地国家的全球吸引力和竞争力稳步提高，现已成为全球旅游市场竞争中的主角之一。2017 年，中国共接待国际入境过夜游客 6 074 万人，排名世界第四，仅次于法国、西班牙和美国。为构建人类命运共同体，中国积极扩大对外开放，为入境游客提供便利。以签证政策为例，京津冀、苏浙沪等地区先后实施了外国人 144 小时过境免签政策，免签时间进一步延长，方便了外国人来华旅行。

As a tourist destination, China has steadily improved its global attractiveness and competitiveness, and has become one of the leading players in the global tourism market competition. In 2017, China received 60.74 million international overnight visitors, ranking fourth in the world, just behind France, Spain and the United States. In order to build a Community of Shared Future for Mankind, China has actively expanded its opening to the world to facilitate inbound tourists. Taking the visa policy as an example, Beijing, Tianjin, Hebei, Jiangsu, Zhejiang and Shanghai have implemented the 144-hour transit visa-free policy for foreigners, which further extended the visa-free time and facilitated foreigners' travel to China.

近年来，中国旅游业在增进中国和全球其他国家之间的友谊和交往中发挥了积极作用，旅游业已成为发出中国声音、讲好中国故事、加强与世界联系的重要平台，旅游外交的独特作用也得到进一步凸显。当下，“旅游年”逐渐成为中国外交和旅游领域的一个热词。

In recent years, China's tourism has played an active role in promoting friendship and association between China and other countries around the world. Tourism has become an important platform to make a Chinese voice, tell Chinese stories well and strengthen ties with the world. The unique role of tourism diplomacy has also been further highlighted. At present, "Visit Year" has gradually become a buzzword in the field of Chinese diplomacy and tourism.

中国与世界其他国家互办“旅游年”一览表

Timetable for China and the Rest of the World to Host "Visit Year"

年份	互办“旅游年”国家 / 地区	“旅游年”
2012	中国与俄罗斯	在中国举办“俄罗斯旅游年”
2013		在俄罗斯举办“中国旅游年”
2015	中国与中东欧	“中国-中东欧国家旅游合作促进年”

续表

年份	互办“旅游年”国家 / 地区	“旅游年”
2015	中国与韩国	在韩国举办“中国旅游年”
2016		在中国举办“韩国旅游年”
2015	中国与印度	在中国举办“印度旅游年”
2016		在印度举办“中国旅游年”
2016	中国与美国	“中美旅游年”
2017	中国与哈萨克斯坦	“中哈旅游年”
2018	中国与欧盟	“中国–欧盟旅游年”

中国不仅是世界旅游市场最重要的目的地之一，同时也是最重要的客源市场之一。自 2012 年起，中国一直是全球最主要的出境旅游消费国之一，为世界旅游市场提供了稳定增长的客流。不仅如此，中国还引领了旅游支付新时代，推动全球旅游消费体验升级。2017 年下半年，中国银联卡受理网络已延展到 168 个国家和地区，境外超过 2 300 万家商户可受理银联卡。随着中国出境旅游增长，境外移动支付推广迅速。2018 年，全球已有 80 多个机场支持支付宝实时退税，扫完码钱直接退回游客的支付宝。

China is not only one of the most important destinations in the world tourism market, but also one of the most important tourist source markets. Since 2012, China has been one of the most important outbound tourism consumers in the world, providing a steady growth of passenger flow for the world tourism market. China has also led a new era of tourism payment and promoted the upgrading of global tourism consumption experience. The acceptance network of China UnionPay Card has been extended to 168 countries and regions at the end of 2017. Over 23 million overseas merchants can accept UnionPay Card. With the growth of China's outbound tourism, the mobile payment abroad has been promoted rapidly. In 2018, there are more than 80 airports in the world supporting Alipay's real-time tax rebate, and the money is directly returned to Alipay after scanning the QR code.

（二）旅游攻略 Travel Guide

1. 旅游注意事项 Travel Tips

中国有很多城市、古镇、乡村以及自然风光值得大家前去参观、体验。不过风景再好，如果旅行时间没选对的话，那么体验也会大打折扣。一般来说，在计划旅行时，最好错过中国的春运和小长假，因为这是中国人出行的高峰期，这个时候交通和景点都会异常拥挤。

There are many cities, ancient towns, villages and natural scenery worth visiting and experiencing in China. But no matter how beautiful the scenery is, if the travel time is not chosen correctly, the experience will be greatly watered down. Generally speaking, when planning a trip in China, it's better to stagger the Spring Festival and the Minor vacation. Because it's the peak time for Chinese people to travel, the traffic and scenic spots will be extremely crowded.

在中国旅行，请记得随身带好护照等有效身份证件。因为很多地方实行实名制购票，对于外国游客来说，很多景点都需要出示护照，这样才可以买票进入参观。如果没带护照，很可能就只能扫兴而归了。

When traveling in China, please remember to take your passport or other valid identity documents with you. Since many places implement the real-name purchasing system. For foreign tourists, passports are required in many scenic spots. If you don't take your passport, you'll probably have to leave disappointingly.

在中国，不光是购买飞机票需要有效身份证件，购买火车票（包括动车票、高铁票）和长途汽车票也需要出示有效身份证件才可以购买。并且，中国实行比较严格的安检制度，乘坐火车和长途汽车也需要接受安全检查。因此，旅行时计算好时间，提前到达火车站和长途汽车站很有必要。

In China, not only air tickets, but also train tickets (including high-speed rail tickets) and long-distance bus tickets require valid identity documents. Moreover, China has a stricter security inspection system, even traveling by train or coach also requires security inspection. Therefore, it is necessary to calculate the time and arrive at the railway station or the long distance bus station in advance.

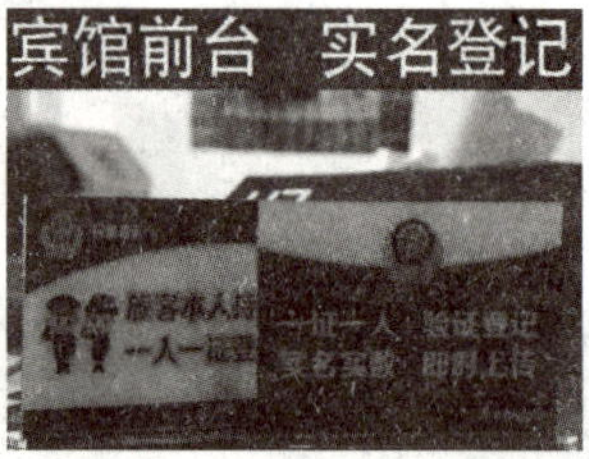

当然了，在中国住宿也需要实名登记，需要注意的是，并不是所有的旅馆都有接收外国人的资质。一般来说，国际青年旅社、快捷酒店和高档酒店都支持外国人持护照入住，因此，外国游客应尽量选择这样的地方住宿。

Of course, accommodation in China also requires real-name registration. It should be noted that not all hotels are qualified to receive foreigners. Generally speaking, international youth hostels, fast hotels and high-end hotels all support foreigners to stay with passports. Therefore, foreign tourists should try to choose such places for accommodation.

2. 旅游小助手
Travel Assistant

在中国，比起谷歌地图，百度地图的使用更加频繁。在手机上下载百度地图，输入本地的一个目的地，它将引导你前往该目的地。

In China, Baidu Map is more frequently used than Google Map. You can download Baidu Map on your mobile phone and try entering a local destination to see how Baidu Map guides you there.

du 百度地图

现在是网络旅游时代，通过互联网和手机软件（App），可以方便快捷地查询或者订购旅游产品。在中国，订机票和酒店，大家常用的是去哪儿网、携程网；

订高铁票、动车票、火车票，大家会用 12306 中国铁路网；想要寻找特色景点、美食、旅游攻略时，美团、大众点评、马蜂窝便派上了用场。

Today is the era of online tourism. With the Internet and mobile application, you can easily and quickly inquire or order tourism products. In China, to book air tickets and hotels, we often use Qunar and Ctrip; to book high-speed rail tickets, train tickets, we will use 12306 China Railway; when we want to find special scenic spots, delicious food, tourism strategies, Meituan, Dazhongdianping, Mafengwo will be used.

去哪儿? Qunar.Com 聪明你的旅行	Ctrip 携程	中国铁路12306 12306 CHINA RAILWAY
美团 美团	大众点评 dianping.com	马蜂窝

课后练习题
Practice

一、选择题
Multiple-choice

1. ______是中国第一大河，是横贯我国东西的水运大动脉，货运量位居全球内河第一，素有“黄金水道”之称。

   ______ is the largest river in China. It is the main water transport artery across China’s east and west. The volume of freight transportation ranks first in the world’s inland rivers, known as the “Golden Waterway”.

   A. 长江　B. 黄河　C. 大运河　D. 珠江
   A. The Yangtze River　B. The Yellow River　C. The Grand Canal　D. The Pearl River

2. 中国有______个直辖市。

   There are ______ municipalities directly under the Central Government in China.

   A. 1　B. 2　C. 3　D. 4

3. 香港和澳门是中国的两个______。

   Hong Kong and Macao Special Administrative Region are China’s two ______.

A. 省
A. provinces

B. 市
B. cities

C. 特别行政区
C. special administrative regions of China

D. 直辖市
D. municipalities directly under the Central Government

4. ______是中国的首都。
______ is the capital of China.

A. 北京 B. 上海 C. 西安 D. 广州
A. Beijing B. Shanghai C. Xi'an D. Guangzhou

5. 在______南部边缘，还耸立着世界上最高大、最雄伟的喜马拉雅山，藏语意为“雪的故乡”。
On the southern edge of ______, there stands the world's tallest and most magnificent Himalayas, which means "home of snow" in Tibetan.

A. 安徽 B. 广州
A. Anhui B.Guangzhou

C. 青藏高原 D. 云南
C. the Qinghai-Xizang Plateau D. Yunnan

二、填空题
Fill-in-the-blanks

1. 中国有______个省级行政区，包括______个省、______个自治区、______个直辖市和______个特别行政区。
At present, there are ______ provincial administrative regions in China, including ______ provinces, ______ autonomous regions, ______ municipalities directly under the Central Government and ______ special administrative regions.

2. “五岳归来不看山，______归来不看岳”

"No more mountains after visiting the Five Great Mountains, and no more Great Mountains after visiting ____________"

3. 古中国的文明中心是____________流域和____________流域。
The center of civilization in ancient China was the ____________ Basin and the ____________ Basin.

4. ____________ 从开凿至今已有 2 000 多年的历史，对沟通中国南北交通曾起过重大的作用。
________________ has a history of more than 2,000 years since its excavation. It has played an important role in the communication between North and South China.

5. 封禅，封为"______"，禅为"______"，是指中国古代帝王在太平盛世或天降祥瑞之时祭祀天地的大型典礼。
Imperial mountain-top worship of Heaven and Earth is called "Fengshan" in Chinese. "Feng" means "______________" and "shan" means "____________".

三、判断题

True or False

1. 中国是世界上河流最多的国家之一。
China is one of the countries with the most rivers in the world.

2. 华山在山东省，称"东岳"。
Mount Hua is called "Dongyue (East Great Mountain)" in Shandong Province.

3. 中国是一个幅员辽阔的国家，国土面积约 960 万平方千米，排在世界第三位。
China is a vast country with an area of 9.6 million square kilometers, ranking third in the world.

4. 很多地方实行实名制购票，对于外国游客来说，很多景点都需要出示护照，这样才可以买票进入参观。
Many places implement the real-name purchasing system. For foreign tourists, passports are required in many scenic spots.

5. 黄河干流自西而东横贯中国中部，最后注入东海。
The main stream of the Yellow River runs through central China from west to east, and finally into the East Sea.

四、简答题

Short-answer Questions

1. “五岳”指哪五座山？

   Which five mountains do the “Five Great Mountains” refer to?

2. 中华民族的“母亲河”是什么？

   Which river is called “Mother River” by Chinese people?

3. 请谈谈中国的气候特征。

   What are the features of China’s climate?

第二章

中国的对外交流

International Communication

课前思考

Lead-in Questions

1. 你听说过丝绸之路吗？
   Have you ever heard of the Silk Road?
2. 你了解中国的“一带一路”倡议吗？
   Do you know the Belt and Road Initiative in China?

一、丝绸之路
The Silk Road

（一）丝绸之路名称的由来
The Term of the Silk Road

“丝绸之路”一词的首创者是德国旅行家和地理学家费迪南·冯·李希霍芬男爵。实际上，冯·李希霍芬在1877年的一次讲座上，以及他的多卷本历史地理学著作《中国》（1877）中，同时使用了这个词的单数（Seidenstrasse）和复数（Seidenstrassen）形式。他用这个词指代中国的丝绸离开汉王朝（公元前206年—公元220年）抵达中亚的多条路线。

It was a German traveler and geographer, Ferdinand von Richthofen, who coined the term “the Silk Road”. Actually, von Richthofen used the term in both singular (Seidenstrasse) and plural (Seidenstrassen) in a lecture in 1877 and in his multivolume historical geography work *China* (1877). For him the term referred to the routes along which Chinese silk moved from the Han Empire (206 B.C.–220 A.D.) to Central Asia.

Ferdinand von Richthofen
费迪南·冯·李希霍芬
(1833—1905)

（二）丝绸之路简介
About the Silk Road

自从张骞通西域以来，中国和中亚及欧洲的商业往来迅速增加。通过这条贯穿亚欧的大道——丝绸之路，中国的丝、绸、绫、缎、绢等丝织品源源不断地输向中亚和欧洲。

丝绸之路，概括地讲，是自古以来，从东亚开始，经中亚、西亚进而联结欧洲及北非的这条东西方交通路线的总称。丝绸之路在世界史上有重大的意义。它是欧亚大陆的交通动脉，是中国、印度、希腊三种主要文化交汇的桥梁。

Since Zhang Qian traveled to the Western Regions, the business communication between China, Central Asia and Europe has increased rapidly. Through the Silk Road which is the main road throughout Asia and Europe, China's silk, silk fabric, thin silk, satin, tough silk and other silk products are exported to Central Asia and Europe.

Generally speaking, the Silk Road is the general name of the East-West transportation route that starts from East Asia and connects Europe and North Africa through Central Asia and West Asia since ancient times. The Silk Road is of great significance in world history. It is the transport artery of Eurasia and the intersection bridge of China, India and Greece.

狭义的丝绸之路，作为位于中国和罗马之间的东西方路线，还掩盖了另一个事实，即它不是一条“路”，而是将许多货仓连接起来的一系列路线。史学家们更倾向于把丝绸之路看作一个网络，而非一条线状的道路。

The narrow conception of the Silk Road as an East-West route between China and Rome likewise obscures the fact that there was not one "road" but rather a skein of routes linking many warehouses. Historians think of the Silk Road more as a network than as a linear route.

丝绸之路的起点一般被认为是西安，其实它随着朝代更替和政治中心转移而变化。西安、洛阳、开封、北京等都曾为丝路起点。

The starting point of the Silk Road is generally considered to be Xi'an. In fact, it changed with the change of dynasties and the shift of political center. Xi'an, Luoyang, Kaifeng and Beijing were all the starting points of the Silk Road.

陆上丝绸之路分为南线和北线，北线自中国北部的商业中心穿过保加利亚钦察地区到达东欧和克里米亚半岛，再从那里穿过黑海、马尔马拉海和巴尔干半岛到达威尼斯；南线穿过土耳其斯坦-呼罗珊地区和伊朗到达美索不达米亚和安纳托利亚，再经过安纳托利亚南部的安提俄克到达地中海或者是经过黎凡特到达埃及和南非。这些交流不仅对于罗马、中国和印度文明的发展与形成异常重要，还为我们的现代世界奠定了基础。当物品和宗教信仰在丝绸之路上传播时，古老的贸易可能也在这条路线上进行着，也许很少有商人和旅行者能够由陆路走遍丝绸之路上的每一个地方——欧洲或是中东和中国。

The continental Silk Road diverges into North and South routes as it extends from the commercial centers of north China, the North route passing through the Bulgar-Kypchak zone to Eastern Europe and the Crimean peninsula, and from there across the Black Sea, Marmara Sea and the Balkans to Venice; the South route passing through Turkestan-Khorasan, through Iran into Mesopotamia and Anatolia, and then through Antioch in southern Anatolia into the Mediterranean Sea or through the Levant into Egypt and South Africa. These exchanges were critical not only for the development and flowering of the great civilizations of Rome, China and India, but they laid the foundations of our modern world. While goods and religious ideas may have travelled the whole way, ancient trade was probably conducted over sections of the routes and it is probable that merchants and travelers very rarely, if ever, covered the whole distance between Europe, or the Middle East, and China, by land.

公元前 139 年，汉武帝派遣张骞作为使者出使西域两次，并在过程中自长安起，穿过新疆和中亚，以地中海东岸为终点开辟丝绸之路。根据张骞的使团和报告，在公元前 1 世纪左右，中国派出大量使团以发展丝绸之路，中国和中亚与西亚之间的商业关系繁荣发展。公元 9—23 年，丝绸之路中断。公元 97 年，将军班超带领 7 万人马西行至里海，与帕提亚帝国建立了直接的军事联络，还派甘英出使罗马帝国。甘英到伊拉克遇波斯湾而返，这是汉代沿丝绸之路西行最远的地方。罗马紧接着自公元 166 年向中国派遣使团。对中国丝绸、非洲象牙和罗马香料的交换加强了东西方之间的联系。与贵霜帝国之间的联系使得佛教在 1 世纪时传入中国。丝绸之路的重要性在唐朝达到顶峰，唐朝时，中国在历经了自汉朝时起的分裂状态后达到了国内相对的稳定。7 世纪时，玄奘穿过此路去印度求取佛教真经。丝绸之路的文化与文明在唐朝时达到新高度。然而，唐朝以后，丝绸之路上的旅行、石窟建筑和艺术都沉寂了下来。五代时期没有维持住唐朝时的国内稳定，因此邻近的地区再次开始抢劫旅行队。中国在宋朝时期再次得到统一，可那时的丝绸之路已经不如唐朝时期那么重要了。海上丝绸之路逐渐取而代之。

From 139 B.C., Emperor Wu of Han dispatched Zhang Qian to the Western Regions twice as his envoy, and in the process pioneered the route known as the Silk Road from Chang'an, through Xinjiang and Central Asia, and on to the east coast of the Mediterranean Sea. Following Zhang Qian's embassy and report, commercial relations between China and Central as well as Western Asia flourished, as many Chinese missions were sent throughout the 1st century B.C., initiating the development of the Silk Road. From A.D. 9 to A.D. 23, the Silk Road was interrupted. In A.D. 97 the Chinese general Ban Chao went as far west as the Caspian Sea with 70,000 men and established direct military contacts with the Parthian Empire, also dispatching an envoy Gan Ying to Rome. Gan Ying arrived at Iraq and returned when he met the Persian gulf, which was the westernmost traveling along the Silk Road in the Han Dynasty. Several Roman embassies to China soon followed from A.D. 166 Good exchanges such as Chinese silk, African ivory, and Roman incense increase the contacts between the East and West. Contacts with the Kushan Empire led to the introduction of Buddhism to China from India in the first century. The height of the importance of the Silk Road was during the Tang Dynasty, with relative internal stability in China after the divisions of the earlier dynasties since the Han. In the seventh century, the Chinese traveler Xuan Zang crossed the region on his way to obtain Buddhist scriptures from India. The art and civilization of the Silk Road achieved its highest point in the Tang Dynasty. After the Tang, however, the traffic along the road subsided, along with the grotto building and art of the period. The Five Dynasties period did not maintain the internal stability of the Tang Dynasty, and again neighboring states started to plunder the caravans. China was partially unified again in the Song Dynasty, but the Silk Road was not as important as it had been in the Tang. The Maritime Silk Road gradually took its place.

地方频道 Local Channel

西安频道 Xi'an Channel

张骞 Zhang Qian

张骞（公元前 164—公元前 114 年），中国汉代杰出的外交家、旅行家、探险家，丝绸之路的开拓者。西汉建元二年（公元前 139 年），奉汉武帝之命，张骞率领一百多人出使西域，打通了汉朝通往西域的南北道路，即赫赫有名的丝绸之路。

Zhang Qian (164 B.C.— 114 B.C.), an outstanding diplomat, traveler and explorer in the Han Dynasty, was a pioneer of the Silk Road. In the second year of Jianyuan (139 B.C.) in the Western Han Dynasty, under the order of Emperor Wu of the Han Dynasty, Zhang Qian led more than 100 people to the Western Regions and opened the South-North road leading to the Western Regions in the Han Dynasty, the famous Silk Road.

张骞被誉为“第一个睁开眼睛看世界的中国人”“东方的哥伦布”。他将中原文明传播至西域，又从西域诸国引进了汗血马、葡萄、苜蓿、石榴、胡麻等物种，促进了东西方文明的交流。

Zhang Qian is known as “the first Chinese to open his eyes to the world” and “Columbus of the East”. He spread the civilization of the Central Plains to the Western Regions, and introduced such species as Ferghana horse, grape, alfalfa, pomegranate and flax from the Western Regions to the Central Plains, which promoted the exchange of eastern and western civilizations.

二、海上丝绸之路
The Maritime Silk Road

我国海上丝绸之路的形成及发展至今已经有几千年的历史了，从先秦时代的少数海上活动，到秦汉以后的规模化海上贸易，从生存化的海上迁徙，到经济化的贸易往来，我国的海上丝绸之路经历了一段不寻常的历程。

The formation and development of China’s Maritime Silk Road has a history of several thousand years. From a few maritime activities in the Pre-qin Period to large-scale maritime trade after Qin and Han Dynasties, from maritime migration for survival to economic trade, China’s maritime Silk Road has experienced an unusual course.

（一）海上丝绸之路的形成
The Formation of the Maritime Silk Road

在秦汉时期，对于刚刚统一成为中央集权的封建国家来说，社会安定与发展成为当时统治者最重视的问题。在此时期，社会生产力有了很大的进步，其中造船技术和航海技术相对于之前而言得到了飞跃式的发展。也就是在这个时期，中国沿海的航海路线全都畅通无阻，甚至出现了抵达日本的远航舰队以及驶过马六甲海峡抵达印度半岛南端的远洋舰队。在此基础上形成了从中国南海到印度洋的中国史上也是世界上的第一条远洋航线，被称为海上丝绸之路。

During the Qin and Han Dynasties, social stability and development became the most important issues for the feudal state which had just been unified into a centralized state. During this period, social productive forces made great progress, among which shipbuilding technology and navigation technology were developed by leaps and bounds compared with before. It was during this period that all the navigation routes along the Chinese coast were unimpeded, even with the appearance of a fleet of voyages to Japan and an ocean-going fleet sailing through the Strait of Malacca to the southern tip of the Indian peninsula. On this basis, China formed the first ocean route in the world, which was from the South China Sea to the Indian Ocean in the history and known as the Maritime Silk Road.

（二）海上丝绸之路的繁荣
The Prosperity of the Maritime Silk Road

公元 6 世纪，隋朝统一了全国，隋炀帝继位之后，发展了海外贸易，并与海外国家和地区友好往来，但朝代历时较短，没有更加深入的发展。

In the 6th century, the Sui Dynasty unified the whole country. After Emperor Yang of Sui Dynasty inherited the throne, he developed overseas trade and made friendly exchanges with countries and regions which had economic relations with each other. But the dynasty lasted for a short time and did not develop further.

唐朝延续了南北朝前期发展的兴旺之势，生产发展、海外贸易空前发达。朝廷特别设置了市舶使专门负责管理海外贸易的相关事宜，如征收航海相关的税款，设立仓库，保护外商的正当权益，制裁违法人员，等等。在政府的保护之下，商船在南海和印度洋来往，络绎不绝。广州、泉州、宁波、扬州更是成为当时的国际四大贸易港。相比之前中原王朝海上丝绸之路航线的规模，唐代的海上丝绸之路航线更加繁盛兴旺。

The Tang Dynasty, with great development of production and overseas trade, continued the prosperity of the early development of the South and North Dynasties. The imperial government specially assigned an officer of commerce to manage overseas trade, such as collecting taxes related to navigation, setting up warehouses, protecting the legitimate rights and interests of foreign merchants, and punishing illegal persons. Under the government protection in this dynasty, merchant ships came and went in an endless stream in the South China Sea and the Indian Ocean. Guangzhou, Quanzhou, Ningbo and Yangzhou became the four international major trade ports in that time. Compared with the scale of the Maritime Silk Road of Central Plain Dynasties before, the Maritime Silk Road in the Tang Dynasty was more prosperous.

（三）海上丝绸之路的繁盛
The Flourishing of the Maritime Silk Road

在10世纪中叶，宋朝结束了五代十国的分裂格局，完成了对长期混乱局面的统一。宋朝占据了江南地区，并借助地理位置的优势，继续发展海外贸易。陶瓷和香药贸易量的加大，直至占据主导地位，是唐宋海上丝绸之路的重要特征之一。因此海上丝绸之路又有“陶瓷之路”“香药之路”之称。宋代瓷器业十分发达，所拥有的品种繁多。由于海上丝绸之路的发达，宋朝出现了不少专供海外出口销售的窑厂。宋代官、哥、钧、汝、定五大名窑，除官窑专供宫廷、皇室使用外，其余的四个窑厂产品均有出口。

In the middle of the 10th century, the Song Dynasty ended the division of the Five Dynasties and Ten Kingdoms and completed the unification of the long period of chaos. The Song Dynasty occupied the south part of China and continued to develop overseas trade with the advantage of its geographical position. One of the important characteristics of the Maritime Silk Road in Tang and Song Dynasties was that the trade volume of ceramics and perfumery increased until it became dominant status. Therefore, the Maritime Silk Road is also known as the “Ceramic Road” and “Incense Road”. The porcelain industry in the Song Dynasty was greatly developed and had a wide variety. Thanks to the development of the Maritime Silk Road, many kilns were set up for overseas export. Royal Kiln, Ge Kiln, Jun Kiln, Ru Kiln and Ding Kiln are the five famous kilns in Song Dynasty, in addition to the Royal Kiln products being for the palace and royal, the other four kilns products were for exportation.

元朝政府对于海外贸易依旧十分开放，并且有很多鼓励政策，在广州设置市舶司，推进国家海运的发展。除了商贸往来，西方基督教士也纷纷在这一时期通过海上丝绸之路来到中国。

The government of Yuan Dynasty was still open to foreign trade and had many incentives, and set up the specialized division named Shibosi in Guangzhou in order to promote the development of national marine. In addition to business and trade, the western Christians also came to China from the Maritime Silk Road in this period.

（四）海上丝绸之路的顶峰
The Summit of the Maritime Silk Road

在中国历史上，明朝政府曾多次组织庞大船队往返于海上丝绸之路，对海上丝绸之路带上的国家进行友好访问与通商贸易活动。明朝的造船业与前代相比发达很多，在各地出现了很多著名的造船厂，例如当时极负盛名的“宝船厂”。当时郑和船队以海上为贸易基地，派出船队分赴各地进行贸易。

In the history of China, there were many large fleets, which were organized by the government of the Ming Dynasty, traveled to and from the Maritime Silk Road, and had friendly visits and trade activities to countries along the Maritime Silk Road. The shipbuilding industry in the Ming Dynasty was much more developed than that of the previous generation. Many famous shipyards appeared in various places, such as the famous “Bao Shipyard” at that time. At that time, Zheng He’s fleet took the sea as its trading base and sent the fleets to various places for trade.

（五）海上丝绸之路的衰落
The Decline of the Maritime Silk Road

到了明宣德年间，由于倭寇侵扰，明朝曾中断海外贸易，重申海禁。嘉靖年间，倭寇对中国沿海的侵扰加剧，海禁更严。直到隆庆元年平定倭寇，开始放松海禁，海外贸易又有所发展。

During the reign of Emperor Xuande of the Ming Dynasty (1426–1435), the overseas trade was interrupted due to invasion by Japanese pirates. And the maritime ban was reaffirmed. During the reign of Jiajing (1522–1566), the invasion of Japanese pirates intensified and the ban on maritime trade became more severe. Until the first year of the reign of Longqing (1567) that Japanese pirates were defeated and the maritime ban was lifted.

此后，随着欧洲资本主义的兴起，从 16 世纪开始，西方的殖民者、商人、传教士、探险家等来到东方。1498 年，达·迦马发现东方航线之后，葡萄牙人首先来到中国，其后有西班牙人和荷兰人，再后有英国人、法国人和美国人。清朝的对外关系发生了极大变化，传统的海上丝绸之路贸易被冲破，面对着西方的商业、传教、殖民、炮舰、掠夺和战争的挑战，以及不堪台湾明朝残余势力不断对其沿海地区的骚扰，清朝初期实行海禁和闭关政策，禁止外商到江苏、浙江、福建等地进行贸易，广州再次成为唯一的对外贸易口岸。到了康熙二十四年，清朝政府下令开放海禁，指定广州、漳州、宁波、云台山（今连云港）四个地方为通商口岸。为加强管理沿海的对外贸易，同年创立粤海关、闽海关、浙海关和江海关。到乾隆四十年清政府又撤销了漳州、宁波和云台山通商口岸，广州又一次成为唯一的对外贸易口岸。嘉庆之后，随着国力日衰，海上丝绸之路昔日盛况不再，在清朝后期快速走向衰落。

Since then, with the rise of European Capitalism, from the 16th century on, western colonists, merchants, missionaries and explorers came to the east. After Vasco da Gama discovered the Eastern Route in 1498, the Portuguese first came to China, followed by the Spanish and Dutch, then the English, French and Americans. Great changes have taken place in Qing Dynasty's foreign relations. The traditional trade on the Maritime Silk Road was broken. Facing the challenges of western business, missionaries, colonial, gunboats, looting and the war and under the harassing to coastal region by the remnants of Ming Dynasty who lived in Taiwan, the early Qing Dynasty adopted a policy of seclusion and ban on the foreign trade. Foreign merchants were forbidden to trade in Jiangsu, Zhejiang, Fujian and other places. Guangzhou had once again become the only foreign trade port in this period. In the 24th year of the reign of Kangxi (1685), the government of Qing Dynasty ordered the opening of the ban on maritime trade and designated Guangzhou, Zhangzhou, Ningbo and Yuntai Mountain (Lianyungang) as trading ports. In order to strengthen the management of coastal foreign trade, Guangdong customs, Fujian customs, Zhejiang customs and Jianghai customs were established in the same year. By the 40th year of the reign of Qianlong (1775), the government of Qing Dynasty had canceled the trading ports of Zhangzhou, Ningbo and Yuntai Mountain, and Guangzhou once again came to the only foreign trade port. After the reign of Jiaqing, with the decline of national power, the Maritime Silk Road was not as prosperous as before and it declined rapidly in the late Qing Dynasty.

（六）海上丝绸之路的意义
The Significance of the Maritime Silk Road

实际上，不管是陆上丝绸之路还是海上丝绸之路，都是东西方经济与文化交流的代名词。自秦汉以来，这一通道不仅对我国，同时也对世界诸多国家的经济和文化发挥了极大的促进作用。

As a matter of fact, both Continental Silk Road and Maritime Silk Road stand for the East-West cultural and economic communication. Since the time of Qin and Han Dynasties, the Maritime Silk Road has significantly stimulated the economic and cultural development of China as well as many other countries in the world.

首先，海上丝绸之路对东西文化交流起到了重要的促进作用。通过海上丝绸之路，我国古代的四大发明（指南针、火药、造纸术、印刷术），纺织、陶瓷等工艺技术，绘画、戏曲、舞蹈、音乐、建筑等艺术技法，天文、算术、历法、医药等科技知识，儒家、道家、兵家、墨家、法家等文化思想，道教、佛教等宗教文化都传播到了海外。其中，中国的人文思想通过海上丝绸之路传播到了欧洲，为欧洲文艺复兴的人文思潮奠定了一定的基础并起到了推动与促进的作用，另外明朝灭亡后，我国著名学者朱舜水（1600—1682）流亡日本，他提倡的实学实理的学风给日本的国民意识带来了深远影响，间接推动了日本的明治维新，被尊称为“日本孔夫子”。与此同时，其他国家的天文、算术、医药等科技知识，音乐、舞蹈、雕塑、绘画、建筑等艺术技法，早期佛教、伊斯兰教、基督教等宗教文化也通过海上丝绸之路传入我国，并对我国的文化发展起到了积极的促进作用。

First of all, the Maritime Silk Road has greatly increased the cultural communication between western and eastern world. Bridged by the Maritime Silk Road, the four great inventions of ancient China (Compass, Gunpowder, Paper-making and Printing); techniques of textile and ceramics; arts of painting, traditional Chinese opera, dancing, music and architecture; knowledge of astronomy, mathematics, medicine and calendar; cultural thoughts of Confucianism, Taoism, Militarism, Mohism and Legalism; as well as the religious culture of Taoism and Buddhism had all spread to other countries. Among them, it is worth to mention that the humanistic thought from China also traveled to Europe by the Maritime Silk Road, which later helped to lay the foundation and further stimulated the prevailing of Humanism in the Renaissance. Also after the collapse of Ming Dynasty, a famous Chinese scholar named Zhu Shunshui (1600–1682) was exiled to Japan, in there, his advocacy for practicality and pursuit in truth exerted a profound influence on the formation of Japanese national consciousness, this influence indirectly motivated the Meiji Restoration of Japan, and thus he was respectfully addressed as “Japanese Confucius”. In the meantime, technologies from other countries including astronomy, mathematics and medicine; arts of music, dancing, sculpture, painting and architecture; religious culture of early stage of Buddhism, Islam and Christianism had contrarily spread to China and played a positive role in the development of Chinese culture.

其次，海上丝绸之路为东西方贸易往来带来了深远影响。我国是东方文明古国，从古至今，我国商品在世界上始终深受各国欢迎，在国际市场上受到一致好评，例如唐代出口的丝绸及黄金，在各国大受欢迎，而以香料、珠玑、翠羽、犀角、象牙、玳瑁、琉璃、玻璃、玛瑙及各种宝石等奢侈品为主的进口商品的引入也大大丰富了唐代时期我国人民的物质文化生活。唐代以后，陶瓷变成了主要输出商品，深受海外市场青睐；明末，茶叶传入欧洲，成为当时中国在国际上最具影响力的商品，进口的商品除了传统的南洋诸地土特产外，还增加了西洋货物，如毛织品、棉织品、钟表、香水、皮毛、金属等。就是因为海上丝绸之路等渠道的贸易，为东西方国家经济和人民生活带来了良好的刺激作用，给包括我国在内的世界各国物质文明带来了深远影响。

Secondly, the Maritime Silk Road exerts a far-reaching influence in East-West trade history. As an ancient oriental country, products made in China enjoy a great popularity and reputation all the time. The silk and gold merchandises in Tang Dynasty sold well in overseas market, correspondingly, imported products mainly dominated by luxury merchandises including spices, pearl, blue jade, rhinoceros horn, ivory, hawksbill, colored glaze, glasses, agate, as well as all kinds of gems, had significantly enriched the Chinese people's life in Tang Dynasty. Right after the Tang Dynasty, ceramics became the main exporting products; At the end of Ming Dynasty, Chinese Tea was brought to European market and then became the most popular and influential Chinese product in that era. In regard of imported products, in addition to the traditional local special merchandises from Southeast Asia, more and more western merchandises such as wool and cotton fabrics, clock, perfume, fur and metal products had also introduced to Chinese market. These communications greatly improved the economy and living standard of eastern and western countries and further exerted a profound influence on the material civilization development of the entire world. All of the above could attribute to the Maritime Silk Road.

最后，海上丝绸之路为东西方友好往来提供了便利条件。海上丝绸之路开辟了中国与海外国家友好往来的道路，南洋诸国通过派遣使节来到中国，在唐朝以后，中国历代王朝在广州等港口设置市舶使主管海路邦交外贸，设立馆驿接待外国使节，承担系列外交事务，这为东西方友好往来奠定了基础，进一步加深了各国友好交往的氛围。

At last, the Maritime Silk Road makes the friendly political communications between western and eastern world become possible. The Maritime Silk Road finds a way for

China to initiate the friendly intercourse with overseas countries. Southeast Asian countries dispatched their envoys to China by this road. Every empire after Tang Dynasty had set up an unique official post in all major trade ports in China, which called Director of Shiboshi, who in charge of all the foreign trade via the Maritime Silk Road. At the same time, they built up courier stations to host the foreign envoys and conduct foreign affairs; all these actions laid a solid foundation for East-West friendly communication, and further deepened the friendly atmosphere among different countries.

海上丝绸之路不仅是东西方经济的交流、文化的交融，还更清晰地展示出了人类文明进程运行的轨迹。

The Maritime Silk Road is not only the bridge for the communication between Eastern and Western world, it also clearly exhibits the trail of the entire human civilization history.

三、“一带一路”倡议
The Belt and Road Initiative

“一带一路”倡议是通过陆上丝绸之路经济带和海上丝绸之路两个部分来推动跨国经济发展。2013 年 9 月和 10 月，中国国家主席习近平在出访中亚和东南亚国家期间，先后提出共建“丝绸之路经济带”和“21 世纪海上丝绸之路”（以下简称“一带一路”）的重大倡议，得到国际社会的高度关注。中国国务院总理李克强在参加 2013 年中国—东盟博览会时强调，铺就面向东盟的海上丝绸之路，打造带动腹地发展的战略支点。加快“一带一路”建设，有利于促进沿线各国经济繁荣与区域经济合作，加强不同文明交流互鉴，促进世界和平发展，是一项造福世界各国人民的伟大事业。

The Belt and Road Initiative is intended for promoting multinational economic development through two component plans, the land-based Silk Road Economic Belt and Maritime Silk Road. When Chinese President Xi Jinping visited Central Asia and Southeast Asia in September and October of 2013, he raised the initiative of jointly building the Silk Road Economic Belt and the 21st-Century Maritime Silk Road (hereinafter referred to as the Belt and Road), which have attracted close attention from all over the world. At the China-ASEAN Expo in 2013, the Chinese Premier Li Keqiang emphasized the need to build the Maritime Silk Road oriented toward ASEAN, and to create strategic propellers for hinterland development. Accelerating the Belt and Road can help promote the economic prosperity of the countries along and regional economic cooperation, strengthen exchanges and mutual learning between different civilizations, and promote world peace and development. It is a great undertaking that will benefit people around the world.

（一）共建原则 Principles

恪守联合国宪章的宗旨和原则。遵守和平共处五项原则，即尊重各国主权和领土完整、互不侵犯、互不干涉内政、和平共处、平等互利。

The Belt and Road Initiative is in line with the purposes and principles of the UN Charter. It upholds the Five Principles of Peaceful Coexistence: mutual respect for each other's sovereignty and territorial integrity, mutual non-aggression, mutual non-interference in each other's internal affairs, equality and mutual benefit, and peaceful coexistence.

坚持开放合作。"一带一路"相关的国家基于但不限于古代丝绸之路的范围，各国和国际、地区组织均可参与，让共建成果惠及更广泛的区域。

The Initiative is open for cooperation. It covers, but is not limited to, the area of the ancient Silk Road. It is open to all countries, and international and regional organizations for engagement, so that the results of the concerted efforts will benefit wider areas.

坚持和谐包容。倡导文明宽容，尊重各国发展道路和模式的选择，加强不同文明之间的对话，求同存异、兼容并包、和平共处、共生共荣。

The Initiative is harmonious and inclusive. It advocates tolerance among civilizations, respects the paths and modes of development chosen by different countries, and supports dialogues among different civilizations on the principles of seeking common ground while shelving differences and drawing on each other's strengths, so that all countries can coexist in peace for common prosperity.

坚持市场运作。遵循市场规律和国际通行规则，充分发挥市场在资源配置中的决定性作用和各类企业的主体作用，同时发挥好政府的作用。

The Initiative follows market operation. It will abide by market rules and international norms, give play to the decisive role of the market in resource allocation and the primary role of enterprises, and let the governments perform their due functions.

坚持互利共赢。兼顾各方利益和关切，寻求利益契合点和合作最大公约数，体现各方智慧和创意，各施所长，各尽所能，把各方优势和潜力充分发挥出来。

The Initiative seeks mutual benefit. It accommodates the interests and concerns of all parties involved, and seeks a conjunction of interests and the "biggest common denominator" for cooperation so as to give full play to the wisdom and creativity, strengths and potentials of all parties.

（二）合作重点
Cooperation Priorities

沿线各国资源禀赋各异，经济互补性较强，彼此合作的潜力和空间很大。以政策沟通、设施联通、贸易畅通、资金融通、民心相通为主要内容，在这五方面加强合作。

Countries along the Belt and Road have their own resource advantages and their economies are mutually complementary. Therefore, there is a great potential and space for cooperation. They should promote policy coordination, facilities connectivity, unimpeded trade, financial integration and people-to-people bonds as their five major goals, and strengthen cooperation.

课后练习题
Practice

一、选择题
Multiple-choice

1. 狭义的丝绸之路，是位于中国和（　　）之间的东西方路线。

   The narrow conception of the Silk Road, is an East-West route between China and (　　).

   A. 中国　　B. 南非　　C. 罗马　　D. 韩国
   A. China　　B. South Africa　　C. Rome　　D. South Korea

2. 汉武帝派遣张骞作为使者出使西域两次，并在过程中自长安起，穿过新疆和中亚，以（　　）为终点开辟丝绸之路。

   Emperor Wu of Han dispatched Zhang Qian to the Western Regions twice as his envoy, and in the process pioneered the route known as the Silk Road from

Chang'an, through Xinjiang and Central Asia, and on to (　　).

A. 罗马
A. Rome

B. 地中海东岸
B. The east coast of the Mediterranean Sea

C. 中国
C. China

D. 地中海西岸
D. the west coast of the Mediterranean Sea

3. 丝绸之路的重要性在（　　）达到顶峰。
The height of the importance of the Silk Road was during (　　).

A. 宋朝
A. the Song Dynasty

B. 明朝
B. the Ming Dynasty

C. 唐朝
C. the Tang Dynasty

D. 元朝
D. the Yuan Dynasty

4. 公元前（　　）年，汉武帝派遣张骞作为使者出使西域两次。
From (　　) B.C., Emperor Wu of Han dispatched Zhang Qian to the Western Regions twice as his envoy.

A. 222　　B. 150　　C. 140　　D. 139

5. 共建"一带一路"致力于亚欧非大陆及附近海洋的互联互通，建立和加强沿线各国互联互通伙伴关系，构建全方位、多层次、复合型的互联互通网络，实现沿线各国（　　）的发展。
The Belt and Road Initiative aims to promote the connectivity of Asian, European and African continents and their adjacent seas, establish and strengthen partnerships among the countries along the Belt and Road, set up all-dimensional, multitiered and composite connectivity networks, and realize (　　) in these countries.

A. 自主、平衡、可持续
A. independent, balanced and sustainable development

B. 多元、自主、可持续
B. diversified, independent and sustainable development

C. 平衡、可持续

C. balanced and sustainable development

D. 多元、自主、平衡、可持续

D. diversified, independent, balanced and sustainable development

二、填空题

Fill-in-the-blanks

1. 丝绸之路是自古以来，从 ______ 开始，经 ______ 、西亚进而联结欧洲及北非的这条东西方交通路线的总称。

   The Silk Road is the general name of the East-West transportation route that starts from ____________ and connects Europe and North Africa through ____________ and West Asia since ancient times.

2. “一带一路”倡议是通过 __________ 和 __________ 两个部分来推动跨国经济发展。

   The Silk Road for today is a Chinese framework named One Belt and One Road, which is for organizing multinational economic development through two component plans, ____________ and ____________.

3. 通过海上丝绸之路，______ 和 ______及西方的海上交往日益频繁，既有友好互访，也有物资交流。

   Through the Maritime Silk Road, ______ has frequent increased maritime exchanges with ____________ and the western countries, including friendly visits and material exchanges.

4. 唐代以后，______变成了主要输出商品，深受海外市场青睐。

   Right after the Tang Dynasty, ______ became the main exporting products.

5. “一带一路”共建原则包括：__________、__________、__________、__________。

   The Principles of the Belt and Road Initiative included: __________, __________, __________ and __________.

三、判断题

True or false

1. 丝绸之路的起点一般被认为是开封，其实它随着朝代更替和政治中心转移而变化。西安、洛阳、开封、北京等都曾为丝路起点。

   The starting point of the Silk Road is generally considered to be Kaifeng. In fact, it changed with the change of dynasties and the shift of political center. Xi'an,

Luoyang, Kaifeng and Beijing were all the starting points of the Silk Road.

2. 唐朝延续了南北朝前期发展的兴旺之势，生产发展、海外贸易空前发达。
   The Tang Dynasty, with great development of production and overseas trade, continued the prosperity of the early development of the South and North Dynasties.

3. 不管是陆上丝绸之路还是海上丝绸之路，其实都是东西方经济与文化交流的代名词。
   Both Continental Silk Road and Maritime Silk Road stand for the East-West cultural and economic communication.

4. 广州、泉州、宁波、扬州成为唐朝时期的国际四大贸易港。
   Guangzhou, Quanzhou, Ningbo and Yangzhou became the international four major trade ports in Tang Dynasty.

5. "一带一路"倡议是促进共同发展、实现共同繁荣的合作共赢之路，是增进理解信任、加强全方位交流的和平友谊之路。
   The Belt and Road Initiative is a way for win-win cooperation that promotes common development and prosperity and a road toward peace and friendship by enhancing mutual understanding and trust, and strengthening all-around exchanges.

四、简答题
Short-answer Questions

1. 丝绸之路的路线是什么？
   What's the route of the Silk Road?

   ____

   ____

2. 海上丝绸之路是怎么形成的？
   How did the Maritime Silk Road form?

   ____

   ____

3. 海上丝绸之路的意义是什么？
   What's the significance of the Maritime Silk Road?

   ____

   ____

中国家庭

Chinese Families

课前思考
Lead-in Questions

1. 你在中国参加过婚礼吗？中国的婚礼和你们国家的有什么不同？
   Have you attended a wedding in China? What's the difference between weddings in your country?
2. 为什么中国不再坚持独生子女政策而改变为二孩政策？
   Nowadays, why has China abandoned its one-child policy and begun to carry out the two-child policy?

一、社会变迁中的家庭生活

The Family Concept in Social Change

中国封建社会延续几千年，中国人始终注重家庭观念和家庭关系，并把家庭关系看作是社会关系和人伦秩序的原点。在古代社会，政治、经济、法律和宗教等事务的处理都在家族内进行，强烈的家庭观念深深扎根于中国人的心灵深处，人们把家庭视为生活的依托，家庭不仅是生产、消费单位，也是进行社会活动的中心。

Feudal society in China had continued for thousands of years. The Chinese people have always attached importance to the family concept and family relationships, and regarded family relations as the core of social relations and human relations. In ancient society, the handling of political, economic, legal and religious affairs was carried out within a family. A strong family concept was deeply rooted in the hearts of the Chinese people. People regard the family as the support of life, and the family is not only the unit of production and consumption but also the center of social activities.

（一）中国婚礼
Chinese Wedding

传统的中国婚礼是中国社会中一种隆重的仪式，不仅仅涉及夫妻双方，还关系到双方家庭。

A traditional Chinese wedding is a ceremonial ritual within Chinese societies that involves not only the couple but also the families of both sides.

1. 结婚游行
Wedding Procession

接亲队伍到达前，一位德高望重的老太太会将新娘的头发用棉线束起来。新娘结婚当天通常要穿红色衣服，因为中国人认为红色是吉祥的象征。当接亲队伍到达时，新娘会和她的母亲一同哭泣以表示她对娘家的不舍。接着，新娘将由她的哥哥扶上花轿。至此，结婚游行将从新娘家进行到新郎家，结婚游行包含传统乐队、新娘的花轿、女仆花轿（如果有女仆），以及除了钱财以外的其他嫁妆。嫁妆里通常包含剪刀，因为剪刀像两只蝴蝶，寓意永不分离。

Before the meeting party's arrival, the bride would be helped by a respectable old woman to tie up her hair with colorful cotton threads. She would wear a red skirt because the Chinese believed red symbolizes happiness. When the party arrived, the bride must cry with her mother to symbolize her reluctance to leave home. She would then be led or carried by her elder brother to the sedan. From here, the wedding procession from the bride's home to the groom's home consists of a traditional band, the bride's sedan, the maid of honor's sedans (if there are maids of honor), and bride's dowry in the forms other than money. The most common dowries include scissors which like two butterflies never separating.

2. 迎接新娘
Welcoming the Bride

新娘的家人来到新郎家门口就将止步。新郎在迎亲路上会遇到一系列故意设置的障碍。他只有应对完这些障碍才能看见他未来的妻子。

The wedding procession of the bride's family stops at the door of the groom's home. In the meeting party the groom would meet a series of difficulties intentionally set in his path. Only after coping with these could he pass to see his wife-to-be.

3. 正式的结婚仪式
Formal Wedding Ceremonies

当新娘的花轿抵达婚礼举行的地点，婚礼现场会响起音乐，并燃放烟花爆竹。新娘会在热烈的气氛中被带上红毯。这时，身穿红色衣服的新婚夫妇将向天地、父母和对方行三次叩头礼。接下来，新婚夫妇将进入洞房，而其他宾客将享用盛宴。

On the arrival of the sedan at the wedding place, there would be music and firecrackers. The new couple would be led along the red carpet in a festive atmosphere. The groom, also in a red gown, would kowtow three times with his bride to worship the heaven, parents and spouse. Then, the new couple would go to their bridal chamber and guests would be treated to a feast.

4. 中式婚宴

Wedding Banquets in Chinese Society

在中国，婚宴被称为喜酒，有时候婚宴比结婚仪式还重要。举行婚宴是为了向养育新郎新娘的长辈（如：祖父母、父母、叔叔婶婶等）表达谢意，也是为了让双方的亲戚互相认识。因此，婚宴通常举行得传统而正式。新婚夜晚，有些地方有亲戚朋友闹洞房的习俗。尽管有些吵闹，但会让夫妻双方变得不那么羞怯，彼此更加熟悉。

The wedding banquet is known as joyful wine, and is sometimes far more important than the actual wedding itself. The wedding banquets are a gesture of thanks and appreciation, to those who have raised the bride and groom (such as grandparents, parents and uncles). It also ensures that the relatives on each side meet the relatives on the other side. Thus, wedding banquets are usually done formally and traditionally. On the night of the wedding day, there was a custom in some places for relatives or friends to banter the newlyweds. Though this seemed a little noisy, both of them dropped shyness and got familiar with each other.

5. 现代婚礼的变化

Changes in Modern Chinese Weddings

改革开放以后，中国婚礼经历了几十年的变化，加上西式婚礼的强大冲击，传统婚礼礼仪越来越淡化，没有过去传统婚俗那样繁杂的过程。很多年轻人追求的是中西合璧式的婚礼，讲求浪漫、时尚，而不是在礼仪和礼节上的至臻完美。

Due to the Reform and Opening-up policy, Chinese weddings have undergone decades of changes. With the strong impact of western-style weddings, traditional Chinese wedding etiquette has become more and more diminished, and the complicated process of traditional marriage customs has gradually faded. Many young people are pursuing a wedding combining Chinese styles and western styles, which emphasizes romance, fashion without the perfection of etiquette.

古代婚礼中有“一拜天地、二拜高堂、夫妻对拜”的拜堂仪式，而现代人往往最重视最后一拜，把新人的宣誓仪式作为婚礼的重点。

In ancient weddings, there was a kowtow ceremony of “The first kowtow is for the heaven and earth, the second kowtow is for the parents and the third kowtow is for each other”, while modern people tend to pay the most attention to the last kowtow, and the new couple’s oath ceremony was the focus of the wedding.

"合卺"指的是新婚夫妇在洞房内共饮合欢酒。"卺"是一种瓠瓜,可以做成瓢。在古代,结婚时人们在仪式中把一个瓠瓜剖成两个瓢,新郎新娘各拿一个饮酒。随着时代的变化,婚礼中新郎新娘喝交杯酒这一环节始终存在着,但其形式比古代要简单得多。

"Hejin" means the bride and groom drink the cross-cupped wine in their bridal chamber. "Jin" is a kind of melon, which can be made into a scoop. In ancient times, when a couple got married, people would cut a melon into two scoops at the ceremony, and the bride and groom each took a scoop and drank the wine contained in the scoops. With the changes of time, the bride and groom have a cup and drink, but the form is much simpler than it was in ancient times.

按照结婚习俗,新婚夫妇通常还需要举行结发之礼,即新婚夫妻同坐于床,男左女右,取新婚男女的头发打结,捆绑在一起,结发象征着夫妻永不分离。但后来这一习俗逐渐消失,现代新婚夫妇很少举行这样的仪式。

According to the marriage customs, newly-married couples usually need to knot their hair. Newly-married couples sit in bed, male on the left side and female on the right, and the newly married man and woman's hair would be taken, knotted and tied together, which symbolizes that the husband and wife would never separate. However, this custom has gradually disappeared, and in modern weddings couples rarely hold such etiquette.

现代中国的婚礼结合了中国传统以及西方影响的元素,婚礼上新娘可以穿旗袍,也可以穿白裙婚纱。而且现代婚礼中最重要的一环是拍婚纱照记录新婚的幸福时刻。

The modern Chinese wedding combines the elements of Chinese tradition and western influence. At the wedding, the bride can wear a cheongsam, or a white wedding dress. And the most important part of modern weddings is to take wedding photos to record the happy moments of the wedding.

(二)从"独生子女"政策到"二孩"政策的转变
The Shift from One-child Policy to Two-child Policy

1."独生子女"政策产生的背景
The Background of One-child Policy

中国婴儿死亡率从 1949 年的 227‰下降到 1981 年的 53‰,而中国人的预期寿命却从 1948 年的 35 岁左右急剧增加到 1976 年的 66 岁。20 世纪 60 年代以前，中国政府鼓励家庭尽可能多地生孩子。于是，中国人口从 1949 年的约 5.4 亿猛增到 1976 年的 9.4 亿。直到 1970 年，国家开始鼓励公民延迟结婚，只生两个孩子。

In China infant mortality declined from 227 per thousand births in 1949 to 53 per thousand in 1981, and life expectancy dramatically increased from around 35 years in 1948 to 66 years in 1976. Until the 1960s, the government encouraged families to have as many children as possible. The population grew from around 540 million in 1949 to 940 million in 1976. Beginning in 1970, citizens were encouraged to marry at later ages and have only two children.

尽管生育率开始下降，但是中国政府始终关注着关于人口过剩成为灾难的全球辩题。为了发展国家经济，1978 年，政府开始鼓励一家只生一个孩子，到 1979 年独生子女政策正式宣布。在 20 世纪 80 年代，这项政策又做了一些修改，允许农村父母在一孩是女儿的情况下再生一个小孩。从此以后独生子女政策推行了 30 多年，直到 2015 年才废止。

Although the fertility rate began to decline, the Chinese government observed the global debate over a possible overpopulation catastrophe. It thus began to encourage one-child families in 1978 in order to develop the economy of the country, and then announced in 1979 its intention to advocate for one-child families. It was modified in the mid-1980s to allow rural parents a second child if the first was a daughter. From then on it lasted three more decades before being eliminated at the end of 2015.

2. 独生子女政策的影响
The Influence of One-child Policy

中国的生育限制从 1970 年到 2015 年，大约为中国减少了 5 亿人口，而其中 4 亿人口的减少都要归功于计划生育政策。生育限制也带来了一些意想不到的结果，其中一个结果就是使中国人口老龄化问题日益突出。此外，当第一代独生子女成为父母时，一对夫妇不仅要赡养四个老人，还要抚养一个孩子。所谓的“421”问题就是年轻的夫妇要承受巨大的压力，而年老的一代需要获得退休金和社会福利的支持才能帮助年轻人减轻负担。

China’s fertility restrictions likely averted over 500 million births between 1970 and 2015, with the portion caused by one-child restrictions possibly totaling 400 million. Fertility restrictions also had other unintended consequences, such as the acceleration of the aging of China’s population. Besides, as the first generation of law-enforced only children came of age for becoming parents themselves, one pair of couple were left with having to provide support for their four parents and raise their only child. The so-called “4-2-1 Problem” creates enormous pressure to young couples and the older generation needs support on retirement funds or charity in order to reduce load of the younger generation.

3. 二孩政策的实施

The Implementation of Two-child Policy

2015 年 10 月，中国新闻机构新华社宣布中国政府将废除独生子女政策，允许所有家庭生育两个孩子，“以改善人口的均衡发展”——这显然是为了应对男女比例失调的问题以及人口老龄化的问题。新法律于 2015 年 12 月 27 日在全国人民代表大会常务委员会通过后于 2016 年 1 月 1 日正式生效。改革以后，中国的出生人数在 2016 年短暂回升，2016 年中国妇女生育了 1 786 万名婴儿（是 21 世纪的最高纪录），但是出生率在 2017 年又下降了 3.5%，2017 年新生儿数量是 1 723 万，2018 年为 1 523 万。

In October 2015, the Chinese news agency Xinhua announced plans of the government to abolish the one-child policy, now allowing all families to have two children. This plan helps to improve the balanced development of population to deal

with the country's female-to-male sex ratio and an aging population. The new law took effect on 1 January 2016 after it was passed in the Standing Committee of the National People's Congress on 27 December 2015. After the reform, China saw a short-lived boost in fertility rate for 2016. Chinese women gave birth to 17.86 million babies in 2016 (a record value in the 21st century), but the number of births declined by 3.5% to 17.23 million in 2017, and to 15.23 million in 2018.

（三）中国人的餐桌文化 Chinese Table Culture

民以食为天，中国人的家庭生活离不开餐桌文化。同其他国家的文化一样，在中国，无论是在餐馆还是在家，用餐时也有很多禁忌。适当了解中国的餐桌礼仪，有利于人们入乡随俗，融入当地的生活。有些餐桌礼仪是随着传统延续下来的，绝不能违反。如果不了解这些餐桌礼仪并且破坏了这些规矩，可能会得罪厨师，扫兴而归。

In China, Chinese family life cannot be separated from table culture. The same with any culture, there are rules and customs that surround what is appropriate and what is not when dining, whether it is in a restaurant or in someone's home. Learning the appropriate way to act and what to say will not only help you feel like a native, but will also make those around you more comfortable. The customs surrounding Chinese table manners is ingrained with tradition, and some rules are not to be broken. Failing to understand and follow all of the rules could result in offending the chef and ending the night in an unfavorable way.

1. 座次 Order of Seats

总的来讲，座次是"尚左尊东""面朝大门为尊"。若是圆桌，则正对大门的为主客，主客左右手边的位置，则以离主客的距离来看，越靠近主客位置越尊，相同距离则左侧尊于右侧。若为八仙桌，如果有正对大门的座位，则正对大门一侧的右位为主客。如果不正对大门，则面东的一侧右席为首席。

In general, seating arrangements follow the rule that the seats on the left side and east side are for honored guests. If the table is round, the seat facing the door is the most glorious one. The superiority of the seats to the left and right of the main guest depends on the distance to the main guest. The closer to the main guest, the more superior the seat is. If the distances are the same, the left one is more superior to the right one. As for old-fashioned square table for eight people, if there is a seat directly facing the door, the right one of such seats is for the main guest, if not, the seat on the east is for the most honored guest.

如果为大宴，桌与桌间的排列讲究首席居前居中，左边依次为 2、4、6 席，右边为 3、5、7 席，根据主客身份、地位，亲疏分坐。

In a feast, there is a definite order to arranging tables. The seats for honor should be arranged in the front and in the center, and the second, fourth and sixth tables should be placed on the left while the third, fifth and seventh are on the right. The seats for main guests are varied from their identity, status and closeness.

如果你是主人，你应该提前到达，然后在靠门位置等待，并为来宾引座。如果你是被邀请者，那么就应听从东道主的安排入座。

If you are the host, you should arrive at the banquet hall in advance, then wait for guests at the door and introduce the quests to their seats. If you are an invitee, you should follow the host's arrangement and take a seat.

还有一点需要注意的是，点菜时不应该问服务员菜肴的价格，或是讨价还价，这样会让你在宾客面前显得有点小家子气，而且客人也会觉得不自在。一顿标准的中式大餐，通常先上冷盘，接下来是热炒，随后是主菜，然后上汤，如果感觉吃得有点腻，可以点一些餐后甜品，最后上果盘。

Another point to note is that you should not ask the waiters the dishes' price or bargain with them when you order food, which shows you are not generous in front of guests, and customers will feel uncomfortable. On a standard Chinese meal, usually, the cold dishes will be served firstly, followed by hot dishes, then the main dishes and soup. If guests are tired of the dishes, ordering some dessert is the best way to adjust the taste. Assorted fresh fruit is always the final one.

2. 吃菜

Having a Meal

中国人很讲究吃，同时也很讲究吃相。中餐宴席进餐伊始，服务员送上的第一道湿毛巾是擦手的，不要用它去擦脸。上龙虾、鸡、水果时，会送上一只小小的水盅，其中漂着柠檬片或玫瑰花瓣，它不是饮料，而是洗手用的。洗手时，可两手轮流沾湿指头，轻轻涮洗，然后用小毛巾擦干。

Chinese people are generally very particular about eating, but also very particular about eating manners. At the beginning of the Chinese banquet, the wet towel sent by the waiter firstly is for wiping hands. Don't use it to wipe the face. When lobster, chicken, and fruit are served, the waiter will also serve a small water basin, in which lemon slices or rose petals float. It is not the beverage, but for hand washing. When washing your hands, you should wet your fingers in both hands, gently wash them, and then dry them with a small towel.

用餐时的文明礼貌非常重要。对宾客不要反复劝菜，可向对方介绍菜的特点，吃不吃由他。同时替宾客夹菜也是不礼貌的行为，因为你并不确定他喜不喜欢吃这道菜。如果你是客人，也不要指望主人会反复给你让菜。你要是等别人给自己布菜，那就只好饿肚子。

Good manners are very important when having a meal. It is impolite to urge guests to take the dish or drink, but it is acceptable to introduce the specialty of the dish. Whether the guests eat or not depends on themselves. It is also rude to take a dish for guests, because you are not sure if he likes to eat this dish. If you are a guest, don't expect the owner to pick food for you repeatedly. If you wait for someone to serve you a dish, then you have to stay hungry.

地方频道
Local Channel

（1）北京频道
Beijing Channel

最难拿户口的城市
Cities Where to Get Household Registration Most Hard

根据《中国社会体制改革报告》，中国 10 大最难拿户口的城市为北京市、上海市、三亚市、广州市、深圳市、海口市、天津市、苏州市、青岛市和西安市。

According to the *Report on China's Social System Reform*, the top 10 cities where people get their household registration most hard in China are Beijing, Shanghai, Sanya, Guangzhou, Shenzhen, Haikou, Tianjin, Suzhou, Qingdao and Xi'an.

（2）重庆频道
Chongqing Channel

零彩礼
Zero Bride-price

如今，中国很多地方有送彩礼的习俗，随着经济的发展和生活水平的提高，彩礼也在不断提高。尤其是农村的彩礼一路攀升，特别是一些贫困山区，从最初的几万上涨到十几万，甚至几十万元的屡见不鲜。而重庆是全国彩礼界的一股清流，很多重庆人表示，彩礼并不是必需的。相比彩礼，重庆女性更看重男性有无才华、性格是否合得来、能力强不强、相貌是否端正，以及交往中感觉是否被尊重、是否有幸福感等方面。

Nowadays, many places in China have the custom of giving betrothal gifts by the bridegroom. With the development of economy and the improvement of living standard, the bride-price is also increasing. Especially in rural areas, the bride-price has been rising all the way, in some poor mountainous areas, from tens of thousands at the beginning to more than one hundred thousand, or even hundreds of thousands yuan. Chongqing is a clear stream in the national bride-price industry. Many Chongqing people say that the bride-price is not necessary. Compared with the bride-price, women in Chongqing pay more attention to men's talent, personality, ability, appearance, feeling respected and happiness.

二、中国人的现代生活
The Modern Life of Chinese People

（一）5G 生活
5G Life

5G 技术是移动通信发展的下一步。5G 不仅可以提供语音和数据通信，还可以提供诸如物联网等新技术的能力。5G 不再局限于为语音和数据通信提供更快的移动服务，而是将为垂直行业提供服务，这将促进一种新的服务形式。新的网络技术，如软件定义的网络（SDN）/ 网络功能虚拟化（NFV）将进一步提升 5G 能力，为新的服务 / 企业的蓬勃发展提供一个有效的平台。业内专家解释了 5G 网络功能如何能够提供更快的服务、更少的延迟，并使更多的设备能够连接到全球。5G 基本上融合了所有的无线技术，现有网络——2.5G、3G、4G、LTE 或 Wi-Fi 的融合将会改变我们与世界沟通和互动的方式。

5G technology is the next step in the development of mobile communication. 5G will not only provide voice and data communication but also provide capabilities for new technologies such as Internet of Things. 5G is no longer confined to provide faster mobile services for voice and data communication but instead it will serve vertical industries, which will foster a new form of services. The new networking technologies such as Software Defined Network (SDN)/Network Functions Virtualization (NFV) will further enhance the 5G capability to provide an effective platform for new services/ businesses to flourish. Industry experts explain how 5G network capabilities will allow for faster service, less latency and enable more devices to be connected across the globe. 5G is basically the fusion of all of the wireless technology, and this convergence of existing networks—2.5G, 3G, 4G, LTE or Wi-Fi—will transform the way we communicate and interact with the world.

说起来 5G 技术可能非常深奥，但无论如何，我们至少知道，5G 网络的速度会非常快，预计会比 4G 快上 100 倍，让你可以在一秒钟内下载整部影片。延迟现象（数据开始传送所需的缓冲时间）会大幅减少，也就是说只要一按播放键，影片便会立即开始播放。5G 的网络频宽也会变大很多，让更多使用者可以同时使用网络，也可能让电信服务商不用再限制网络用量。

It seems that 5G technology can be very esoteric, but at least we know that 5G networks are going to be very fast, and 100 times faster than 4G, so you can download the whole movie in a second. Latency, which refers to the amount of time it takes for data to start being transmitted, is greatly reduced, meaning that the movie starts playing as soon as the play button is pressed. 5G's network bandwidth will also be much larger, allowing more users to use the network at the same time, and possibly also allowing telecom service providers to no longer limit the amount of network usage.

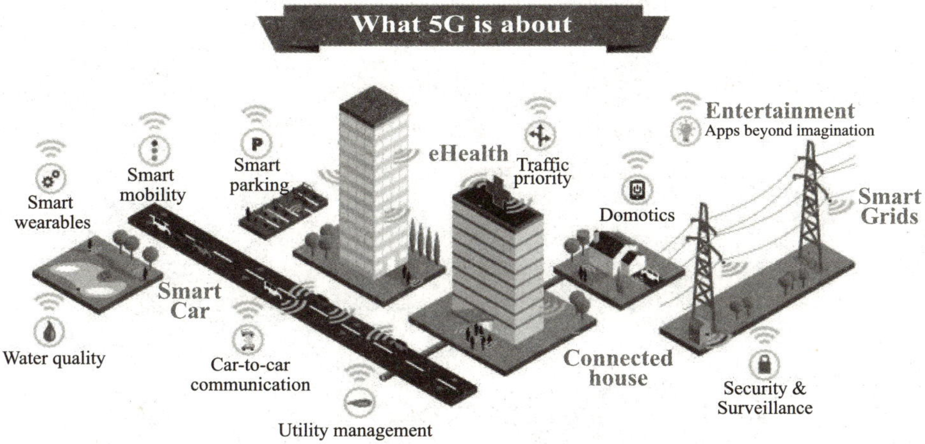

2019 年 4 月，上海已宣布成为中国首个 5G 城市。5G 到来后，中国即将变得万物互联！ 5G 将使物联网更有效、更高效。中国三大电信运营商，在 5G 基础设施上的总投入，在 7 年内预计将达到 1800 亿美元。作为世界最大移动网络运营商的中国移动在 2017 年 3 月份宣布，从 2018 年开始，在主要城市建设试点 5G 网络，并在 2020 年，推出全面的商业服务。中国三大运营商，都在迅速推动 5G 全国覆盖。其中，中国移动很可能在 2021 年实现这一目标。

In April 2019, Shanghai has been announced as China's first 5G city. With 5G coming, China is going to become all things connected. 5G will make the Internet of Things more effective and efficient. China's three major telecom operators are expected to spend $180 billion over seven years on 5G infrastructure. China Mobile, the world's largest mobile network operator, announced in March 2017 that it would build a pilot 5G network in major cities on the Chinese starting in 2018 and launch a comprehensive commercial service in 2020. The Chinese three major operators are all rapidly pushing for nationwide 5G coverage. Among them, China Mobile is likely to achieve this goal in 2021.

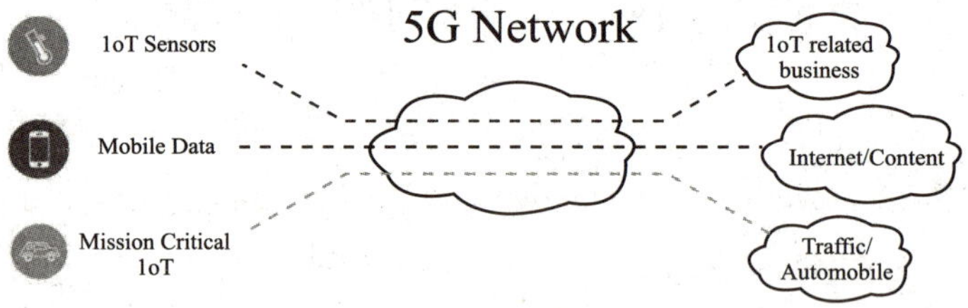

1. 5G 家居：家居方面，原先我们只能在家里遥控的家居，包括空调开关、窗帘开关、除湿器，以后我们出门在外也一样可以做到千里遥控。下班前，手指轻轻一按，扫地机、空调、窗帘就自动在家开始井然有序地工作了。

5G households: In the perspective of households previously, we could only use remote control in our home, including an air conditioner switch, a curtain switch and dehumidifier. In the near future, when we go out, the remote control can realize the same work. Before going off duty, we just need to press the button gently, the sweeper, the air conditioner and the curtain begin orderly working the home functions automatically.

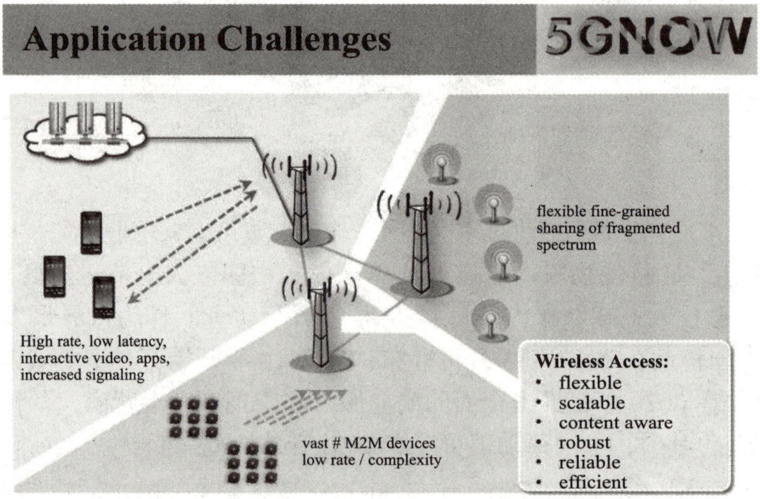

2. 5G 超高清视频会议：超高清视频会议如身临现场，人们相隔万里，也能无障碍“面对面”沟通交流。

5G ultra high definition video conference: as the ultra-high definition video conference is on the spot, people can communicate face to face without barriers even though they are thousands of miles away.

3. 5G AR/VR 全景直播：5G 让高清晰度、高码率的全景直播成为可能。

5G AR/VR panoramic broadcasting: 5G makes it possible to broadcast panoramic broadcasting with high definition and high bit rate.

4. 5G 平安校园：5G 远程教学、5G 夜视无人机校园巡逻等新应用都将在校园内实现，学生的人身安全将得到更加全面的保障。

5G safe campus: 5G remote teaching, 5G night vision drone campus patrol and other new applications will be realized on campus, and students' personal safety will be more comprehensively guaranteed.

5. 5G 远程教学：5G 的引入会颠覆传统教育方式。未来，将能够随时随地地视频学习，学习不再需要以教室为基础系统。同时，在线学习的方式，打破了教育资源的界限，让教育变得更加公平。

5G remote teaching: the introduction of 5G will subvert the traditional way of education. In the near future, video learning will be able to be conducted anytime and anywhere, so that learning no longer needs to be based on the classroom system. At the same time, online learning breaks the boundaries of educational resources and makes education fairer.

6. 5G 远程医疗：5G 能让病人和千里之外的医生直接互动，医生也可以远程操刀。中国已经做了第一场 5G 远程手术，而且非常顺利。这也将打破传统的医疗资源限制，使就医环境更加公平。

5G telemedicine: 5G allows patients to directly interact with doctors thousands of miles away, and doctors can also operate remotely. China has conducted the first 5G telemedicine operation successfully. This will also greatly break the limitation of traditional medical resources and make the medical environment fairer.

7. 5G 自动驾驶：5G 将让自动驾驶顺利实现。

5G autonomous driving: 5G will enable the smooth realization of autonomous driving.

8. 5G 无人机巡线： 5G 将让无人机达到全方位无死角的安防布控。控制人员通过 5G 远程控制无人机摄像头的转向、无人机的飞行状态及路线，进一步追踪锁定目标，实时获得回传高清视频。

5G UAV patrol: 5G will enable the UAV to achieve all-around security control without dead angle. The controller can remotely control the UAV camera's steering, UAV flight status and route through 5G, further track and lock the target, and get the real-time high-definition video being returned.

9. 5G 质量检测： 5G 产品质量云端智能检测，让产品检测更加精准，产品瑕疵的概率大大降低，品质得到充分保证。

5G quality detection: 5G product quality cloud intelligence detection makes product detection more accurate, greatly reduces the probability of product defects, and fully guarantees the quality.

（二）微信
WeChat

微信是中国腾讯公司研发的一款集通信、社交、移动支付为一体的多功能手机应用。它于 2011 年首次发布，到 2018 年，按每月活跃用户计算，它是世界上最大的独立移动应用程序之一，每月活跃用户超过 10 亿。《福布斯》称其为全球最强大的应用程序之一，因其功能和平台广泛，被称为中国的“万能应用”和“超级应用”。

WeChat (literally: “micro-message”) is a Chinese multi-purpose messaging, social media and mobile payment app developed by Tencent. It was first released in 2011, and by 2018 it was one of the world's largest standalone mobile apps by monthly active users, with over 1 billion monthly active users. Described as one of the world's most powerful apps by *Forbes*, it is also known as China's “app for everything” and a “super app” because of its wide range of functions and platforms.

1. 发送消息

Messaging

微信提供文本消息、语音消息、群聊（一对多）、视频电话和会议、视频游戏、发送照片和视频以及位置共享。可以通过蓝牙与附近的人取得联系，如果人们愿意，还可按照条件随机搜索朋友。照片也可以经微信的滤镜和字幕功能加以修饰，文字可使用自动翻译服务。

WeChat provides text messaging, hold-to-talk voice messaging, broadcast (one-to-many) messaging, video calls and conferencing, video games, sharing of photographs and videos, and location sharing. It can exchange contacts with people nearby via Bluetooth, as well as providing various features for contacting people at random if desired (if people are open to it). Photographs may also be embellished with filters and captions, and an automatic translation service is available.

微信用户可以注册公众号，这样他们就可以向订阅者推送新闻，与订阅者互动，并为他们提供服务。公众号有三种类型：服务号、订阅号和企业号。一旦用户作为个人或组织设置了一种类型的账号，他们就不能将其更改为另一种类型。截至 2014 年底，微信官方账号已达 800 万个。组织创建的公众号可申请验证（费用为 300 元人民币或约 45 美元）。公众号可以作为医院预挂号、签证续签、信用卡等服务的平台。

WeChat users can register as an official account, which enables them to push feeds to subscribers, interact with subscribers and provide them with services. There are three types of official accounts: a service account, a subscription account and an enterprise account. Once users such as individuals or organizations set up a type of account, they cannot change it to another type. By the end of 2014, the number of WeChat official accounts had reached 8 million. Official accounts of organizations can apply to be verified (cost 300 RMB or about USD $45). Official accounts can be used as a platform for services such as hospital preregistrations, visa renewal or credit card service.

2. 朋友圈

Moments

“朋友圈”是微信社交平台上用于好友更新状态的栏目。朋友圈允许用户发布图片、文字、评论、分享音乐、分享文章和点“赞”。2017 年，微信的政策是每天最多给用户的朋友圈投放两个广告。

“Moments” is WeChat’s brand name for its social feed of friend updates. Moments allows users to post images, post text, post comments, share music, share articles and post "likes". In 2017 WeChat had a policy of a maximum of two advertisements per day per user.

3. 微信支付
WeChat Pay

在中国，只要提供银行账户信息，用户就可以使用微信支付账单、订购商品和服务，以及向其他用户转账。如果商店可提供微信支付，还可以在商店付款。微信支付是一项整合到微信中的数字钱包服务，它允许用户进行移动支付，并在联系人之间互相转账。截至 2016 年 3 月，微信支付拥有超过 3 亿用户。据报道，大约 80% 的微信用户尝试过支付服务。

In China, users who have provided bank account information may use the app to pay bills, order goods and services, transfer money to other users, and pay in stores if the stores have WeChat option. WeChat Pay is a digital wallet service incorporated into WeChat, which allows users to perform mobile payments and send money between contacts. By March 2016, WeChat Pay had over 300 million users. It has been reported that about 80 percent of WeChat users have tried the payment services.

2014 年春节期间，微信推出了虚拟红包分发功能，模仿中国传统节日期间朋友和家人之间互送红包的习俗。该功能允许用户将钱作为礼物发送给好友和群组。发红包时，这些钱（"压岁钱"）可以平均分配给好友，也可以随机分配给好友。这一功能是在中国中央电视台万众瞩目的春节联欢晚会期间推出，在晚会邀请观众在直播过程中摇一摇手机，以获得抢红包的机会。红包功能显著增加了对微信支付的使用。2016 年，春节期间共发送了 32 亿个红包，仅在除夕夜当晚就发送了 40.9 万个。

In 2014 for Chinese New Year, WeChat introduced a feature for distributing virtual red envelopes, modelled after the Chinese tradition of exchanging packets of money among friends and family members during holidays. The feature allows users to send money to contacts and groups as gifts. When sent to groups, the money is distributed equally, or in random shares ("Lucky Money"). The feature was launched through a promotion during China Central Television's heavily watched New Year's Gala, where viewers were instructed to shake their phones during the broadcast for a chance to win sponsored cash prizes from red envelopes. The red envelope feature significantly increased the adoption of WeChat Pay. In 2016, 3.2 billion red envelopes were sent over the holiday period, and 409,000 alone were sent on the eve of Chinese New Year.

2017 年，腾讯报告称，微信已经超过阿里巴巴，拥有 6 亿活跃的微信移动支付用户，而阿里巴巴的支付宝拥有 4. 5 亿活跃用户。然而，2017 年阿里巴巴在中国移动在线支付市场的份额为 54%，而微信的份额为 37%。同年，腾讯推出了“香港微信支付”，这是一款面向香港用户的支付服务，交易以港元进行。

In 2017 Tencent reported that WeChat had overtaken Alibaba with 600 million active WeChat mobile payment users versus 450 million for Alibaba's Alipay. However, Alibaba had a 54 per cent share of the Chinese mobile online payments market in 2017 compared to WeChat's 37 per cent share. In the same year, Tencent introduced "WeChat Pay HK", a payment service for users in Hong Kong. Transactions are carried out with Hong Kong dollar.

4. 城市服务

City Services

2015 年，微信在北京、上海、广州、深圳等 27 个城市推出了城市服务功能。城市服务包括预约医生、支付电费或交通罚款，以及预订交通工具。

In 2015 WeChat launched the City Services feature in 27 cities across China, including Beijing, Shanghai, Guangzhou and Shenzhen. City Services included booking doctor appointments, paying electricity fees or traffic fines, and booking transportation.

2017 年，微信推出了一项名为“迷你程序”的功能。企业主可以使用专有应用程序界面在微信系统中创建小型应用程序。用户只要在微信应用程序中安装这些程序即可。2018 年 1 月，微信宣布了创纪录的 58 万个微型程序即小程序。有了微信小程序后，微信游戏大受欢迎，其“Jump Jump”游戏在不到 3 天的时间内就吸引了 4 亿玩家，仅两周时间内就获得了 1 亿的每日活跃用户。到目前为止，微信小程序允许用户在不下载微博、小红书、腾讯游戏等其他社交媒体应用和游戏应用的情况下访问这些应用，提高了可访问性和便利性。

In 2017, WeChat launched a feature called “Mini Programs”. Business owners can create mini apps in the WeChat system, with JavaScript and a proprietary API. Users may install these inside the WeChat app. In January 2018, WeChat announced a record of 580,000 Mini Programs. After the birth of WeChat Mini Program, WeChat Games have received huge popularity, with its “Jump Jump” game attracting 400 million players in less than 3 days and attaining 100 million daily active users in just two weeks after its launch. Up to now, the WeChat Mini Program allows user to access other social media apps and game apps such as Weibo, RED, Tencent Games, and many others without downloading them on the phone, which improves accessibility and convenience.

（三）支付宝

Alipay

支付宝于 2004 年推出，是一个建立在第三方托管系统上的在线支付平台，是在淘宝进行交易的首选支付方案，也是在中国使用最广泛的第三方在线支付解决方案。为了确保交易安全，支付宝使用第三方托管系统，只有在买家收到满意的商品后，支付宝才会向卖家支付款项。阿里巴巴集团网站称，支付宝与多家金融机构以及维萨和万事达合作，为中国和海外的支付提供便利。

Launched in 2004, Alipay, an escrow-based online payment platform, is the preferred payment solution for transactions on Taobao Marketplace. It is the most widely used third-party online payment solution in China. To ensure safe transactions, Alipay uses an escrow system through which payment is only released to the seller once the buyer has received his or her goods in satisfactory condition. According to the Alibaba Group website, Alipay is partnered with multiple financial institutions as well as Visa and MasterCard to facilitate payments in China and abroad.

三、中国人的业余生活
The Spare Time of Chinese People

1. 广场舞
Square Fitness Dance

广场健身舞蹈源于社会生活，产生于人民群众之中，群众是广场健身舞的创作者和表演者。人民群众不仅创造了广场健身舞蹈，而且发展了中老年广场健身舞，使这一民间艺术之花深深扎根于广大群众的社会生活之中。

Square fitness dance originates from social life and comes from the masses, who are the creators and performers of square fitness dance. The people not only created square fitness dance, but also developed square fitness dance for middle-aged and elderly people, making this unfailing flower of folk art deeply rooted in the social life of the masses.

广场舞具有体育锻炼的价值，经常进行练习，心血管和呼吸系统都能得到良好的锻炼，可以改善心肺功能，加速新陈代谢过程，促进消化，消除大脑疲劳和精神紧张，从而达到增强体质、增进健康、延缓衰退、提高人体的活动能力等良好的健身作用。广场舞还可以调节情绪、调节生活、调节人际关系，使人们的文化生活更加充实。

With the value of physical exercise, regular square dance practice can adjust the cardiovascular and respiratory system, improve cardiopulmonary functions, accelerate the metabolism process, promote digestion, eliminate brain fatigue and mental stress, so as to achieve the goal of enhancing physique, improving health, slowing decline, increasing the ability of human activities and other good fitness functions. Square dance can also adjust emotions, life and interpersonal relations, so that people's cultural life could be more colorful.

2. 麻将

Mahjong

麻将是一个基于麻将牌的游戏。自中国清朝时期开始发展，至 20 世纪初已传遍世界。它通常由四个人玩（在日本、韩国和东南亚有一些三人版本）。麻将是一种技巧、策略和计算的游戏，涉及一定程度的运气。

Mahjong is a tile-based game that was developed in China during the Qing Dynasty and has spread throughout the world since the early 20th century. It is commonly played by four players (with some three-player variations found in Japan, the Republic of Korea and Southeast Asia). Mahjong is a game of skill, strategy, calculation and involves a degree of luck.

麻将玩法种类繁多，中国麻将的玩法大致分为：广东麻将、杭州麻将、南昌麻将、营口麻将、贵州麻将、江南麻将、台湾麻将、合肥麻将、成都麻将、四川麻将等。多样的玩法、极高的娱乐性和互动性，使麻将成为家喻户晓的娱乐活动，被称为民间“国粹”。麻将不仅具有独特的游戏特点，而且是集益智性、趣味性、博弈性于一体的运动，魅力及内涵丰富、底蕴悠长。

There are many kinds of mahjong playing methods, including Guangdong mahjong, Hangzhou mahjong, Nanchang mahjong, Yingkou mahjong, Guizhou mahjong, Jiangnan mahjong, Taiwan mahjong, Hefei mahjong, Chengdu mahjong and Sichuan mahjong. They contain various playing methods, extremely high entertainment and interactivity which made mahjong become a household entertainment activity, known as the folk “quintessence”. Mahjong is not only a game, but also a sport, getting mathematics, enjoyment, gambling, and altogether with a rich charm, connotation and long heritage.

课后练习题

Practice

一、选择题

Multiple-choice

1. 古代婚礼中有“一拜天地、二拜高堂、夫妻对拜”的拜堂仪式，而现代人最重视哪一拜？（　　）

In ancient weddings, there was a kowtow ceremony of "The first kowtow is for the heaven and earth, the second kowtow is for the parents and the third kowtow is for each other". Which kowtow do modern people value most?

A. 最后一次 B. 第一次 C. 不知道 D. 都重视
A. the last B. the first C. unclear D. all

2. 下面二孩政策实施的目的不包括哪一项？（ ）
The purpose of the implementation of the two-child policy does not include ( ).

A. 改善人口的均衡发展
A. to improve the balanced development of population

B. 调节男女比例的问题
B. to adjust the ratio of male to female

C. 解决“421”问题
C. to solve the "421" problem

D. 使中国人口老龄化问题日益突出
D. to accelerate the aging of China's population

3. 若为八仙桌，如果有正对大门的座位，则正对大门一侧的______为主客。如果不正对大门，则面______的一侧右席为首席。
As for old-fashioned square table for eight people, if there is a seat directly facing the door, the ______ one of such seats is for the main guest, if not, the seat on the ______ is for the most honored guest.

A. 右；东 B. 东；右 C. 左；右 D. 左；东
A. right; east B. east; right C. left; right D. left; east

4. 2019 年 4 月，（ ）已宣布成为中国首个 5G 城市。
In April 2019, which city has been announced as China's first 5G city?

A. 北京 B. 上海 C. 广州 D. 天津
A. Beijing B. Shanghai C. Guangzhou D. Tianjin

5. 民间的“国粹”是什么？（ ）
What's the folk "quintessence"?

A. 熊猫
A. Panda

B. 麻将
B. Mahjong

C. 广场舞
C. The Square Dance

D.《红楼梦》
D. *The Dream of Red Mansion*

二、填空题
Fill-in-the-blanks

1. 取新婚男女的头发打结，捆绑在一起，结发象征着________________。
The newly married man and woman's hair would be taken, knotted and tied together, which symbolizes that ______________________.

2. 从 1978 年，政府开始鼓励一家只生一个小孩，到 1979 年独生子女政策正式宣布是为了______________。
It thus began to encourage one-child families in 1978 in order to develop the economy of the country, and then announced in 1979 its intention to advocate for one-child families, due to ____________________.

3. 座位安排的规则是____________________。
The seating arrangement follows the rule that _______________________.

4. 5G 不仅可以提供语音和_____，还可以提供诸如_____等新技术的能力。
5G will not only provide voice and __________ but also provide capabilities for new technologies such as__________.

5. 广场健身舞蹈源于 _______，产生于_______之中，群众是广场健身舞的_____和_____。
Square fitness dance originates from _______ and comes from _______, who are the _______ and _______ of square fitness dance.

三、判断题
True or False

1. 2018 年，按每月活跃用户计算，微信是世界上最大的独立移动应用程序之一。
In 2018, WeChat was one of the world's largest standalone mobile apps by monthly active users.

2. 若是圆桌，则正对大门的为主客，主客左右手边的位置，则以离主客的距离来看，越靠近主客位置越尊，相同距离则右侧尊于左侧。
   The seat facing the door is the most glorious one, if the table is round. The superiority of the seats to the left and right of the main guest depends on the distance to the main guest. The closer to the main guest, the more superior the seat is. If the distances are the same, the right one is more superior to the left one.

3. 5G 仅局限于为语音和数据通信提供更快的移动服务。
   5G is confined to provide faster mobile services for voice and data communication.

4. 5G 网络的速度预计会比 4G 快上 200 倍。
   5G networks are going to be 200 times faster than 4G.

5. 麻将全是靠经常性的练习、精准的计算和娴熟的牌技。
   Mahjong is totally about practice, precision, and proficiency.

四、简答题

Short-answer Questions

1. 5G 在生活中的运用有哪些？
   What are the applications of 5G in life?

   ____

   ____

2. 什么是"朋友圈"？
   What is "Moments"?

   ____

   ____

3. 微信用户可以注册的公众号类型是哪三种？
   What are the three types of official accounts that WeChat users can register?

   ____

   ____

第四章

中国的教育

Chinese Education

课前思考

Lead-in Questions

1. 哪一个制度是中国历史上持续时间最长的选拔人才制度？

   Which system is the longest-term system used to select talents in Chinese history?

2. 你们国家需要读几年小学、几年中学？需要参加考试才能读大学吗？

   How many years do you spend on your primary school and secondary school? Do you need to join in the examinations before entering university?

一、中国传统教育

Chinese Traditional Education

（一）科举制度

The Imperial Civil Examination System

科举是通过考试选拔官吏的制度，由于采用分科取士的办法，所以叫作科举。科举制度是中国历史上用于选拔人才延续时间最长的制度。从隋炀帝大业元年（605 年）进士科的创设，到清光绪三十一年（1905 年）废除科举，科举制在中国历史上存在 1 300 年之久。

The Imperial Civil Examination System is an examination system with the purpose of selecting civil servants based on the subjects. The Imperial Civil Examination System is the longest-term system used to select talents in Chinese history, originating from the Chin-shih system in 605 during the reign of Emperor Yang of Sui. In that system, successful candidates would be admitted to the public servant division of the country. The system was abolished by Emperor Guangxu in 1905, and it lasted for 1,300 years.

科举考试最早起源于隋朝，隋朝统一全国后，隋文帝为了适应封建经济的发展和加强中央集权，废除魏晋以来的“九品中正制”，把选拔官吏的权力收归中央，开始采用分科考试的方式选拔官员。大业年间（605—617年），隋炀帝设置明经、进士两科，标志着科举制正式诞生。

The Imperial Civil Examination System dates back to Sui Dynasty, when Emperor Wen of Sui adapted the examination to select public officials after abolishing the "Nine Rank Judging System", the power of selecting officials was transferred to the Central Government, and officials were selected by means of separate examination during Wei Dynasty and Jin Dynasty. The new system was expected to boost economy and enhance central power of emperors. From 605 to 617, Emperor Yang of Sui set two categories, namely, Mingjing and Jinshi, which symbolized the formal establishment of the Imperial Civil Examination System.

宋代的科举放宽了录取的范围。宋代进士分为三等：一等称进士及第，二等称进士出身，三等赐同进士出身。由于扩大了录取范围，名额也成倍增加。

宋朝确立了三年一次的三级考试。宋初科举，仅有两级考试。一级是由各州举行的取解试，另一级是礼部举行的省试。宋太祖为了选拔真正有才干的人担任官职，于开宝六年实行殿试。自此以后，殿试成为科举制度的最高一级的考试，并正式确立了州试、省试和殿试的三级科举考试。

The Imperial Civil Examination in the Song Dynasty reduced the admission requirements. In the Song Dynasty, Jinshi was divided into three categories: first-class scholars, second-class scholars, third-class scholars. Due to the expansion of the admission, the number of learners admitted has also increased exponentially.

The Song Dynasty established a three-year third-level examination. At the beginning of the Song Dynasty, there were only two levels of examinations. The one level is the deliberation test held by the states, and the other level is the provincial test held by the Ministry of Rites. In order to select a truly talented person as an official, Song Taizu practiced the palace test in the sixth year of Kaibao. Since then, the palace test has become the highest level of examination in the Imperial Civil Examination System, and officially established the three-level examinations for the state, provincial and palace examinations.

19 世纪 80 年代后，随着西学的传播和洋务运动的发展，科举制度发生了改变。1888 年，清政府准设算学科取士，首次将自然科学纳入考试内容。1898 年，加设经济特科。同时，应康有为等人的建议，废八股文改试策论，以时务策命题，严禁凭楷法优劣定高下。戊戌变法失败后，慈禧下令所有考试悉照旧制。

1901 年 9 月清廷实行“新政”后，各地官员纷纷上奏，重提改革科举，恢复经济特科，因为科举成为人们向往的能通往功名利禄的途径，而新式学校难以发展，因此清廷诏准袁世凯、张之洞所奏，将育人、取才合于学校一途。至此，在中国历史上延续了 1 300 多年的科举制度最终被废除，科举取士与学校教育实现了彻底分离。

After the 1880s, with the spread of western studies and the development of the Westernization Movement, the Imperial Civil Examination System was changed. In 1888, the Qing government approved the calculate discipline to take the examination, and for the first time included the natural sciences into the examination content. In 1898, an economic special section was added. At the same time, Kang Youwei and other scholars suggested abolishing eight shares of the text to begin the discourse on politics. After the failure of the Reform Movement of 1898, the Empress Dowager ordered all the examinations to take its older form.

After the “New Deal” was implemented in the Qing court in September 1901, the Officials from different places of China played on it, revisiting the reform of the imperial examinations and restoring the economic specialties. Because the imperial examinations became the way for people to gain the fame and fortune, the new schools were difficult to develop, so the Qing court Yuan Shikai and Zhang Zhidong applied to combine school and examinations together. At this point, the Imperial Civil Examination System, which lasted more than 1,300 years in Chinese history, was finally abolished, and the imperial examinations and school education were completely separated.

科举制度与之前的选拔人才制度相比，具有相对公平公正公开的优点，打破了关于选拔的出身限制，是我国选拔人才制度上的巨大进步，主要有以下方面的影响。

首先是对于社会和国家而言，科举制度大大拓宽了选拔人才的基础，为选人任人开辟了空间，使拥有才识的读书人有机会进入各级政府任职，促进了国家的发展，减少了社会等级矛盾激化的可能。科举制使用功读书的风气盛行，促进了教育事业、文化艺术事业的发展，留下了灿烂的文化遗产。

Compared with previous selecting systems, the Imperial Civil Examination System promoted equality better, regardless of the family backgrounds and other factors of participants. The system marks made great progress in the history of selecting talented people.

First of all, the system was helping to recruit more competent participants of various social backgrounds. Besides, it enabled learners with knowledge and virtues to work in government and in turn make contributions to society as a whole. Since the system was not a biased one, it reduced the conflicts caused by low mobility of social class. Because of the importance attached to education in the system, people in the society studied hard. As a result, the culture and arts prospered.

我国的科举制度从宋元以后外传越南、日本、韩国、朝鲜等国，这些国家都较长时间仿照中国推行过科举制度；16 至 17 世纪，欧洲传教士在中国了解了科举取士制度，在他们的游记中把它介绍到欧洲。18 世纪时启蒙运动中，不少英国和法国思想家都推崇中国这种公平和公正的制度。西方现代的文官选拔制度、我国现代的教育制度和干部选拔制度都是对中国科举制度的继承和发展。西方人将中国的科举制度称为“中国第五大发明”。它无疑对中华民族，对全人类都是一个了不起的贡献。

The system not only impacted China, but also influenced its neighboring countries including Vietnam, Japan, South Korea and the Democratic People's Republic of Korea, which promoted the system within their own borders. Some western preachers in China of the 16th to 17th century introduced the system to their home countries through their travel journals. In the 18th century during the Enlightenment Movement, many French and English greater minds praised the system as a fair and impartial system. The western modern civil service selection system, China's modern education system and cadre selection system were inheritance and development of Chinese Imperial Examination System. Westerners used to call the system “the Fifth Great Invention of China”. There is no doubt that the system led to the progress of the society and the world.

科举制度也存在不足。由于单一的形式和考试内容，科举制度也有负面影响。由明代开始，科举的考试内容陷入僵化，变成只要求考生能造出合乎形式的文章，反而不注重考生的实际学识。大部分读书人为应对科考，思想渐被四书五经、迂腐的八股文所束缚；无论是眼界、创造能力还是独立思考能力都被大大限制，导致从事科学技术研究的人才力量相对薄弱。

考试形式单一固定，考中实在不容易，导致许多人费尽心机，不择手段，这就不利于国家建立一个公正、公平、公开的良好社会制度，造成了官场的黑暗和社会的混乱。

The negative influence of the Imperial Civil Examination System was caused by its rigid form and testing content. From the beginning of the Ming Dynasty, the examination did not test participants' actual competency. It only focused on a standard answer. To succeed in the exam with high scores, participants spent all their time on rote learning, reciting poems and classics without actual understanding and reflective thinking, which in turn constrained the development of their intelligence and horizons. Furthermore, the system failed to encourage the development of science among participants.

Due to the rigid structure of the examination, it was extremely difficult for participants to stand out. As a result, some participants resorted to bribery and cheating, which made the examination less equal and caused chaos in society.

（二）四大书院
Four Major Academies

由于国家的逐步统一和安定，而且读书成为获取功名的途径，书院逐渐兴盛起来，成为我国古代教育的一种特殊形式。书院有点类似于今天的私立大学，最有名的是四大书院。

The academy has gradually prospered and became a special form of ancient education in China, due to the gradual unification and stability of the country, as well as reading becoming a way to obtain fame. The academy was a bit like today's private university. The most famous ones are "Four Major Academies".

中国古代四大书院，即应天书院、岳麓书院、白鹿洞书院、嵩阳书院。

The Four Major Academies in ancient China were Yingtian Academy, Yuelu Academy, Bailudong Academy, and Songyang Academy.

1. 应天书院
Yingtian Academy

应天书院又名睢阳书院、应天府书院，是我国北宋时期的最高学府。大文学家范仲淹曾在此求学、执教达八年之久。现在的应天书院坐落在商丘古城南湖湖畔。

Yingtian Academy is also known as Chuyang Academy. Yingtian Academy was the highest institution of learning in Northern Song Dynasty. Great literateur, Fan Zhongyan had studied and taught here for nearly 8 years. The present Yingtian Academy is located on the bank of Nanhu Lake in the ancient city of Shangqiu.

2. 岳麓书院

Yuelu Academy

岳麓书院位于湖南省长沙市湘江西岸秀丽的岳麓山下，创建于北宋开宝九年（976 年），历经宋、元、明、清，一直绵延办学，历时千年，弦歌不绝，世称“千年学府”。2009 年岳麓书院开始招收历史学本科生。今天的岳麓书院已经形成从学士、硕士、博士到博士后科研流动站的办学格局，传承和弘扬中华文化。

Yuelu Academy is located at the beautiful Yuelu Mountain on the west bank of Xiangjiang River in Changsha City, and was founded in the Northern Song Dynasty in the ninth year (976 A.D.). It has been running for a long time through Song, Yuan, Ming and Qing Dynasties. It lasted for a thousand years. So it is called the “Millennium School”. In 2009, it began to enroll undergraduate students majoring in history. Today Yuelu Academy has formed a school-running pattern from bachelor’s, master’s, doctoral to post-doctoral research stations, and carries forward the Chinese culture.

3. 白鹿洞书院

Bailudong Academy

白鹿洞书院位于江西省九江市，享有“海内第一书院”的赞誉。因为南宋著名学者朱熹的关系，白鹿书院影响后世几百年。清嘉庆后，白鹿洞书院日益衰败，失去了文化中心的地位。新中国成立后白鹿洞书院得到了很好的维护，如今已成为江西省的著名旅游景点。

The Bailudong Academy is located in Jiujiang, Jangxi province. It enjoys the praise of "the First Academy in China". Because it had strong connection with scholar Zhu Xi in Southern Song Dynasty, Bailudong Academy influenced the later generations for hundreds of years. After the Emperor Jiaqing, it became increasingly declining and lost its status as a cultural center. The Bailudong Academy was well maintained and now it became a famous tourist attraction in Jiangxi, after the founding of the People's Republic of China.

4. 嵩阳书院

Songyang Academy

嵩阳书院位于河南省，坐落在嵩山之阳。嵩阳书院从五代后唐清泰元年（934年）已经成为读书人文化活动的教育场所，距今已经有 1 085 年的历史。宋朝1035 年，皇帝赐名嵩阳书院。宋代理学的“洛学”创始人程颢、程颐兄弟都曾在嵩阳书院讲学，此后，嵩阳书院成为宋代理学的发源地之一。

Songyang Academy is located in the south of Mount Song, Henan Province. It has become a place for scholars to carry out cultural activities since the later Tang Dynasty (in 934). It already was 1,085 years old. In 1035, the emperor gave the name to the Songyang Academy. Cheng Hao and his brother Cheng Yi, the most famous scholars of the Song Dynasty, had lectured at the Songyang Academy. Since then, the Songyang Academy has become one of the birthplaces of rationalistic Confucianism of the Song Dynasty.

二、当代中国教育
Chinese Contemporary Education

（一）九年义务教育制度
The Nine-year Compulsory Education System

义务教育又称免费教育，是根据宪法规定，适龄儿童和青少年都必须接受，国家、社会、家庭都必须予以保证的国民教育。义务教育具有强制性、免费性、普及性的基本特点。实施九年义务教育，就是适龄儿童、少年开始接受教育的九年不收学费、杂费。九年义务教育制度是我国现行的教育制度。

Compulsory education, also known as free education, is a national education that must be accepted by school-age children and adolescents according to the constitution, and must be guaranteed by the state, society and family. Compulsory education has the basic characteristics of compulsory, free and universal. The implementation of nine-year compulsory education means that school-age children and adolescents will not pay tuition fees and miscellaneous fees for nine years. The current education system in China is the nine-year compulsory education system.

根据2006年6月由中华人民共和国全国人民代表大会常务委员会修订通过的《中华人民共和国义务教育法》（简称《义务教育法》），凡具有中华人民共和国国籍的适龄儿童、少年，不分性别、民族、种族、家庭财产状况、宗教信仰等，依法享有平等接受义务教育的权利，并履行接受义务教育的义务。该制度从1986年7月1号开始施行。

According to "The Compulsory Education Law of the People's Republic of China" (hereinafter referred to as "The Compulsory Education Law"), which was amended and passed by the Standing Committee of the National People's Congress in June 2006, all school-age children and adolescents who own the nationality of the People's Republic of China, regardless of gender, nation, ethnicity, or family property status, religious beliefs, etc, have the right to accept compulsory education on an equal footing and fulfill the obligation to accept it. The system was implemented on July 1, 1986.

《义务教育法》确认并保障适龄儿童、少年接受义务教育的各项权利，包括入学的权利、接受规定年限教育的权利、就近入学的权利、免交学费的权利等。

"The Compulsory Education Law" recognizes and guarantees the rights of school-age children and adolescents to receive compulsory education, including right to enroll, right to receive education for a prescribed period, right to be admitted to the neighborhood school, and right to have free tuition, ect.

（二）高考制度
The National College Entrance Examination

高考，一般指高等教育入学考试，现有普通高校招生考试、自学考试和成人高考三种形式。它是对中国学生高中三年学业水平的一次总结，是一种相对公正、公平、公开的人才选拔形式。以此次成绩为依据，国家按照学习能力的差异将学生分进与其自身学习能力相当的学府。高考是考生选择大学和进入大学的资格标准，也是国家教育考试之一。每年 6 月 7 日、6 月 8 日为考试日，部分省区高考时间为 3 天。

"Gaokao", the college entrance examination for China's high school students, generally refers to the entrance examination for higher education, and there are three forms of admission examinations for colleges and universities: national college entrance examination and self-study exams and the national higher education exams for self-taught adults. It is a summary of the three-year academic level of Chinese students in high school. It is a relatively fair, equitable and open method of talent selection. Based on their grades of the exam, the state distributes students into institutions equivalent to their own learning ability. The college entrance examination is a qualification for candidates to choose and enter a university. It is also one of the national education exams. Gaokao takes place on June 7th and June 8th each year, and some provinces and districts have three days for it.

2018 年 11 月，江苏、湖北、福建、辽宁、广东、重庆、河北、湖南八个省（市）经教育部评估，达到新高考启动条件，被批准启动。新高考改革主要体现在学生的选科和录取形式上，不再分文理科，而是实施“3+1+2”模式：“3”为全国统考科目语文、数学、外语，所有学生必考；“1”为首选科目，考生须在高中学业水平考试的物理、历史科目中选择一科；“2”为再选科目，考生可在化学、生物、思想政治、地理四个科目中选择两科。

In November 2018, Eight provinces (cities), including Jiangsu, Hubei, Fujian, Liaoning, Guangdong, Chongqing, Hebei, and Hunan, were evaluated by the Ministry of Education to meet the conditions for the start of the new college entrance examination and were approved for initiation. The reform of the new college entrance examination is mainly reflected in the selection of students and the form of admission. Instead of dividing the Arts and Sciences, it implements the “3+1+2” model: “3” refers to Chinese, mathematics, and foreign language, which are compulsory examination subjects; “1” is the preferred subject. Candidates must choose one subject between physical and historical subjects; “2” is the re-selected subject. Candidates can choose two subjects among the four subjects: chemistry, biology, ideological politics and geography.

从 2021 年起，普通高校将依据 3 门全国统考科目成绩和 3 门普通高中学业水平选考科目成绩，参考普通高中学生综合素质评价，择优录取学生，即通常所说的“两依据、一参考”。

Starting from 2021, ordinary colleges and universities will select students according to the scores of 3 national unified examination subjects and 3 general high school level examination subjects, and refer to the comprehensive quality evaluation of ordinary high school students, which is commonly referred to as “two basis, one reference”.

自 1977 年恢复高考以来，我国对于高考所做的改革从未停止。从全国统一试卷到全国多份试卷，从单一选拔到多元录取，回溯这 43 年间的高考制度，一直在争议中变革和前行。新世纪高考改革的各项思路已逐渐清晰，一项更为全方位、系统的高考改革正在渐次展开。

Since the resumption of the college entrance examination in 1977, China’s reforms to the college entrance examination have never stopped, from the national unified test papers to multiple national examination papers, from single selection to multiple admissions in the past 43 years; it has been changing and moving forward in controversy. The ideas of the college entrance examination reform in the new century have gradually become clear, and a more comprehensive and systematic college entrance examination reform is gradually unfolding.

此外，针对听力残疾考生，经申请批准后可免除外语听力考试。免除外语听力考试考生的外语科成绩，按“笔试成绩 × 外语科总分值 / 笔试部分总分值”计算。

In addition, the hearing-impaired candidates can exempt the listening test upon approval of the application. The scores of the foreign language subjects of the disabled candidates who are exempted from the listening test are calculated according to the “written test score × foreign language total score / written test total score”.

2015 年 5 月 21 日，北京教育考试院召开高考考务工作会。2015 年高考，考生依然必须携带准考证和身份证入场，如果考生忘记或者遗失了身份证（或准考证），监考员可以先验证考生相貌，如果与准考证存根上的照片相符，可以先安排考生进场考试，要求考生下一科考试时带来。

The Beijing Education Examinations Institute held a college entrance examination work meeting on May 21, 2015. In the college entrance examination in 2015, candidates must bring the admission ticket and ID card to enter the examination room. If the candidate forgets or loses the ID card (or the admission ticket), the invigilator could verify the appearance of the candidate firstly. The candidate could enter the room and promised to bring them in the next exam, if he or she was matching to the photo on the admission ticket stub.

（三）中国的大学 Chinese University

截至 2017 年 5 月 31 日，全国高等学校共计 2 914 所，其中：普通高等学校 2 631 所（含独立学院 265 所），成人高等学校 283 所。

As of May 31, 2017, there were 2,914 colleges and universities nationwide, including 2,631 ordinary colleges and universities (including 265 independent colleges) and 283 adult higher education institutions.

在 2017 年 9 月 21 日教育部公布外界期待已久的“双一流”建设高校名单和“双一流”建设学科之前，全国的大学分为若干批次，主要有“提前批”（军事类院校）、“第一批”（一本大学，包括全国重点大学、普通一本大学）、“第二批”（普通二本大学，包括公二本、民二本）、“第三批”（三本，主要包括独立学院、中外合作办学本科院校）、“第四批”（高职高专学校，即专科）。

On September 21, 2017, the Ministry of Education announced the long-awaited list of “double first-class” universities and “double first-class” disciplines. The universities nationwide were divided into several batches, mainly “advance approval” (military schools), “the first batch” (including national key universities) “the second batch” (including provincial institutions), “the third batch” (mainly including independent colleges, Sino-foreign cooperative undergraduate colleges), and “the fourth batch” (higher vocational colleges, i.e. junior college).

世界一流大学和一流学科建设，简称“双一流”。建设世界一流大学和一流学科，是中国高等教育领域继“211 工程”“985 工程”之后的又一国家战略，有利于提升中国高等教育综合实力和国际竞争力，为中华民族伟大复兴的中国梦提供有力支撑。

The construction of world-class universities and first-class disciplines, referred to as “double first-class”. Building world-class universities and first-class disciplines was another national strategy in China’s higher education sector following the “211 Project” and “985 Project”, which was conducive to upgrading China’s higher education, comprehensive strength and international competitiveness, providing strong support for the Chinese dream of the great rejuvenation of the Chinese nation.

“双一流”与“985”“211”一个显著的区别就在于，建设重点是学科而非学校，“一流”与“非一流”之间流动性显著增强，原先较为固化的高校生态格局将逐渐被打破。

A significant difference between the “double first-class” initiative and the “985” and “211” projects lies in the fact that the focus of construction is on disciplines rather than schools. The mobility between “first-class” and “non-first class” is significantly enhanced, and the ecological structure of the previously solidified universities will gradually be changed.

（四）来华留学生制度
System for International Students in China

来华留学生制度是为规范学校招收、培养、管理国际学生的行为，为国际学生在中国境内学校学习提供便利，增进教育对外交流与合作，提高中国教育国际化所制定的相关管理制度。来华留学生是指不具有中国国籍且在中国接受教育的外国学生。

System for international students in China is a management system which aims at regulating the behavior of recruiting, cultivating and managing international students, facilitating the international students in China, promoting educational exchanges and cooperation internationally, and improving the internationalization of Chinese education. International students refer to the students studying in China without Chinese nationality.

培养留学生最终要达到的目标有：来华留学生应当熟悉中国历史、地理、社会、经济等中国国情和文化基本知识，了解中国政治制度和外交政策，理解中国社会主流价值观和公共道德观念，形成良好的法治观念和道德意识。语言方面，以中文为专业教学语言的学科本科生毕业时中文能力应当达到《国际汉语能力标准》五级水平。以外语为专业教学语言的学科本科生毕业时，中文能力应当至少达到《国际汉语能力标准》四级水平。在跨文化交际能力上，来华留学生应当具备包容、认知和适应文化多样性的意识、知识、态度和技能，能够在不同民族、社会和国家之间的相互尊重、理解和团结中发挥作用。

The final training objectives for international students: the international students should be familiar with China's history, geography, society, economy and other general conditions and cultural knowledge, and understand China's political system and foreign policies. Besides, they should understand Chinese mainstream values and public moral values, which help to form good concept of the law and moral awareness. In terms of language skill, the students taught in Chinese should reach the fifth level of the International Chinese Proficiency Standard when graduate. While those taught in foreign languages shall reach the fourth level when accomplishing the undergraduate course. As for intercultural communication skills, international students in China should have the awareness, knowledge, attitudes and skills to be inclusive, cognizant and adaptive to cultural diversity, and play a role in mutual respect, understanding and solidarity among different peoples, societies and nations.

中国政府为外国留学生来华学习设立"中国政府奖学金"，类别有：本科生奖学金、研究生奖学金和进修生奖学金等。地方人民政府和高等学校可以根据需要单独或联合为外国留学生设立奖学金。

Chinese government provides Chinese Government Scholarship for foreign students as follows: undergraduate scholarship, postgraduate scholarship, and scholarship for advanced non-degree students. Local governments, colleges and universities may set up scholarships for foreign students, individually or jointly, as needed.

校内管理制度对留学生参加文艺活动、公益活动等进行规范，规定外国留学生在校学习期间不得就业、经商，或从事其他经营性活动，但可以按学校规定参加勤工助学活动。

In-campus management system regulates foreign students' participation in literary and artistic activities and public welfare activities. However, foreign students are not allowed to obtain occupation, do business, or engage in other business activities during their studies. They can participate in work-study activities as required by the school.

来华留学生的宗教活动，可依据《中华人民共和国境内外国人宗教活动的管理规定》进行管理。学校管理层面应当持有的最基本态度为：尊重外国留学生的民族习俗和宗教信仰，但不提供举行宗教仪式的场所。校内严禁进行传教及宗教聚会等活动。

The religious activities of foreign students in China must be managed in accordance with "The Regulations on the Administration of Religious Activities of Foreigners in the People's Republic of China". The most basic attitude that should be held at the school management is to respect the national customs and religious beliefs of foreign students, but not to provide places for religious ceremonies. Missionary and religious gatherings are strictly prohibited on campus.

《中国政府奖学金来华留学生管理工作手册》由国家留学基金委员会颁布，面向的管理对象是政府奖学金留学生。中国政府奖学金来华留学项目，是我国政府为增进中国人民与世界各国人民的相互了解与友谊，设立的来华留学生全额奖学金和部分奖学金项目，国家留学基金委员会受委托具体负责中国政府奖学金来华留学生的招生及日常管理工作。这部规定是管理工作的依据。

Workbook of Chinese Government Scholarships for International Students was promulgated by the China Scholarship Council and aimed at government scholarship students. The Chinese Government Scholarship Program is a full scholarship and partial scholarship program for international students to promote mutual understanding and friendship between Chinese people and people around the world. The China Scholarship Council is entrusted with students' enrollment and daily management. This provision is the basis of management work.

（五）孔子学院
Confucius Institute

1. 孔子
Confucius

孔子（公元前 551 年 9 月 28 日—公元前 479 年 4 月 11 日），中国古代著名

的思想家、教育家、政治家，是当时社会上最博学的学者之一，被后世统治者尊为孔圣人、万世师表。其儒家思想对中国和世界都有深远的影响，被联合国教科文组织评为“世界十大文化名人”之首。孔子是中国传统文化的代表人物，选择孔子作为汉语教学品牌是中国传统文化复兴的标志。

Confucius (September 28, 551 B.C. –April 11, 479 B.C.), was a famous thinker, educator, and politician in China. He was one of the most knowledged scholars in the society at that time, and he was honored as a Confucius and a Master of the World by the rulers of later generations. His Confucianism had a profound influence on China and the world, and it is ranked first among the "Top Ten Cultural Celebrities in the World" by UNESCO. Confucius is the representative figure of Chinese traditional culture, and the choice of Confucius as the brand of Chinese teaching is the symbol of the revival of Chinese traditional culture.

2. 孔子学院简介
Introduction to Confucius Institute

孔子学院（Confucius Institute），它并非一般意义上的大学，而是推广汉语和传播中国文化的交流机构，是一个非营利性的社会公益机构，一般都是下设在国外的大学和研究院之类的教育机构里。孔子学院最重要的一项工作就是给世界各地的汉语学习者提供规范、权威的现代汉语教材；提供最正规、最主要的汉语教学渠道。

The Confucius Institute, which is not a university in the general sense, is a communication institution that promotes Chinese and spreads Chinese culture. It is a non-profit social welfare institution and generally located in universities and research institutes abroad. One of the most important tasks of the Confucius Institute is to provide Chinese learners around the world with standardized and authoritative modern Chinese textbooks and to provide the most formal and major Chinese teaching channels.

3. 孔子学院标识
The Logo of Confucius Institute

孔子学院标识使用简体中文“汉”字的变体，融合昂首高飞的和平鸽和地球两种图案；简洁明快，刚柔并济，动感有力，既充分体现了中国传统的语言文化，又体现了快速向现代化迈进的时代步伐，与中国国家语言推广机构——国家汉办的标志有一定的传承性，是国家汉办“创新、集成、跨越”工作方针的生动体现。

The Confucius Institute logo uses a variant of the simplified Chinese character “汉” (Han), which combines the peace dove and the Earth. With the characteristics of simple and clear, soft and flexible, dynamic and powerful, it not only fully reflects the traditional Chinese language and culture, but also reflects the pace of the rapid development of modernization. It has a certain inheritance with the logo of the Office of Chinese International Promotion Leading Group, Hanban. It is a vivid embodiment of the Hanban’s work guidelines “innovation, integration, and leapfrogging”.

4. 孔子学院的建立与发展

Establishment and Development of Confucius Institute

从 2004 年 11 月全球首家孔子学院在韩国成立，到 2018 年 12 月 31 日，全球 154 个国家（地区）建立了 548 所孔子学院和 1 193 个孔子课堂。孔子学院 147 国（地区）共 548 所，其中，亚洲 34 国（地区）126 所，非洲 43 国 59 所，欧洲 41 国 182 所，美洲 24 国 160 所，大洋洲 5 国 21 所。孔子课堂 83 国（地区）共 1 193 个（缅甸、瓦努阿图、格林纳达、莱索托、库克群岛、安道尔、欧盟只有孔子课堂，没有孔子学院），其中，亚洲 22 国 114 个，非洲 18 国 41 个，欧洲 30 国 341 个，美洲 9 国 595 个，大洋洲 4 国 102 个。除海外孔子学院之外，体验基地和特色孔院正逐渐兴起。

Since the founding of the world’s first Confucius Institute in the Republic of Korea in November 2004, 548 Confucius Institutes and 1193 Confucius Classrooms were established in 154 countries around the world as of December 31, 2018. There are 548 Confucius Institutes in 147 countries (regions), including 126 in 34 Asian countries (regions), 59 in 43 countries in Africa, 182 in 41 countries in Europe, 160 in 24 countries in the America, and 21 in Oceania. 83 countries (regions) (Myanmar, Vanuatu, Grenada, Lesotho, Cook Islands, Andorra, EU only classroom, no institute) have a total of 1193 Confucius Classrooms, of which 114 in 22 Asian countries, 41 in 18 African countries, 341 in 30 European countries, 595 in 9 American countries, and 102 in 4 countries in Oceania. In addition to the overseas’ Confucius Institute, the experience base and the special Confucius Institute are gradually emerging.

5. 汉语桥中文比赛

Chinese Bridge—Chinese Proficiency Competition

“汉语桥”中文比赛是国家汉办主办的大型国际汉语比赛项目，是世界人文交流领域的知名品牌活动，共分为“汉语桥”世界大学生中文比赛、“汉语桥”世界中学生中文比赛和“汉语桥”在华留学生汉语大赛三项比赛。每年一届，由汉语桥比赛组委会进行项目的具体组织和实施。近年来，“汉语桥”中文比赛项目采取汉办与地方政府合作的方式，并结合电视呈现，取得了较好效果。

The “Chinese Bridge”, a Chinese Contest, is a large-scale international Chinese language competition sponsored by Hanban. It is a well-known brand activity in the field of humanities communication in the world. “Chinese Bridge” competition is divided into the Chinese Proficiency Competition for college students, foreign secondary school students and Chinese Proficiency Competion for international students in China. Every year, the “Chinese Bridge” Competition Organizing Committee will carry out the specific organization and implementation of the project. In recent years, the “Chinese Bridge” competition project has adopted the cooperation between Hanban and local governments, and combined with television presentation, achieved good results.

课后练习题

Practice

一、选择题

Multiple-choice

1. 科举制最早起源于（　　）

   The earliest origin of imperial examination is (　　).

   A. 隋　　B. 元　　C. 宋　　D. 清

   A. Sui Dynasty　　B. Yuan Dynasty　　C. Song Dynasty　　D. Qing Dynasty

2. 西方人称中国的什么为中国的第五大发明？（　　）

   What is called China’s fifth largest invention by westerners? (　　)

   A. 马车

   A. Carriage

B. 中国的科举制度
B. China's imperial examination system

C. 造纸术
C. Papermaking

D. 水利工程
D. water conservancy project

3. 中国的九年义务教育制度是从什么时候开始实施的？（　　）
When did China's nine-year compulsory education system come into force? (　　)

A. 1986 年 7 月 1 日
A. July 1, 1986

B. 1986 年 6 月 1 日
B. June 1, 1986

C. 1987 年 7 月 1 日
C. July 1, 1987

D. 1987 年 7 月 2 日
D. July 2, 1987

4. 岳麓书院何时开始招收历史学本科生？
When did Yuelu Academy begin to enroll undergraduate students majoring in history? (　　)

A. 2009　　B. 2001　　C. 1999　　D. 1998

5. 高考必考的学科有多少个？
How many subjects are required for the college entrance examination? (　　)

A. 3　　B. 4　　C. 5　　D. 6

二、填空题
Fill-in-the-blanks

1. 以中文为专业教学语言的学科毕业时，本科生中文能力应当达到《国际汉语能力标准》______水平。
In terms of language skill, the students taught in Chinese should reach the ______ level of the International Chinese Proficiency Standard when graduate.

2. 来华留学生制度是为规范学校______、______、______国际学生的行为。
System for international students in China is a management system which aims at regulating the behavior of ______, ______, ______ international students.

3. 在培养留学生跨文化交际能力上，来华留学生应当具备包容、认知和适应文化多样性的______、______、______和技能，能够在不同民族、社会和国家之间的______、理解和团结中发挥作用。

As for intercultural communication skills, international students in China should have the________, ________, ________and skills to be inclusive, cognizant and adapt to cultural diversity, and play a role in ____________, understanding and solidarity among different peoples, societies and nations.

4. 孔子学院的承办体现了国家汉办的______、______、______的工作方针。

The undertaking of Confucius Institute reflects the policy of Hanban in terms of ______, ______ and ______.

5. 现在招收本科、硕士、博士的是______书院。

______ Academy can enroll the undergraduate, graduate students and doctors today.

三、判断题

True or False

1. 九年义务教育具有可选择性。

Free education is optional.

2. 如果你是一位十四岁的拥有中国国籍的女基督教徒，那么你不享有接受义务教育的权利。

If you are a 14-year-old female Christian with Chinese nationality, you are not entitled to compulsory education.

3.《义务教育法》只确认和保障适龄儿童和少年入学的权利、就近入学的权利、免交学费的权利。

"The Compulsory Education Law" recognizes and guarantees only the right to enroll, right to be admitted to the neighborhood school, and right to have free tuition.

4. 每年 7 月 7 日、7 月 8 日为考试日，部分省区高考时间为 3 天。

Gaokao takes place in July 7th and July 8th each year, and some provinces and districts have three days for college entrance examination.

5. 孔子学院并非一般意义上的大学，而是推广汉语和传播中国文化的交流机构。

The Confucius Institute, which is not a university in the general sense, is a communication institution that promotes Chinese and spreads Chinese culture.

四、简答题
Short-answer Questions

1. 科举制度是什么时候建立的？
   When was the Imperial Civil Examination System established?

   ____

   ____

2. 什么是九年义务教育？
   What is the meaning of nine-year compulsory education?

   ____

   ____

3. 外国留学生在校学习期间可以就业、经商，或从事其他经营性活动吗？
   Can foreign students be allowed to obtain occupation, do business, or engage in other business activities during their studies?

   ____

   ____

第五章

中国的哲学家

Chinese Philosophers

课节思考

Lead-in Questions

1. 你知道孔子的故事吗？

   Do you know the story of Confucius?

2. 在庄子的众多故事中，你最喜欢哪一个？为什么？

   Which story of Chuang-tzu do you like best? Why?

一、孔子的故事

The Story of Confucius

孔子，春秋末期鲁国（今山东曲阜）人，是中国著名的哲学家、思想家、教育家。他的故事在中国家喻户晓，可以说他的思想在一定程度上影响了中国的历史进程。

Confucius was a famous Chinese philosopher, thinker and educator. His story was well known in China. To some extent, the historical process of China had been influenced by his thought. What kind of person was he? Let's learn Chinese stories through the stories of Confucius.

（一）学习经历
Study Experience

孔子的祖先是商朝的王室，封地在宋国。因为各种原因，家族辗转到了鲁国。孔氏家族的身份由贵族变成了“士”。

Confucius' ancestors were the royal family of the Shang Dynasty, who lived in a small kingdom called Song. For various reasons, the family moved to another kingdom called Lu. The identity of the family changed from the nobility to the "shi" class which was just formed at that time.

孔子三岁时他的父亲就去世了，他的母亲把他抚养大。孔子 17 岁时，他的母亲因为太过操劳也去世了。孔子主持了母亲的葬礼，并且克服困难将父母合葬。这一系列仪式办得非常合乎礼仪，给当时的人们留下了深刻的印象，并被记载在史书里。这说明 17 岁时孔子已经完成了对“礼”的学习，做好步入成人世界的准备了。

Confucius' father died when he was three years old and his mother raised him. When Confucius was 17, his mother died because she had worked too hard. Confucius was very sad. As a son, he presided over the burial of his mother and had to overcome difficulties to bury his parents together. The series of ceremonies was conducted very formally, leaving a deep impression on the people of the time. This showed that at the age of 17, Confucius had already completed the basic study, and was getting ready to enter the adult world. So what has Confucius learned before 17?

当时的少年学习内容主要有六样，分别是“礼、乐、射、御、书、数”。其中“射、御、书、数”是比较实用的课程，即射箭、驾车、读写和算术。“礼、乐”则更为重要，主要用于外交和祭祀，孔子最重视“礼、乐”。“礼、乐”也是他哲学思想的重要内容。

At that time, the basic learning content mainly included six items, namely, "ritual, music, archery, chariot-riding, reading and writing, arithmetic". Among them, "archery, chariot-riding, reading and writing, arithmetic" were the more practical courses. However, in Confucius' opinion "ritual and music", which were mainly used in diplomacy and sacrifice, were more important. "Ritual and music" were an important part of his philosophy.

（二）教育家孔子
Educator

孔子是中国历史上很有成就的教育家，据说有弟子三千，其中成为知名人士的就有七十二人之多。著名的《论语》是一本记录他及其弟子言行的书。《论语》共 20 篇 492 章，内容涉及政治、教育、文学、哲学以及立身处世的道理等多方面，后来成为儒家经典著作。这本书体现了孔子的思想，是他和弟子们智慧的结晶。

Confucius was a very accomplished educator in Chinese history, and there were three thousand students who studied under him, seventy-two of whom became famous people. *The Analects*, is a book that records the words and deeds of Confucius and his disciples. *The Analects*, a total of 492 chapters, cover politics, education, literature, philosophy and the truth of the world, which later became a Confucian classic. This book, which reflected Confucius' thought, was the crystallization of the wisdom of Confucius and his disciples.

《论语》中提到了"仁""礼""乐"三个重要概念。这是三个既各自独立又紧密相依的范畴。其中"仁"主要涉及伦理道德范畴，"礼"是对人的外在规约，作用于社会政治范畴，"乐"是内心的和谐。三个概念有着密切的关系。

The important concepts of "benevolence", "ritual" and "music" were mentioned in *The Analects*. These are three categories that are independent but also closely dependent on one another. Among them, "benevolence" mainly involved the category of ethics and morality; "ritual" represented the order and the limits of the social structure. "Music" referred to the inner harmony. So ritual is outside and music is inside harmony. The three concepts were closely related.

孔子因材施教，对不同的弟子采用不同的教育方法。《论语》中既有名言警句又有针对具体事件的评价，至今读来还很生动。从书中可以感受到孔子的形象及其与弟子的关系。他并不是一个板着面孔教训人的先生，而更像一个亲切的老人。他与学生的关系更为微妙，有时像学生的朋友，有时又像是他们严厉的父亲。学生们不仅向孔子学习知识和思辨的能力，也被孔子的魅力所折服。孔子去世后，很多弟子为他守孝三年，而子贡则为他守孝六年，从中可以看出孔子在弟子们心中的地位。

Confucius taught different kinds of disciples in various ways according to their different talents. *The Analects* contained a lot of famous phrases, as well as some comments of specific events, so even nowadays reading this book is still very enjoyable. The relationship between Confucius and his disciples could be seen in the book. He was not just serious, but more like a kind old man. His relationship with his students was more subtle, sometimes like a friend, and sometimes like their stern father. Students learned not only knowledge from him but were also impressed by his charm. After the death of Confucius, many disciples voluntarily lived beside his grave for three years, and Zi Gong did that for six years, and one can see Confucius' place in the hearts of his disciples.

（三）周游列国
Traveling around the Kingdoms

孔子所处的时代是中国历史上十分混乱的时期，战乱纷仍、礼崩乐坏。上面提到的“仁”“礼”“乐”就是孔子给当时的社会开的药方。孔子希望他的思想能被国君采用，从而给人民带来和平的生活。为了达到这个目的，五十五岁的孔子带着几个学生离开家乡去各个国家推行他的理想。前后整整十四年！

Confucius lived in a very chaotic period in Chinese history, for war was still a great deal, and every kingdom wanted to annex other kingdoms. The concepts of "benevolence", "ritual" and "music" mentioned before were the prescriptions that Confucius gave to the society at that time. Confucius hoped that his thoughts would be adopted by the king of the kingdom, thus bringing peace and security to the people.

In order to achieve this goal, at the age of fifty-five, Confucius left his hometown with several disciples to carry out his ideals in various kingdoms. He did not know that it would take him fourteen years to come back home.

然而，这漫长而艰苦的旅行并没有让孔子的梦想成真。他的思想并没有被当时的国君们所采用，但是他的思想得到了进一步的发展，还在路上收了更多弟子。他的很多弟子后来都成了重要的政治人物，发扬了孔子的思想。孔子回到家乡后，用剩下的生命编订、整理了《诗经》《尚书》等前代典籍，特别是整理了《春秋》这本中国历史上第一部编年体史书。

However, this long and arduous journey did not make Confucius' dream come true. His ideas were not adopted by the kings of the time, but instead his ideas were further developed by him and he accepted many disciples on the journey. Many of his disciples later became important political figures, carrying forward Confucius' ideas. Confucius returned to his hometown, spending the rest of his life compiling *The Book of Poems*, *Shang Shu* and other classic books. In particular, *The Spring and Autumn,* which is a history book that focuses on kingdom Lu. It was the first chronological history book in China.

这就是孔子一生的故事，他并不是圣人更不是神人，而是一个有责任感的普通人。《论语》里的道理是朴素的，孔子的理论并不是逻辑严密、深刻难懂的真理，而是从人们的日常生活中而来，是每个人都可以做到的。道不远人，孔子像一位亲切的老者，又是伟大的理论创作者。他乐于学习、善于学习的态度，让中华民族的文化成为一种兼容并包的文化。他第一个提出“有教无类”，让所有人都能通过学习提升自己，有能力管理国家、服务人民。后来，他的思想和他的教育理念经由官方的推崇整整影响中国长达 2 500 年。即使在今天，我们仍能从他的故事中了解中国精神、寻找中国力量。从汉代起儒家思想就被历代统治者所推崇，从而成了中国最主要的传统思想。人们为了纪念孔子，在他的家乡建立了孔庙、孔府、孔林。

This was the Confucius' life story. He is not a saint nor god, but a responsible ordinary person. The theory in *The Analects* was simple, and Confucius's theory was not a logical, profound truth but something from the people's daily life. Being a kind old man and a great theoretical creator, Confucius was willing to learn about different ways of thought and teach others. So the Chinese culture is an inclusive culture. Confucius was the first one to propose that everyone who is willing to learn could be allowed to improve themselves through learning and to participate in the brilliant cause of running the country for the benefit of the people. His educational ideas have influenced China for 2,500 years by offical endorsement. Even today, we can learn about the Chinese spirit from his stories. Confucianism has been respected by emperors of almost all generations since the Han Dynasty, thus becoming the most important traditional thought in China. In honor of Confucius, Chinese people established the Temple of Confucius, Kong Family Mansion and Cemetery of Confucius in his hometown.

二、老子的故事
The Story of Lao-tzu

（一）"老子"其人
The Profile of Lao-tzu

"老子"，是一个充满神秘色彩的名字。很多中国人听到这个名字就会联想到一位白发苍苍、慈眉善目的老者。"老"字不是他的姓，在中文中"老"是年纪大、晚年、经常的意思，也可以作为词头表示排行，"子"是古人对有道德、有学问的人的尊称，"老子"这个称呼既可以指他这个人，也可以说是其学说的简称。

The name of Lao-tzu is full of mystery. When many Chinese hear the name, they associate it with a white-haired, kind-looking elderly man, but "Lao" is not his last name. In Chinese culture, "lao" means "old", "later in life" and "often". It can also be used as a prefix to indicate seniority. "Tzu" is a respectful title for moral and learned people in ancient times. Lao-tzu is not only a reference to a name, but also an abbreviation of Lao-tzu's theory.

老子的思想在中国哲学、艺术、文学、医学等多个领域都存在着深远的影响。在汉初，老子无为而治的思想被作为治理国家的学说，和“黄帝”一起合称“黄老之术”；作为哲学思想流派，他与后世的庄子被人合称为“庄老”；在中国本土的道教中，老子被不断神化，被道教徒尊称为“道祖”。受此影响，人们常会把老子想象成一位仙风道骨的老人。

Lao-tzu's thoughts have a profound influence on Chinese philosophy, art, literature, medicine and other fields of Chinese culture. In the early period of Han Dynasty, Lao-tzu's thought of non-interference was regarded as the theory of governing a country. His thoughts, together with the Yellow Emperor's, are called the "art of Huang and Lao", As a school of philosophy, Lao-tzu and the later Chuang-tzu are known as the "Chuang and Lao". In China, Lao-tzu is constantly deified and referred to by Taoists as the ancestor of Taoism. Accordingly, people often think of Lao-tzu as an old man with an immortal spirit.

那么老子到底是什么样的人呢？庄周（约公元前369—前286）在《庄子》中以“寓言”的笔法写了一些老子的故事。学者们则普遍相信西汉司马迁（公元前145或前135—？）在《史记》里的记载：老子是楚苦县（今河南陈州）人，姓李，名耳，字聃。他在周王朝做官，相当于今天的国家图书馆馆长。据司马迁的记述，他的年纪比孔子大，孔子曾经前往周朝都城向老子请教有关“礼”的问题。关于“问礼”的对话记载简略，老子却让孔子非常钦佩。

So what kind of person is Lao-tzu? There are some fable stories of Lao-tzu in the book of *Chuang-tzu.* Generally, scholars believe what Sima Qian has recorded in *Shih Chi (Historical Records)* in 145 B.C. or 135 B.C. In *Shih Chi*, Lao-tzu was born in Chuku County, now in Chenzhou County, Henan Province and his surname was "Li", his given name was "Er" and his courtesy name was "Dan". Lao-tzu was an official in the Zhou Dynasty, equivalent to being the head of the National Library today. Sima Qian reported that Lao-tzu was elder than Confucius, and Confucius once went to the capital to ask him questions about "ritual". Although the record of their dialogues is brief, it shows that Confucius admires Lao-tzu very much.

司马迁称老子为“隐者”。这位令人钦佩的老者在周室衰微之后，骑青牛来到了函谷关，打算出关过隐逸的生活。结果函谷关的守备请求他著书。老子无法推辞，于是便有了蜚声中外的《道德经》。老子出关后就不知所终，传说他活到了一百六十岁或二百岁。

Sima Qian called Lao-tzu a hermit. This admirable old man, after the decline of the Zhou Chamber, rode a blue ox to Hangu Pass, intending to leave it for a secluded life. As a result, the officer of Hangu Pass was a fan of him, and asked him to write a book. Lao-tzu could not refuse his request, so the *Daodejing* came into being, which is famous at home and abroad. Lao-tzu has disappeared after he left Hangu Pass, and legend has it that he lived to 160 or 200 years old.

司马迁还提出老子身份的另外两种可能：与孔子同时的老莱子以及比孔子晚的周太史儋。这一线索曾引起了学者们的争论。但大部分人还是认同老子就是那个曾经被孔子请教过的李耳。

Sima Qian put forward two other possibilities of Lao-tzu's indentity. One is the Lao Laitzu, who was at the same time as Confucius, and the *taishi* Dan in Zhou, who was later than Confucius. This clue has caused controversy among scholars. But most people agree that Lao-tzu is Li Er, who was once consulted by Confucius.

（二）《老子》其书
The Book of *Lao-tzu*

老子的著作《老子》，也叫《道德经》，是一部非常伟大的作品。因为只有五千字，所以也被称作《五千言》。早在 18 世纪，西方一些国家就有了《老子》的多种文字版本。据联合国教科文组织统计，《老子》一书是当今除《圣经》外，在全世界出版发行数量最多的一本书，单是日本就有 300 多种版本。到 20 世纪四五十年代，欧洲共有 60 多种《道德经》译文，德国哲学家黑格尔、尼采，俄罗斯大作家托尔斯泰等世界著名学者对《道德经》都有深入的研究。

The book *Lao-tzu*, also known as *Daodejing*, is a great work. It is also called *Five Thousand Words* because it has only five thousand words. As early as the 18th century, some western countries had several versions of *Lao-tzu*. According to the UNESCO, *Lao-tzu* is the most widely published book in the world second to the Bible, with more than 300 editions in Japan alone. By the 1940s and 1950s, there were more than 60 versions of *Daodejing* in Europe, and world-known scholars such as German philosopher Hegel, Nietzsche and Russian writer Tolstoy had made in-depth studies of this book.

老子的思想深远玄妙。其以“道”为中心概念和最高范畴。老子的哲学思想是以“道”建立起来的完整的智慧哲学体系，在这个体系中，老子提出了世界本源的命题。“道”不是具体的“人间之道”“可言之道”，而是“恒常之道”，是一个超越了相对的绝对本体。

Lao-tzu's thoughts are profound and mysterious and "Tao" is the central concept and the highest category in his thoughts. Lao-tzu's philosophical thought is a complete system of wisdom based on "Tao", in which Lao-tzu has put forward the proposition of the origin of the world. "Tao" is not the concrete thing of the world or something spoken, but the theory of constancy, which is a transcendent absolute noumenon.

老子说:“道可道，非常道。”它将“道”看作是不可用语言来加以限制的纯粹空无的思维起始状态。“道生一,一生二,二生三,三生万物……”，“道”是抽象的绝对，是一切存在的根源，是自然界中最初的动力和创造力。

Lao-tzu once said, the essence of "Tao" cannot be gained in ordinary ways. It regards "Tao" as a pure and empty state of mind which cannot be restricted by language. Tao gives birth to one, the one gives birth to two, the two gives birth to three, and the three gives birth to all things. "Tao" is the abstract absoluteness, the root of all existents, the original power and creativity in nature.

老子说:“道法自然。”老子在书中强调遵循自然规律，与自然和谐相处。他主张“无为”“不争”“无名”，就是说一切皆要顺势而为，反对“知其不可为而为之”的做法。在今人看来，这不失为一种智慧。

Lao-tzu once said, "Tao" is a natural thing. In his book, Lao-tzu emphasized that people should obey the laws of nature and live in harmony with nature. He advocated being free, true and unknown, which emphasized that one should follow the trend of the times rather than disobeying the rules. In our eyes, this is a kind of wisdom.

老子认为世界上的任何事物都是相互依存的。美丑、善恶、有无、难易、长短——有此才有彼，有是才有非，有善才有恶。表面看来，正相反的两个方面是相互对立的，而实际上又是相互包含、相互渗透的。他说:“祸兮，福之所倚;福兮，祸之所伏。”

Lao-tzu believed that everything in the world is interdependent. Beauty and ugliness, good and evil, being and not being, difficulty and easiness, length and shortness, each pair of them is interdependent. If one of them disappears, the other does not exist correspondingly. On the surface, the two are opposite, but in fact they are mutually contained and permeated. Just as he said, where there is the misfortune, there is the fortune and vice versa.

老子认为任何事物都不是一成不变的。《道德经》第四十章提出“反者道之动”。这就是说，事物发展到一定程度，必然会向相反的方面转化，所谓“物壮则老，兵强则灭”。同时，事物的发展、事物向反面的转化，并不是一下子实现的，这需要经历一个数量上不断积累的过程。他说：“合抱之木，生于毫末；九层之台，起于累土；千里之行，始于足下。”

Lao-tzu believed that nothing is immutable. In Chapter 40 of the *Daodejing*, it explained the meaning of “the movement of the backward”. That is to say, when things develop to a certain extent, they will inevitably turn to the opposite direction. As the saying goes, if things are extremely strong, they are going to die; if soldiers are strong to the extreme, they will perish. At the same time, the development and transformation of things are not realized all at once, for it takes time and needs to go through a process of continuous accumulation of quantity. He said that, a tree is born in little, a tower rises from the earth and a journey of a thousand miles begins with the first step.

老子的智慧也是处世之道、养生之道。他说“上善若水”，水最为柔弱却又最有力量。他主张为人要柔弱、谦虚、知足。柔弱是保存力量因而成为刚强的方法；谦虚表明极限远远没有达到；知足的人不会走向极端。《道德经》第四十四章：“知足不辱，知止不殆。”

Lao-tzu’s wisdom is also the way to live and keep healthy. He said, the highest level of ethics is like water, which is the most weak but the most powerful. He advocated weakness, modesty, and contentment. Weakness is the preservative of strength, and therefore of strength; modesty shows that the limit is far from being reached; contented people do not go to extremes. In Chapter 44 of the *Daodejing*, there is a saying that knowing contentment will not be humiliated, and knowing when to stop would not be in danger.

三、庄子的故事

The Story of Chuang-tzu

庄子姓庄，名周，战国时期宋国蒙人，是道家思想的代表人物，他是中国历史上著名的哲学家、思想家。据司马迁的《史记》记载，他和梁惠王、齐宣王同时代，学识渊博，但拒绝做高官，只做过蒙邑的漆园吏。

庄子留下了一本著作，也就是《庄子》这本书。书中有内篇 7 篇，外篇 15 篇，杂篇 11 篇。这些内容有的是庄子写的，有的是他的学生写的。我们可以从《庄子》这本书中寻找他的故事。

Chuang-tzu, whose surname was Chuang and whose given name was Zhou, was a native of Song during the Warring States Period. He was a representative figure of Tao. He was a famous philosopher and thinker in Chinese history. According to *Shih Chi* written by Sima Qian, he was at the same time as King Hui and King Xuan of Qi. He is a man of great learning. However, he refused to be a high official and only served as a small officer.

Chuang-tzu left behind a work, namely *Chuang-tzu*. There were 7 inner chapters, 15 outer chapters and 11 miscellaneous chapters in the book. Now we know that part of the book was written by Chuang-tzu, while the other part might have been written by his students.

（一）会讲故事的《庄子》
The Story-telling *Chuang-tzu*

《庄子》一书中讲述了很多美妙的故事。庄子的思想大多在《庄子》这本书中体现出来。这本书的开篇是《逍遥游》，使人大开眼界。

Chuang-tzu told us many wonderful stories in his book. Most of Chuang-tzu's thoughts were embodied in the book *Chuang-tzu*. The book began with *A Happy Excursion*. This was an eye-opening article.

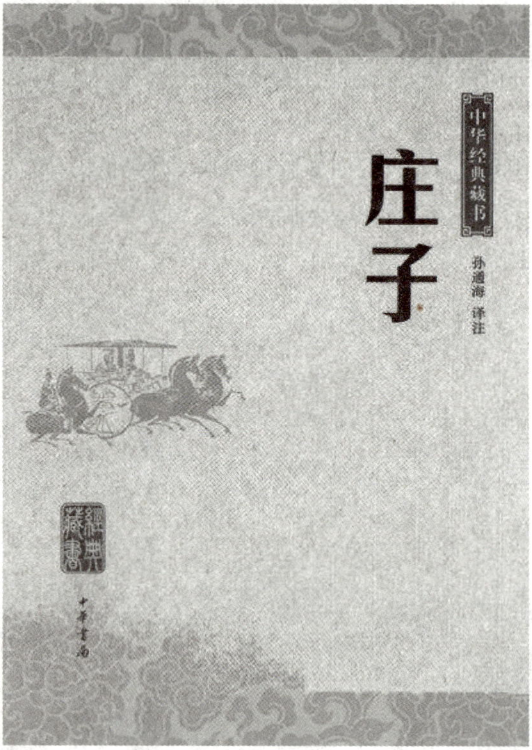

在《逍遥游》里，庄子描绘了这样的画面：北方的大海里有一条鱼，它的名字叫鲲。鲲的体积，不知道有几千里；变化成为鸟，它的名字就叫作鹏；鹏的脊背，真不知道有几千里；当它奋起而飞的时候，那展开的翅膀就好像遮天蔽日的云。鹏往南方的大海迁徙的时候，翅膀拍打水面，能激起三千里的浪涛，环绕着旋风飞上了九万里的高空……

这些描写都深深地印在了后人的头脑中，出现在后人的诗歌和文学作品中。这些意象带我们脱离了纷繁困扰的日常生活，体会与天地精神相往来的无我境界。“天”在儒家超越人生且具有人格性的力量；在《庄子》里，“天”则是广阔无垠的时空，甚至是无垠的宇宙，能够任凭心灵自由翱翔。

In this article, Chuang-tzu depicted a picture of a big fish. He wrote that:

In the northern ocean there is a fish, called the k'un, and I do not know how many thousand li (1 li=0.5km) in size. This k'un changes into a bird, called the p'eng. I do not know how many thousand li of its back. When it flies, its outstretched wings are like clouds that blot out the sky and cover the sun. When it flies to ocean in the south, its wings strike the water to arouse three thousand li of roaring waves. It flies to ninety thousand li in the sky with whirlwind.

These images deeply impressed Chinese writers, which appeared constantly in the poetry and literature of later writers. These images took the followers out of their complicated and troubled daily life and enables them to experience the non-ego realm, which connected the spirit of heaven and earth. In Confucianism, "heaven" transcended life and had the power of personality. In *Chuang-tzu*, "heaven" referred a vast space and time, and even an infinite universe where the mind can soar freely.

庄子在开篇所塑造的浪漫的世界让我们看到外在于人与社会的自然本质。庄子所秉承的境界是精神的绝对自由。逍遥于无何有之乡，无用于世。做到无己、无功、无名。

The romantic world created by Chuang-tzu in the beginning of the book made people see the natural world which was beyond human beings and societies. Chuang-tzu's realm needed absolute freedom of spirit. He had highly praised people who could do all the things without considering themselves, their merits, and their reputations.

从《庄子》中，我们能看到崇尚自然、反对人为的准则。

Chuang-tzu advocated nature and opposed man-made principles.

《庄子·应帝王》中讲过一个故事。"南海帝王叫倏，北海帝王叫忽。他们俩是好朋友。因为两个人的国家相聚太远，他们经常会在中间的一个国家相聚。这个国家的帝王叫混沌。混沌的脾气很好，经常款待他们。他们受了混沌的热情招待总想要找机会报答他。混沌的帝国是个很富裕的帝国，并不缺少什么，可是混沌自身却是一个大肉球没有七窍。倏和忽常常很为混沌感到遗憾。于是他们决定帮助他们的朋友凿出七窍，让他们的朋友混沌和他们一样，可以看见、听见这个世界的美好，品尝到各种美食。于是他们日夜工作，帮助混沌开窍，每天开一窍，连续开了七天。可惜，到了第七天，混沌有了七窍，却一命呜呼了！”庄子似乎用这个故事告诉人们，外在的世俗标准不一定适合每个人，每个人都是独特的。人要尊重自己的本性。

Chuang-tzu told a story in the book.

"The name of the king of South ocean was Shu, and the name of the king of north ocean was Hu. They were good friends. Because of the two countries were far away from each other, so they used to meet in the middle of the two places. The king of the middle country they met was called Hundun. Hundun had a good temper and treated them very well. They were always looking for a chance to reciprocate Hundun's hospitality. Hundun's country was a rich one and lacked nothing, but Hundun himself was a big ball of flesh without eyes, nose, ear and mouth. Shu and hu often felt sorry for him. So they decided to help their friend chisel out the seven orifices so that their friend Hundun could see and hear the beauty of the world and taste all kinds of delicious food. So they worked day and night to help Hundun unlock his riddle. Unfortunately, Hundun died on the seventh day with his eyes, nose, ears and mouth." Chuang-tzu seemed to be telling people with this story that the external secular standards were not necessarily suitable for everyone, and everyone is unique. Man must respect his own nature.

《庄子》里描述了对自由的崇尚。

Chuang-tzu advocated freedom.

《庄子》里曾经讲了一个这样的故事：一天天气很好，庄子正兴高采烈地在濮水钓鱼。有两个穿着十分得体的人找到了他。原来他们是当时的大国楚国国君的使者，想邀请庄子去楚国做宰相，治理楚国。庄子看都没有看他们一眼，问来人说："听说你们楚国有一只神龟，已经死了三千年，楚王用珍贵的盒子把它供起来了。你们说，这只龟是愿意死后让别人供奉起来，还是愿意拖着尾巴在泥里游来游去呢？"来人说，它当然愿意在泥里游来游去了。于是庄子说："你们去吧，我要在泥里多游一阵子。"在庄子看来，做官、治理国家并不能体现生命的价值，反而损害了生命。

There was another story in *Chuang-tzu that one day the weather was fine and Chuang-tzu was happily fishing in a river. He was found by two well-dressed men. It turned out that they were emissaries of the sovereign of Chu, a big state at that time.*

They wanted to invite Chuang-tzu to be the prime minister of Chu. However, Chuang-tzu did not even look at them. He asked the messenger, "I heard that there was a god turtle in your state of Chu. It has been dead for three thousand years. Do you think this turtle would choose to die and be worshiped or swim about in the mud with its tail?" The messenger said, "of course he would like to swim about in the mud". Then Chuang-tzu said, "Go away, I will swim in the mud for a longer time". According to Chuang-tzu, being an official and governing a country did not reflect the value of life, but instead diminished it.

庄子认为人的智慧和生命是有限的，而知识是无穷的，用有限的生命去追随无限的知识是对生命的消耗。人应该依照自然的规律去养生。

Chuang-tzu believed that human wisdom and life were limited, while knowledge was infinite. So to follow infinite knowledge with limited life is the consumption of life. On the contrary, people should maintain their health according to the law of nature.

《庄子 · 养生主》里面写了一位庖丁为梁惠王杀牛。梁惠王发现，他杀牛不但不费力气，整个过程就像是舞蹈一样。梁惠王很高兴，觉得看他杀牛是一种享受，就问他原因。他说："因为我喜欢的是'道'，做事要找到事物的规律。我在杀牛时不是用我的感官在看这头牛，而是用我的心在看，我能清楚每头牛的身体结构，能够让薄薄的刀片在筋骨的缝隙间游走，所以根本不会费力 。我杀了 19 年牛，而刀还像新的一样。 这就是我杀牛的奥秘。"梁惠王从他的话里听出了养生的真谛。

There was a story about the law of nature. It was about a butcher, killing an ox for a king. The whole process was like a dance. It was a pleasure to watch him kill an ox. The king was very happy and asked him why. "Because I like Tao," he said. "When I kill an ox, I do not look at the ox with my senses, but with my heart. I can clearly understand the body structure of each ox, and I can make the thin knife swim between the gaps of the bones and muscles, so it is not difficult at all. I have killed oxen for 19 years, and the knife is as good as new. This is my secret of killing the ox." The king found the true meaning of following the law of nature and understanding one's health and body from his words.

《庄子》中还存在着辩证思想。

There was dialectical thought in *Chuang-tzu*.

（二）辩证的《庄子》
Dialectical *Chuang-tzu*

《庄子》里讲了一个匠人去齐国，在曲辕这个地方他看见一棵被世人当作树神的栎树。这棵栎树的树冠大到可以遮蔽数千头牛。人们在树下乘凉、嬉戏。到底是什么让这棵树如此壮美呢？

匠人明白其中的原因，那竟然是：这是一棵什么用处也没有的树！用它做成船定会沉没、用它做成棺椁定会很快朽烂、用它做成器皿定会很快毁坏，这是不能取材的树，没有什么用处，所以它才能长到这么大。

匠人回到家里，梦见了这棵树，树对他说："那些长果子的树，果实成熟就会被打落在地，打落果子以后枝干也就会遭受摧残。这就是因为它们能结出鲜美的果实才苦了自己的一生，是它自身招来了人们的打击，各种事物莫不如此。而我正因为无用，才保全了性命。无用也就成了我最大的用处。假如我有用，又怎么会成为树神让世人瞻仰呢？ 无用之用才是大用。"

Chuang-tzu told a famous story about a craftsman who went to the state of Qi. He saw an oak tree which was regarded as a shrine by the world. The crown of the oak tree was large enough to shelter thousands of cattle. People enjoyed the shade and played under the trees. What made this tree so great? The craftsman understood the reason, and it was as follow: This had been a tree of no use! If made it into a ship it would sink. If made it into a coffin, the coffin would rot. If made it into a vessel, it would perish. That's why it's so big. When the craftsman came home, he dreamed of the oak tree, and the tree said to him, "the trees that bear fruit will fall to the ground, when their fruit is ripe, and when the fruit has fallen, their branches will be destroyed. They suffer their own life because they can produce delicious fruit. And it is because I am useless that I can save my life. Being useless has become my greatest virtue. If I was useful, how could I become a magical tree to be worshiped? What is useless is useful."

以上就是中国三位历史人物的故事。希望他们的故事能够帮助大家了解中国哲学、理解中国人的想法和做法。林语堂说:"道家及儒家是中国人灵魂的两面。"如果大家对儒家思想、道家思想以及其他哲学思想感兴趣,可以读一下冯友兰的《中国哲学史》。

These are the stories of three Chinese historical philosophers. We hope their stories will help you understand Chinese philosophy, and understand Chinese people's thinking and behaviors. Lin Yutang said, Taoism and Confucianism are the two sides of the Chinese soul. If you are interested in Confucianism, Taoist thought or other philosophical ideas, you should read Feng Youlan's book *A Brief history of Chinese Philosophy*.

课后练习题
Practice

一、选择题
Multiple-choice

1. 以下不是对孔子的描述的是（　　）。
   Which of the following is not the description of Confucius? (　　)

   A. 哲学家　B. 思想家　C. 军事家　D. 教育家
   A. philosopher　B. thinker　C. militarist　D. educator

2. 道家思想的代表人物是（　　）。
   The representative figure of Taoism is (　　).

   A. 庄子　B. 孔子　C. 孟子　D. 墨子
   A. Chuang-tzu　B. Confucius　C. Mencius　D. Mo-tzu

3. 道家认为世界的本源是（　　）。
   Taoism considers the origin of the world is (　　).

   A. 法　B. 仁　C. 道　D. 物
   A. law　B. benevolence　C. Tao　D. goods

4. 庄子的思想通过（　　）体现出来。
   Chuang-tzu's thoughts can be embodied through (　　).

   A.《论语》　B.《庄子》
   A. *The Analects*　B. *Chuang-tzu*
   C.《大学》　D.《中庸》
   C. *The Great Learning*　D. *The Doctrine of Mean*

5. 从《逍遥游》中我们能看出庄子对（　　）的向往。
   We can see from *A Happy Excursion* that Chuang-tzu is looking for (　　).

   A. 自由　B. 秩序　C. 责任　D. 仁爱
   A. freedom　B. order　C. response　D. kindness

二、填空题

Fill-in-the-blanks

1. 孔子学习的比较实用的课程分别为________，________，________，________。

   The much more practical courses Confucius learned are ________, ________, ________, ________.

2. “礼”“乐”分别用于________和________。

   “Ritual and music” were mainly used in ________ and ________.

3. 根据司马迁的记载，老子姓________，名________。

   According to Sima Qian, ________ is Lao-tzu’s surname, while ________ is his given name.

4. 老子的著作叫________，也叫________或________。

   Lao-tzu’s work can be named ________, or ________ or ________.

5. 老子以“________”为中心概念和最高范畴。

   Lao-tzu takes ________ as central concept and the highest category.

三、判断题

True or False

1. 《大学》是在孔子教学过程中产生的著作。

   The Great Learning is the work that emerged in Confucius’s teaching process.

2. 《论语》共 20 篇 492 章，内容涉及政治、教育、文学、哲学以及立身处世的道理等多方面，后来成为儒家经典著作。

   The Analects, a total of 492 chapters, cover politics, education, literature, philosophy and the truth of the world, which later became a Confucian classic.

3. 庄子留下了一本著作，也就是《庄子》这本书。书中有内篇 7 篇，外篇 15 篇，杂篇 11 篇。这些内容都是庄子写的。

   Chuang-tzu left behind a work, namely *Chuang-tzu*. There were 7 inner chapters, 15 outer chapters and 11 miscellaneous chapters in the book. Now we know that the book was written by Chuang-tzu.

4. 司马迁称老子为“隐者”。

   Sima Qian called Lao-tzu a hermit.

5. 庄子姓庄，名周，战国时期宋国蒙人，是道家思想的代表人物，他是中国历史上著名的哲学家、思想家。

Chuang-tzu, whose surname was Chuang and whose given name was Zhou, was a native of Song during the Warring States Period. He was a representative figure of Taoism. He was a famous philosopher and thinker in Chinese history.

四、简答题

Short-answer Questions

1. 人们修建了什么场所来纪念孔子？

What did people establish in honor of Confucius?

____

____

2.《春秋》这本书在历史上有什么样的地位？

What's the important role of *The Spring and Autumn* in history?

____

____

3. 儒家思想和道家思想有什么不同？

What is the difference between Confucianism and Taoism?

____

____

第六章

中国的政治制度

Chinese Political Systems

课前思考

Lead-in Questions

1. 你知道中国的国旗、国徽和国歌吗?

   Do you know about China's national flag, national emblem and national anthem?

2. 你了解中国的政治协商制度吗?

   Do you understand China's political consultation system?

一、国旗、国徽、国歌

National Flag, National Emblem, National Anthem

(一)中华人民共和国国旗

The National Flag of the People's Republic of China

中华人民共和国国旗是五星红旗，是中华人民共和国的象征和标志。五星红旗旗面为红色，长和宽的比例为 3∶2，左上方有五颗黄色五角星，四颗小星环拱在一颗大星的右面，并各有一个角尖正对大星的中心点。其中红色象征革命，五星呈黄色，象征光明。大星代表中国共产党，四颗小星环拱于大星象征中国共产党领导下的人民大团结和人民对党的拥护。

The national flag of the People's Republic of China (PRC) is a five-star red flag and it is a symbol of the PRC. The five-star red flag has a red field with a length to width ratio of 3:2. There are five yellow pointed stars in the upper left, and the four small stars are arched to the right of a large star, each with a pointed tip facing the center of the big star. The red color symbolizes the revolution, and the yellow color of the stars, stands for the light. The big star represents the Communist Party of China, and the arrangement of the smaller stars towards the big one symbolizes great unity of the revolutionary people under the leadership of the Communist Party of China and the people's support for the Party.

1949 年 9 月 25 日，五星红旗得到毛泽东主席的肯定，9 月 27 日中国人民政治协商会议第一届全体会议上一致通过国旗议案，中华人民共和国国旗诞生。

On September 25, 1949, the five-star red flag was approved by Mao Zedong. On September 27, the first plenary session of the Chinese People's Political Consultative Conference unanimously voted for and adopted the national flag bill and the national flag of the PRC was born.

（二）中华人民共和国国徽
The National Emblem of the People's Republic of China

中华人民共和国国徽上的图案都有象征意义。四颗小五角星环绕一个大五角星，象征着中国共产党领导下的全国人民的大团结；齿轮和麦稻穗象征着工人阶级领导下的工农联盟；天安门则体现了中国人民的革命传统和民族精神，同时也是首都北京的象征。国徽在颜色上用正红色和金黄色互为衬托对比，体现了中华民族特有的吉寿喜庆的民族色彩和传统。

The patterns on the national emblem of the People's Republic of China are symbolic. Four small five-pointed stars surround a large five-pointed star, symbolizing the great unity of the people of the country under the leadership of the Communist Party of China. Gears and wheat ears represent the union of workers and peasants under the leadership of the working class. Tian'anmen Square reflects the revolutionary tradition and national spirit of Chinese people, and it is a symbol of the capital Beijing. The national emblem is in red and golden, reflecting the national color and unique tradition of Chinese people.

1950 年 6 月 18 日，中国人民政治协商会议第一届全国委员会第二次会议通过中华人民共和国国徽图案及对该图案的说明。同年 9 月 20 日，公布中华人民共和国国徽。

On June 18, 1950, the second session of the first National Committee of the Chinese People's Political Consultative Conference adopted the national emblem of the People's Republic of China and a description of the pattern. On September 20 of the same year, the national emblem of the People's Republic of China was announced.

（三）中华人民共和国国歌
The National Anthem of the People's Republic of China

中华人民共和国国歌是《义勇军进行曲》。《义勇军进行曲》由田汉作词、聂耳作曲。1934年春，田汉决定写一个以抗日救亡为主题的电影剧本。在他刚完成一个故事梗概和一首主题歌的歌词时，就被国民党反动派逮捕入狱。另一位共产党员、戏剧家夏衍接手将这个故事写成了电影剧本，聂耳主动要求为田汉写的主题歌《义勇军进行曲》谱曲。《义勇军进行曲》由此诞生。

The national anthem of the People's Republic of China is *The March of the Volunteers* written by Tian Han and composed by Nie Er. In the spring of 1934, Tian Han decided to write a film script with the theme of fighting against Japanese aggression and saving the country. When he had just completed a synopsis of the story and the lyrics of a theme song, he was arrested and imprisoned by the Kuomintang reactionaries. Another Chinese Communist Party member and dramatist Xia Yan took over the story into a film script. Nie Er volunteered to compose the theme song *The March of the Volunteers* written by Tian Han. *The March of the Volunteers* was born.

二、人民代表大会制度
The People's Congress System

中国的人民代表大会制度是在中国人民长期革命斗争中产生和发展起来的。《中华人民共和国宪法》规定：中华人民共和国的一切权力属于人民。人民行使国家权力的机关是全国人民代表大会和地方各级人民代表大会。中国国家政权的组织形式是人民代表大会制度。

The people's congress system was born and developed in the long-term revolutionary struggle of Chinese people. China's Constitution stipulates that all power in the People's Republic of China belongs to the people, and the organs through which the people exercise state power are the National People's Congress and the local people's congresses at different levels. The organizational form of Chinese state power is the people's congress system.

人民代表大会制度是中国的根本政治制度。人民代表大会制度是根据民主集中制的原则，通过民主选举产生全国人民代表大会和地方各级人民代表大会，以人民代表大会为基础，组成整个国家机构，实现人民当家作主的一种政权组织形式。人民代表大会的职权主要有立法权、决定权、任免权、监督权等。

The people's congress system is China's fundamental political system. It is based on the principle of democratic centralism, which manifests itself through the democratic voting meetings of the National People's Congress and through the elections for the local people's congresses that are carried out in every administrative division. This forms an entire state institution, a political organization, which is governed by the Chinese people, who are the source of power in the country. The powers of the people's congresses mainly include legislation, decision, appointment, dismissal, and supervision.

全国人民代表大会会议每年举行一次，由全国人民代表大会常务委员会召集。如果全国人民代表大会常务委员会认为必要，或者有五分之一以上的全国人民代表大会代表提议，可以临时召集全国人民代表大会会议。全国人民代表大会举行会议的时候，选举主席团主持会议。全国人民代表大会常务委员会是全国人民代表大会的常设机关，在全国人大闭会期间，行使最高国家权力，对全国人民代表大会负责并报告工作。

The National People's Congress is held once a year and is convened by the Standing Committee of the National People's Congress. If the Standing Committee of the National People's Congress deems it necessary, or if more than one-fifth of the representatives of the National People's Congress propose necessity, it may temporarily convene a meeting of the National People's Congress. When the National People's Congress holds a meeting, the elected presidium will preside over the meeting. The Standing Committee of the National People's Congress is the permanent organ of the National People's Congress. It functions as the highest body of state power and accepts supervision by the National People's Congress when it is not in session.

全国人民代表大会常务委员会委员长、副委员长、秘书长组成委员长会议，处理常务委员会的重要日常工作。全国人民代表大会常务委员会每届任期和全国人民代表大会每届任期相同。全国人大常委会委员长会议负责处理全国人大常委会的重要日常工作，包括决定常委会每次会议的会期，拟定会议议程草案；指导和协调各专门委员会的日常工作；处理常委会其他重要日常工作等。

The Chairmen, Vice-chairmen and Secretary-General of the Standing Committee of the National People's Congress form a chairmen meeting to deal with the important daily work of the Standing Committee. The term office of the Standing Committee of the National People's Congress is the same as the National People's Congress. The chairmen meeting of the Standing Committee of the National People's Congress is responsible for handling the important daily work of the Standing Committee of the National People's Congress, including deciding on the session of the Standing Committee meeting, drawing up the draft agenda of the meeting, guiding and coordinating the daily work of the special committees and handling other important daily tasks of the Standing Committee.

国家的一切权力属于人民，人民当家作主、行使国家权力，是国家的主人，是国家机关权力的来源，这是人民代表大会制度的核心。人民通过民主选举，产生各级人大代表，组成各级人民代表大会，代表人民的利益、按照人民的意志行使国家权力。

All state power belongs to the people who are the masters of the country and exercise state power. They are the source of powers of the state organs. This is the core of the people's congress system. Through democratic elections, people elect deputies to the National People's Congress and form people's congresses at all levels. They also represent the interests of the people, and exercise state powers in accordance with the will of the people.

国家行政机关、审判机关、检察机关都由人民代表大会产生，对人民代表大会负责，受它监督。在中央统一领导下，合理划分中央和地方的国家机构职权，赋予地方依法决定本地事务的权力，充分发挥了地方的主动性、积极性。

The state administrative organs, judicial organs, and prosecutors' offices are all instituted by the people's congresses and are under charge of the people's congresses and subject to its supervision. Under the leadership of the Central Government, powers of central and local institutions are reasonably divided, and the local authorities are given the right to determine local affairs in accordance with laws, and are given the full rein to take the local lead and initiative.

各少数民族聚居的地方实行区域自治，通过民族区域自治制度来管理地方事务，既保证少数民族能够充分享有和行使管理地方事务的权力，又维护民族团结和国家统一。

Regional autonomy is practiced in areas where ethnic groups live, and local affairs are managed through the system of regional ethnic autonomy, which not only ensures that ethnic groups can fully enjoy and exercise the power to manage local affairs, but also safeguard national unity.

三、政治协商与多党合作
Political Consultation and Multiparty Cooperation

政治协商制度是在中国共产党领导下，各政党、人民团体、少数民族和社会各界的代表，以中国人民政治协商会议为组织形式，经常就国家的大政方针进行民主协商的一种制度。

The political consultation system is a system that representatives of political parties, people's organizations, ethnic groups and all walks of life use the Chinese People's Political Consultative Conference as an organizational form to conduct democratic consultations on the country's major policies under the leadership of the Communist Party of China.

中国多党合作制度中包括中国共产党和八个民主党派。八个民主党派是中国国民党革命委员会、中国民主同盟、中国民主建国会、中国民主促进会、中国农工民主党、中国致公党、九三学社、台湾民主自治同盟。

The Chinese multi-party cooperation system includes the Communist Party of China and eight democratic parties. The eight democratic parties are the Revolutionary Committee of the Chinese Kuomintang, the China Democratic League, the China National Democratic Construction Association, the China Association for Promoting Democracy, the Chinese Peasants and Workers Democratic Party, the China Zhi Gong Party, the Jiu San Society, and the Taiwan Democratic Self-Government League.

中国共产党领导的多党合作和政治协商制度是中华人民共和国的一项基本的政治制度。中国共产党是中华人民共和国的唯一执政党，八个民主党派在接受中国共产党领导的前提下，具有参政党的地位，与中国共产党合作，参与执政。政治协商是中国共产党领导的多党合作的最主要的政治内容和组织形式。

The multi-party cooperation and political consultation system under the leadership of the Communist Party of China is a basic state policy of the People's Republic of China. The Communist Party of China is the only party in power in the People's Republic of China while the eight other political parties participate in the discussion and management of the state affairs, in cooperation with the Communist Party of China. The political consultation is the most important political content and organizational form of multi-party cooperation led by the Communist Party of China.

四、中国环保制度

China's Environmental Protection Systems

生态环境是人类生存和发展的基本条件，是经济、社会发展的基础。保护和建设好生态环境，实现可持续发展，是中国现代化建设中必须始终坚持的一项基本国策。

The ecological environment is the basic condition for human survival and development, and the basis for economic and social development. Protecting and building an ecological environment and achieving sustainable development are a basic national policy that must be adhered to in modernization in China.

中国政府十分重视因人口增长和经济发展而出现的环境问题，把保护环境作为提高人民生活水平和生活质量的一个重要方面。为了促进经济、社会与环境的协调发展，中国在 20 世纪 80 年代制定并实施了一系列保护环境的方针、政策、法律和措施。

The Chinese government has paid great attention to the environmental issues arising from the country's population growth and economic development, and has made protecting the environment as an important aspect of the improvement of the people's living standards and quality of life. In order to promote coordinated development between the economy, the society and the environment, China enacted and implemented a series of principles, policies, laws and measures for environmental protection in the 1980s.

确立环境保护为中国的一项基本国策。防治环境污染和生态破坏以及合理开发利用自然资源关系到国家的全局利益和长远发展，中国政府坚定不移地贯彻执行环境保护这项基本国策。

The Chinese government established environmental protection as one of China's basic national policies. The prevention and control of environmental pollution and ecological destruction and the rational exploitation and utilization of natural resources are of vital importance to the country's overall interests and long-term development. The Chinese government is unswervingly carrying out the basic national policy of environmental protection.

制定经济建设、城乡建设和环境建设同步规划、同步实施、同步发展，实现经济效益、社会效益、环境效益相统一的指导方针，实行“预防为主，防治结合”、“谁污染，谁治理”和“强化环境管理”三大政策。

China formulated guidelines for simultaneous planning, simultaneous implementation, and simultaneous development of economic construction, urban and rural construction, and environmental construction, and achieved the guiding principles for the unification of economic, social, and environmental benefits, and implemented "prevention first, prevention and control combination", "who pollutes, who governs" and "strengthening environmental management policies".

为了加强环境保护的国际合作与交流，1973 年国务院环境保护领导小组办公室以中华人民共和国政府的名义，加入了联合国环境规划署，是联合国环境规划理事会 58 个理事国之一。1974 年 5 月，国务院成立了环境保护领导小组，负责统一管理全国的环境保护工作。经过 40 多年的发展，中国的环境保护政策形成了一个完整的体系，具体包括三大政策八项制度。

In order to strengthen international cooperation and exchanges in environmental protection, the Office of the Environmental Protection Leading Group of the State Council joined the United Nations Environment Program in the name of the Government of the People's Republic of China in 1973 and is one of the 58 members of the United Nations Environment Planning Council. In May 1974, the State Council of China established the Environmental Protection Leading Group to be responsible for the unified management of environmental protection throughout the country. After more than 40 years of development, China's environmental protection policy has formed a complete system, including three major policies and eight systems.

1992 年到 2005 年，是中国环保机构和制度建设的重要阶段。其间，环境污染治理全面开展，政府提出了可持续发展的理念，强调保护环境就是保护生产力。1992 年 8 月，联合国环境与发展大会之后，中国政府提出了中国环境与发展应采取的十大对策，明确指出走可持续发展道路是当代中国以及未来的必然选择。

From 1992 to 2005, it was an important stage in the construction of environmental protection institutions and regulations in China. During the period, the environmental pollution control was fully carried out, and the government put forward the concept of sustainable development, emphasizing that protecting the environment means protecting productivity. In August 1992, shortly after the United Nations Conference on Environment and Development, the Chinese government put forward ten major measures that China was to adopt to enhance its environment and development, clearly pointing out that the road of sustainable development was a logical choice for China now and in the future.

1994年3月，中国政府批准发布了《中国21世纪议程——中国21世纪人口、环境与发展白皮书》，从人口、环境与发展的具体国情出发，提出了中国可持续发展的总体战略、对策以及行动方案。有关部门和地方也分别制定了实施可持续发展战略的行动计划。

In March 1994 the Chinese government approved and promulgated *China's Agenda 21—White Paper on China's Population, Environment, and Development in the 21st Century*. This document, proceeding from the country's specific national conditions in the three respects of population, environment and development, put forward China's overall strategy, measures and program of action for sustainable development. The various departments and localities also worked out their respective plans of action to implement the strategy for sustainable development.

2005年到2012年，环保工作的机构不断完善、制度体系逐渐成熟，开展了大规模的城市环境基础设施建设。十八大以后到现在主要以改善环境质量为目标，加强生态文明建设，这是环保体制机制改革力度最大、逐步成形的阶段。环保部门还出台了多个与环境保护相关的法律法规，环境保护的法律体系日趋完善。

From 2005 to 2012, the institutions and regulations for environmental protection continued to be improved, and large-scale urban environmental infrastructure construction was carried out. Since the 18th National Congress of the Communist Party of China, the goal of improving environmental quality has been to strengthen the construction of ecological civilization. This is the stage in which the reform of the environmental protection system is the most intense and gradually shaped. The environmental protection departments have also enacted a number of laws and regulations related to environmental protection, and the legal system for environmental protection has become increasingly improved.

《中华人民共和国环境保护法》规定：保护环境是国家的基本国策。国家采取有利于节约和循环利用资源、保护和改善环境、促进人与自然和谐的经济、技术政策和措施，使经济社会发展与环境保护相协调。明确保护环境是国家的基本国策，也对环境保护与经济社会发展关系做出了规定。

"The Environmental Protection Law of the People's Republic of China" stipulates that protecting the environment is the basic national policy. The state adopts economic and technological policies and measures conducive to saving and recycling resources, protecting and improving the environment, and promoting harmony between mankind and nature, so that economic social development and environmental protection are coordinated. Clearly protecting the environment is the basic national policy, and it also regulates the relationship between environmental protection, economic and social development.

环境是人类赖以生存和发展的基本物质条件，人与自然是生命共同体。大气、水、海洋、土地、森林、草原、湿地、野生生物等自然环境要素，对人类至关重要，缺少其中任何一个，人类都将难以生存，而且会对经济社会发展和人民的生活产生直接或间接的影响。

The environment is the basic material condition for human survival and development. The natural environment elements such as the atmosphere, water, ocean, land, forests, grasslands, wetlands, and wildlife are vital to human beings. Without any of them, humankind would find it difficult to survive, which would have a direct or indirect impact on economic and social development and people's lives.

保护环境具有长期性和持久性。20 世纪 80 年代，中国政府确立了环境保护的基本国策，90 年代又大力实施可持续发展战略。进入 21 世纪后，又强调要树立和落实科学发展观，加快转变经济发展方式，建设生态文明，推动环境保护从认识到实践发生了重要变化。改善环境还是一项系统工程，无论是转变经济发展方式、调整优化产业结构、改变公众的生活方式，还是防治污染和生态破坏，都是十分艰巨的任务。

Protecting the environment is a long-term and long-lasting career. In the 1980s, the Chinese government established the basic national policy of environmental protection. In the 1990s, it vigorously implemented the sustainable development strategy. After entering the 21st century, it also emphasized the need to establish and implement the scientific concept of development, accelerate the transformation of economic development mode, build ecological civilization, and promote environmental protection changes from realization to practice. Improving the environment is still a systematic project. Whether it is to change the mode of economic development, adjust and optimize the industrial structure, change the way of life of the public, or to prevent pollution and ecological damage, it is a very difficult task.

生态建设和环境保护是一项战略任务。环境保护是生态文明建设的主阵地，加强环境保护是推进生态文明建设的根本途径，也是现代化建设中的一项战略任务，对未来的可持续发展具有决定性影响。

Ecological construction and environmental protection are a strategic task. Environmental protection is the main front for the construction of ecological civilization. Strengthening environmental protection is the fundamental way to promote the construction of ecological civilization, and it is also a strategic task in the modernization construction, which has a decisive impact on the future sustainable development.

中国环境保护工作的基本方针是：全面规划、合理布局、综合利用、化害为利、依靠群众、大家动手、保护环境、造福人民。这条方针是 1972 年中国在联合国人类环境会议上提出的，在 1973 年举行的中国第一次环境保护会议上得到了确认，并写入 1979 年颁布的《中华人民共和国环境保护法 (试行)》。

The basic policy of China's environmental protection work is comprehensive planning, rational distribution, and comprehensive utilization, turning harm into profit, relying on the masses, everyone to be involved, protecting the environment, and benefiting the mankind. This policy was proposed by China at the United Nations Conference on the Human Environment in 1972. It was confirmed at the first Environmental Protection Conference held in China in 1973 and was written in "The Environmental Protection Law of the People's Republic of China (Trial)".

中国保护环境相关的法律制度框架已经基本形成，各环境要素主要领域监管已得到基本覆盖。在综合立法方面，制定了环境保护法、环境影响评价法、清洁生产促进法、循环经济促进法等；在污染防治领域，制定了海洋环境保护法、水污染防治法、大气污染防治法、固体废物污染防治法、噪声污染防治法等；在生态保护领域，制定了防沙治沙法、野生动物保护法、水土保持法、自然保护区条例等；在核与辐射安全领域，制定了放射性污染防治法等。

The legal system related to China's environmental protection has been basically formed, and the supervision of the main areas of various environmental factors has been simply covered. In terms of comprehensive legislation, the Environmental Protection Law, the Environmental Impact Assessment Law, the Cleaner Production Promotion Law and the Circular Economy Promotion Law have been formulated. In the field of pollution prevention and control, the Marine Environmental Protection Law, the Water Pollution Prevention Law, the Air Pollution Prevention Law, and the Solid Waste Pollution Prevention and Control Law, the Noise Pollution Prevention and Control Law have been formulated. In the field of ecological protection, the Sand Prevention and Control Law, the Wildlife Protection Law, the Soil and Water Conservation Law and the Nature Reserve Regulations have been formulated. In the field of nuclear and radiation safety, the Radioactive Pollution Prevention and Control Laws have been formulated.

课后练习题

Practice

一、选择题

Multiple-choice

1. 五星红旗旗面的长和宽的比例为（　　）

   The five-star red flag has a length to width ratio of (　　)

   A. 9 : 6　　B. 16 : 9　　C. 3 : 2　　D. 5 : 4

2. 全国人民代表大会会议（　　）举办一次。

   How often is the National People's Congress held? (　　)

   A. 五年　　B. 三年　　C. 两年　　D. 一年

   A. Every five years.　　B. Every three years.　　C. Every two years.　　D. Once a year.

3. 中国多党合作制度包括（　　）党派。

   How many parties are included in China's multi-party cooperation system?

   A. 七个　　B. 八个　　C. 九个　　D. 多个

   A. Seven　　B. Eight　　C. Nine　　D. Some

4. 中国政府把（　　）作为提高人民生活水平和生活质量的一个重要方面。

   What does the Chinese government regard as an important aspect of improving people's living standards and quality of life?

   A. 人口增长　　B. 经济发展

   A. population increase　　B. economic development

   C. 环境保护　　D. 以上都是

   C. environmental protection　　D. All of the above

5. 生态建设和环境保护是（　　）。

   Ecological construction and environmental protection are (　　).

   A. 战略任务　　B. 基本建设

   A. a strategic task　　B. a piece of infrastructure

   C. 主要任务　　D. 十分艰巨的任务

   C. a major task　　D. a very difficult task

二、填空题

Fill-in-the-blanks

1. 中华人民共和国国旗是__________。

   The national flag of the People's Republic of China is ______________.

2. 中国国徽主要是由______色和______色构成。

   The Chinese national emblem is in ______ and ______.

3. 中国国家政权的组织形式是______________。

   The organizational form of Chinese state power is ______________.

4. 人民代表大会的职权归纳起来主要有__________、__________、__________、________等。

   The powers of the people's congresses mainly include ______、________、_______、_________.

5. 《中华人民共和国环境保护法》规定：保护环境是中国的一项___________。

   "The Environmental Protection Law of the People's Republic of China" stipulates that protecting the environment is __________________.

三、判断题

True or False

1. 人民代表大会制度是中国的根本政治制度。

   The people's congress system is China's fundamental political system.

2. 如果有五分之一以上的全国人民代表大会代表提议，可以临时召开全国人民代表大会会议。

   If more than one-fifth of the representatives of the National People's Congress propose it, it may temporarily convene a meeting of the National People's Congress.

3. 1994 年 3 月，中国政府批准发布了《中国 21 世纪议程——中国 21 世纪人口、环境与发展白皮书》。

   In March 1994 the Chinese government approved and promulgated *China's Agenda 21—White Paper on China's Population, Environment and Development in the 21st Century*

4. 中国人民政治协商会议全国委员会和中国人民政治协商会议地方委员会一模一样。

   The National Committee of the Chinese People's Political Consultative Conference is exactly the same as the local committee of the Chinese People's Political Consultative Conference.

5. 中国的环境保护有三大政策八项制度。
China's environmental protection has three major policies and eight systems.

四、简答题
Short-answer Questions

1. 四颗小五角星环绕着一个大五角星象征着什么？
What does the four stars surrounding a large star symbolize?

____

____

2. 中国政治协商会议的主要职能是什么？
What are the main functions of the Chinese People's Political Consultative Conference?

____

____

3. 人民代表大会的职权有哪些？
What are the powers of the people's congresses?

____

____

中国人的生活

Chinese Daily Life

课前思考
Lead-in Questions

1. 你吃过中国菜吗？和你们国家的菜相比，中国菜有什么特点？
Have you ever eaten Chinese food? What are the characteristics of Chinese food comparing to your country's dishes?
2. 中国建筑的特点是什么？
What are the characteristics of Chinese architecture?

一、服饰文化

Costume Culture

“衣食住行”常用来指代人们的日常生活，其中“衣”排在首位。“衣”在一定情况下代表了人的身份地位以及审美品位。代表中国传统元素的服装有汉服、唐装、旗袍。

Clothing, food, shelter and transportation are often used to referred to people's daily life. Among them, clothing ranks first. Clothing in certain circumstances represents the status of people and aesthetic taste. Clothing with traditional Chinese elements are Hanfu, Tang suit and cheongsam.

（一）汉服
Hanfu

汉服又称汉衣冠、汉装、华服。它不是指汉代的服饰，而是指汉民族传统服饰。在古代汉服文化很复杂，包括全套的服装和饰品，不但讲究审美，还要符合礼制，有一套详细的规则，是华夏民族礼仪文化的体现。

Hanfu, also known as Han Crown, Han dress, Chinese clothing, in general refers to the traditional costumes of the Han nationality, and not to the Han Dynasty. In ancient times, clothing culture was very complex. It included a full set of clothing and jewelry, not only paid attention to aesthetic, but was also in line with the ritual, a set of detailed rules, and was the embodiment of the Chinese national etiquette culture.

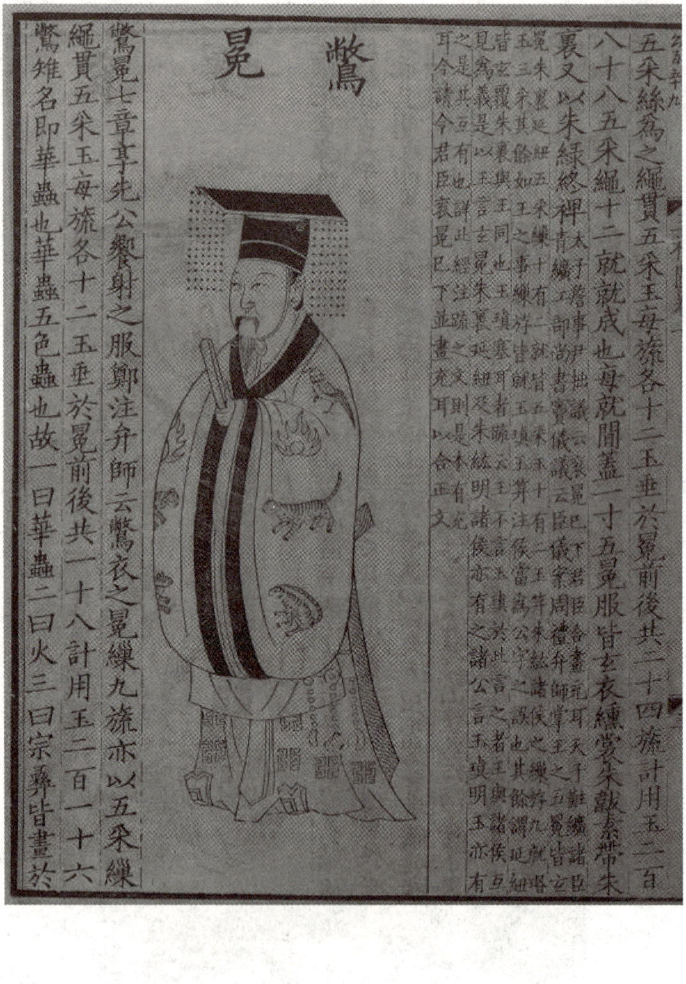
五采絲爲之繩貫五采玉每旒各十二玉垂於冕前後共二十四旒計用玉二百
八十八五采繩十二就就成也每就間蓋一寸五冕服皆玄衣纁裳朱韍素帶朱
裏又以朱綠終裨

鷩冕

鷩冕七章享先公饗射之服鄭注弁師云鷩衣之冕繅九旒亦以五采繅
繩貫五采玉每旒各十二玉垂於冕前後共一百八計用玉二百一十六
鷩雉名即華蟲也華蟲五色蟲也故一曰華蟲二曰火三曰宗彝皆畫於

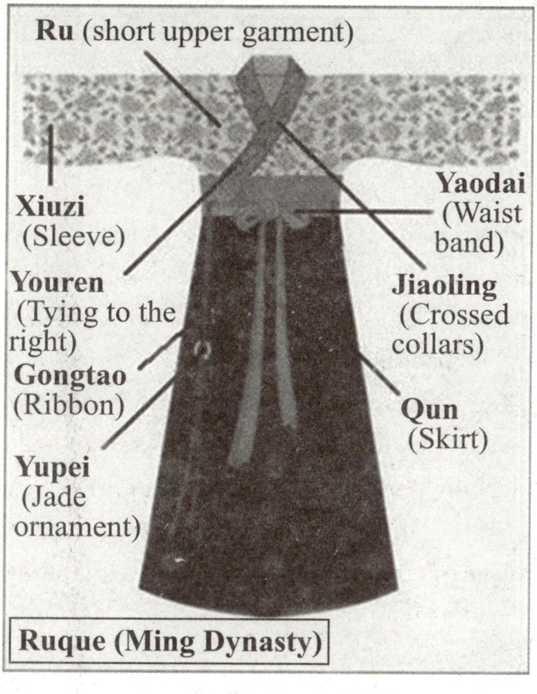

今天人们穿的汉服要简单得多。汉服一般分上下两部分即上衣下裳，衣接近于我们今天的上衣，而裳则是裙裾。现在兴起了一股汉服热，体现出人们复兴传统文化，寻找古典美的热情。

Nowadays, wearing Hanfu is much simpler. Hanfu is generally divided into two parts: an upper part and a lower part. The upper part is similar to a blouse and the lower part is a skirt. The popularity of Hanfu reflects people connecting back with the traditional culture, and their enthusiasm of classical beauty.

（二）唐装
Tang Costume

近年来，唐装在中国非常流行。每到春节，人们喜欢穿唐装去拜年。那么唐装是怎么来的呢？唐装也并不是唐朝的服装，之所以叫唐装是因为人们习惯把一切和中国有关的事物冠以“唐”来形容。其实唐装是以马褂为雏形，加入立领和西式立体裁剪所设计的服饰，是一种现代服饰。

In recent years, Tang costume has become very popular in China. So how did the Tang costume come about? Tang costume is not the clothing of the Tang Dynasty. The clothing is called “Tang dress” because people are used to putting “Tang” before everything related to China. In fact, Tang clothing is influenced by the clothing of Manchu ethnic group (one of Chinese minority groups) and the western suit.

（三）旗袍
Cheongsam

中国的旗袍，在英语中被翻译为 Chinese dress。旗袍原本是“旗人长袍”的简称。旗人指中国的少数民族——满族。旗袍虽然起源于满族，但不仅仅属于满族，随着时代的发展，旗袍的设计也不断地发生变化。

China's *chi-pao* (or cheongsam) is translated to "Chinese dress" in English. *Chi-pao* is short for "*Qiren changpao*", and "*Qiren*" refers to the Manchu ethnic group in China. Although *chi-pao* originated from the Manchu culture, it goes beyond it. With the development of the times , the design of *chi-pao* changes constantly.

旗袍是中国多个民族服饰文化融合的产物。我们现在看到的旗袍，也就是被称作 Chinese dress 的旗袍，实际是指 20 世纪 30 年代的旗袍。它的主要特点是：腰身变瘦了，紧贴皮肤，领子是立着的，下摆可长可短，开衩。

The *chi-pao* (cheongsam) today, is labeled as the “Chinese dress”. It refers to its style during the 1930s. Its main features are as follows: small waistline, skin dress, a stand up collar, and a hemline that can be lowered or raised and slits on the sides.

1925年　　**1927**年　　**1930**年

旗袍带有布条盘成的花儿，叫盘花扣，是中国古代服饰的一大特点，也是旗袍上重要的点缀。由于旗袍线条流畅、典雅，能够很好地体现女性的身体曲线。现在，越来越多的女性喜欢穿旗袍。

The flower-setting button is a unique characteristic of the ancient Chinese clothing and an important ornament on *chi-pao* (cheongsam). Wearing a *chi-pao* could well present the female body, so more and more women like to wear *chi-pao* nowadays.

二、饮食文化

Culinary Culture

（一）筷子

Chopsticks

筷子是中国人发明的进餐用具，大多由竹子做成，也有用金属、象牙、彩漆等原材料制作的。从古代开始，筷子就逐渐流传到中国的周边国家，也成为其他许多东亚国家的进餐工具。

Chopsticks are invented by Chinese people, which are usually made of bamboo, and can also be made of metal, ivory or colored lacquer. Chopsticks are not only found in China. In ancient times they spread to neighboring countries in East Asia.

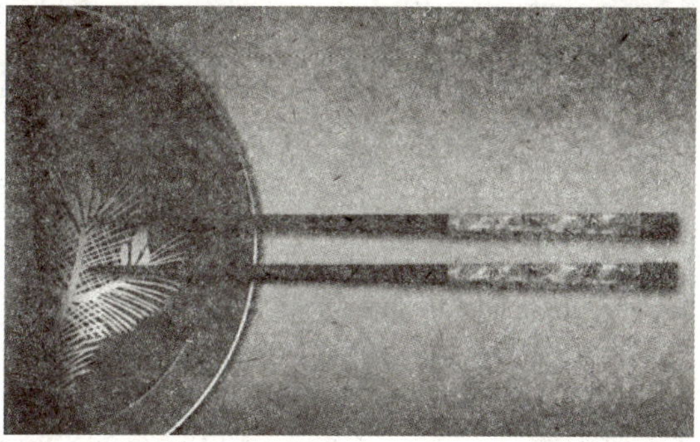

筷子在古代叫“箸”，箸的发音和帮助的“助”一样，意思就是帮助吃饭的工具。但是“箸”又和“住”同音，有缓慢、停下等不吉利的意思，所以人们就用“住”的反义词“快”加上竹字头来称呼这个工具，于是，“筷子”就一直沿用到今天。

In classical Chinese, the word chopsticks are pronounced the same as “zhu” in the word “bangzhu”—assistance, which means “assistance to eating”. There is another “zhu”, but has a different meaning of “slow” or “to stop”. To counteract this ominous meaning, people began to use the antonym “快”, meaning “fast”. With the radical for bamboo added above “快”, it became the character “筷”, pronouncing “kuai”, and it has been the name for chopsticks ever since.

看起来简单的筷子，具备的功能却非常多，两根筷子可以解决大部分进餐的需要。中国的孩子差不多从三四岁开始就要学习使用筷子。研究发现，人们用筷子吃饭，可以锻炼多个关节和多条肌肉。

Chopsticks, though seem quite simple, serve many functions. A pair can serve majority of purposes in eating. Chinese children learn how to use chopsticks when they are three or four years old. Scientists say this is very good for the development of their joints and muscles.

筷子在中国流传了几千年，因此，除了作为每餐必须使用的工具以外，也形成了丰富的筷子文化。对于就餐来说，最重要的就是遵守筷子礼仪。例如，筷子一定要放在筷子架上，不要放在杯子或盘子上；不要用筷子叉取食物；不要把筷子直接放在嘴里；不要把筷子插入米饭中；等等。通过这些礼仪，我们能看到中国人长期使用筷子而积累下来的经验、习惯和禁忌。

Chopsticks have been in China for several thousand years, so it is more than an eating tool, and rich culture has also been formed around it. Certain taboos have become accepted. For example, chopsticks should always be left on their stand when not in use and never on top of a plate or cup; food should never be picked up in the way as with a fork; chopsticks should never be sucked in the mouth; and they should never be placed vertically in rice. These are rules Chinese people have observed in the past and today.

（二）中国菜 Chinese Cuisine

中国菜是中国饮食文化的重要组成部分，讲究色、香、味、形、意俱全，重视选料、刀工、火候和调味四个方面。

Chinese cuisine, as part of China's culinary culture, values the color, fragrance, taste, appearance and connotation of dishes. The selection of the ingredients is considered important, along with the cutting method, the cooking temperature and the choice of condiments.

中国菜的选料非常丰富，也有很多要求，需要区分时令、产地、品种和部位等等。比如北京烤鸭，必须用北京地区的填鸭才行；吃螃蟹，一定要用阳澄湖的大闸蟹；做红烧肉要用五花肉，做京酱肉丝就必须用里脊肉了。

Chinese cuisine uses a wide range of ingredients, often dictated by the season, location and different parts of the animal. Peking roast duck, for instance, uses only ducks from Beijing; freshwater crabs come from Yangcheng Lake in Jiangsu; pork braised in brown sauce uses streaky pork and the shredded pork braised in Peking style, relies on the best tenderloin.

中国菜在烹饪前，大多需要把原料加工成方便食用的尺寸，因此刀工就显得非常重要。刀工需要的主要工具是菜刀和砧板，厨师通常会把原料切成片、丝、条、块、丁、粒等形状。有些原料经过厨师的巧手，就能变成一件精致的工艺品。

Before a dish is cooked, the ingredients are cut to the proper size. The way in which they are cut is very important. When cutting, a knife and a cutting board are needed. The ingredients are cut to different shapes: slices, shreds, strips, chunks, dices or grains. Even before the cooking begins, the ingredients, processed by an expert could become works of art.

中国菜的烹调方法非常多，例如蒸、煮、煎、炒、炸、炖、烧等。无论哪种烹饪方法，火候的掌握都是非常重要的。时间的长短，火的大小往往就能决定菜肴的品质。

There are many ways of cooking Chinese food: steaming, boiling, stir-frying, frying, deep frying, stewing and braising. Each method requires a certain time and temperature. The slightest deviation can make a huge difference in quality.

中国菜的调料很多，不同的地区虽然会有些差异，但也有一些是各地通用的，比如：盐、白糖、酱油、醋、料酒、生姜、蒜、葱、香油、辣椒、胡椒、花椒等。

The various regional styles of Chinese cuisine use numerous condiments. Some of them are universal, such as salt, sugar, soybean sauce, vinegar, wine, ginger, garlic, Chinese onions, sesame oil, hot pepper, pepper and Chinese Sichuan pepper.

（三）四大菜系
Four Different Styles of Cooking

一个地区，经过漫长的历史演变逐渐形成一种独特的烹饪方法和风味，这种独特的风味就形成了菜系。中国有八大菜系和四大菜系的说法。一般来说，四大菜系指的是川菜、鲁菜、粤菜和淮扬菜。

Chinese cuisine is divided into eight different styles of cooking and each has developed over a long period of history to create a special style of cooking and unique flavor. However, some people say it only has four different styles of cooking, Sichuan, Shandong, Guangdong and Huaiyang.

1. 川菜
Sichuan Cuisine

川菜起源于四川，是四大菜系之首，也是中国民间最大的菜系。川菜以“麻辣”为主味，中国各地常见的“麻婆豆腐”“宫保鸡丁”等都是川菜的代表菜品。由于川菜善于吸收其他各家菜系的长处，不断创新，因此最受欢迎，人们常说“食在中国，味在四川”。

The Sichuan cuisine is the most popular of the four. Ma Po Dou Fu (Sauteed Tofu in Hot and Spicy Sauce) and Kung Pao Chicken are two of the most famous Sichuan-style dishes. During its evolution, Sichuan cuisine borrowed from other styles in order to keep up with its popularity. No wonder people say, “The best food in the world is in China and the best food in China is in Sichuan.”

2. 鲁菜
Shandong Cuisine

鲁菜是北方菜肴的代表，历史非常悠久，烹饪手段较多。在长期的历史演变中，主要分成了济南和胶东两种口味。济南菜最擅长制汤，有清汤和奶汤的区别；胶东菜则以海鲜为主。

The Shandong cuisine, with its long history and many different cooking methods, represents the cuisine of northern China. In the course of its development, it has evolved into two styles: Jinan and east Shandong. Jinan style is famous for its soups, the "clear soup" and "milky soup" are the most popular. The east Shandong style relies heavily on seafood.

3. 粤菜

Guangdong Cuisine

粤菜指的是广东一带的风味菜。由于南方气候比较温暖，食物不能存放太久，因此，粤菜对原料的新鲜程度要求比较高。粤菜在海外的影响也是最大的，世界各地的中国餐馆中，粤菜馆最多。

The Guangdong cuisine has been developed in an area where the climate is warm, so food can quickly go bad. For this reason, Guangdong-style cuisine emphasizes the freshness of the ingredients. Guangdong cooking is the best-known style of Chinese food outside the country; many Chinese restaurants abroad offer Guangdong-style, or Cantonese food.

4. 淮扬菜

Huaiyang Cuisine

淮扬菜主要指的是江苏一带的风味菜，口味相对清淡，比较讲究刀工，重视菜的时令特点，在制作上也更加精细一些。其实，除了传统菜系，人们也在不断丰富和发展着更多不同的地方菜肴，许多新的地方菜系正在逐渐形成。

The Huaiyang cuisine refers to the style of cooking popular in Jiangsu, where people prefer a mild taste. Its main feature is the way the ingredients are cut, and the ingredients in season are also emphasized. Besides, the preparation is extremely elaborate. Apart from these four major cooking styles, new ones are continuously emerging and developing from different provinces styles, and even more new ones are still forming.

（四）地方小吃

Snacks

小吃，就是一日三餐之外的食品，一般特色突出，价格便宜。总的来说，中国北方的小吃味重，南方的小吃精致。

Snacks—known in Chinese as *Xiaochi*—are foods that are eaten separately from breakfast, lunch and dinner. They are usually low-priced and have prominent and distinctive characteristics. In general, northern Chinese snacks are characterized by a strong flavor, while southern Chinese snacks are usually delicate and dainty.

西北的传统小吃大都与牛羊肉有关。比如西安的牛羊肉泡馍、兰州的牛肉拉面、乌鲁木齐的烤羊肉串，都是全国有名的小吃。

Most of the traditional snacks of northwestern China are made with beef or mutton. Xi'an's steamed bread dipped in beef or mutton soup, Lanzhou's beef *lamian* (pulled noodles) and Urumqi's lamb kebabs, for instance, are well-known throughout China.

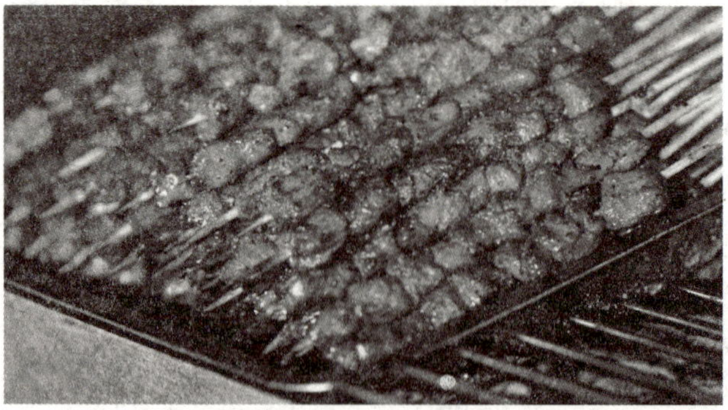

西南小吃与川菜一样，比较麻辣，担担面、凉面、凉粉、夫妻肺片等都是成都的传统小吃。

Snacks of southwestern China, like Sichuan food, are both hot and spicy. Chengdu's traditional snacks include Sichuan-style noodles in hot sauce, cold noodles, bean-starch jelly, and *fuqi feipian* (made of thinly sliced beef in spices).

北京较有地方色彩的小吃有灌肠、爆肚、茶汤、豆汁儿、炒肝、驴打滚、艾窝窝、烧卖等。

Beijing's local-flavor snacks include sausages, quick-fried tripe, *Chatang* (seasoned flour mush), soybean milk, stewed liver, "rolling donkey" (a kind of cake made of bean-flour and glutinous rice flour), glutinous rice balls, and *shaomai*.

还有一些地方小吃也很有特色，比如南京小吃、杭州小吃、福建小吃、广东小吃。中国各地小吃，历史悠久，自成风格，与地方菜肴相互辉映，成为中国饮食文化中的一份宝贵遗产。

There are also many local snacks from other parts of China with their own special characteristics, including those from Nanjing, Hangzhou, Fujian and Guangdong. Like Chinese regional cuisines in general, the snacks of each region have a long history and exhibit their own style. Chinese snacks with local food have become an invaluable part of Chinese culinary culture.

（五）酒文化
Wine Culture

发达的农耕文明提供了大量粮食，中国人很早就学会了用粮食做原料来酿酒，并且在 3 000 多年前就做出了一种叫“酒曲”的原料，用它酿出来的酒口味极佳。“酒曲”是中国人对酿酒技术的一大贡献。

China's advanced agricultural civilization has always provided a large volume of grain. From early times, the Chinese people learned how to use grains as an ingredient in making alcohol. Over 3,000 years ago, they devised a kind of “distiller” (rice that has been cultured predominantly by various molds, yeast and bacteria). This gave the brewed alcohol a superb flavor. The Chinese people's creation of this “distiller” served as a great contribution to liquor-making technology.

中国的酒主要是白酒，白酒的意思就是无色的酒，白酒和法国白兰地、俄罗斯伏特加、苏格兰威士忌并称世界四大蒸馏酒。中国白酒最著名的要数贵州茅台、山西汾酒和四川五粮液。

The main alcoholic beverage in China is Baijiu. The literal meaning of Baijiu is "white liquor." Baijiu is known as one of the world's four great distilled alcohols (the others are French brandy, Russian vodka and Scottish whiskey). China's most famous types of Baijiu are Guizhou Province's Maotai (Moutai), Shanxi Province's Fenjiu, and Sichuan Province's Wuliangye.

"无酒不成席"，中国人待客一定要用酒，用白酒待客则更显郑重。白酒也是中国人互相馈赠的首选，每到春节的时候，市场上的白酒总是有相当多的购买者。

There is a Chinese expression which says, "Without wine, there is no feast." In China, serving alcohol is an absolute custom when entertaining guests; compared with other alcohols, Baijiu is considered more dignified. Baijiu is also a preferred choice for gift-giving among the Chinese people. When the Spring Festival arrives each year, countless people rush to the markets to purchase this important beverage.

（六）茶文化
Tea Culture

中国是茶的故乡，据说从神农时代人们就开始饮茶，至少有 4 700 年的历史了。直到现在，中国各族同胞还有以茶代礼的风俗。

China is the birthplace of tea. It is said that people have been drinking tea since the Shennong era, which has a history of at least 4700 years. Until now, Chinese people still have the custom of giving each other gifts of tea.

中国茶文化是中国制茶、饮茶的文化。作为开门七件事（柴米油盐酱醋茶）之一，饮茶在古代中国是非常普遍的。中国的茶文化不但包含物质文化层面，还包含深厚的精神文明层次。唐朝上元初年（公元 760 年），陆羽隐居苕溪（今浙江湖州），撰《茶经》三卷（世界上第一部茶叶著作）。从此茶的精神渗透了宫廷和社会，进入了中国的诗词、绘画、书法、宗教、医学。几千年来中国不但积累了大量关于茶叶种植、生产的物质文化，更积累了丰富的有关茶的精神文化，这就是中国特有的茶文化，属于文化学范畴。

Chinese tea culture includes making and drinking tea in China. Drinking tea was very common in ancient China. Chinese tea culture contains not only the tea, but also the meaning of the tea. In the early years of Tang Dynasty (A.D. 760), Lu Yu wrote three volumes of *The Classic of Tea* which became the first tea book in the world. From then on, the spirit of tea permeated the court and society, deep into Chinese poetry, painting, calligraphy, religion and medicine. Over the past few thousand years, China has not only accumulated a large number of cultures about tea planting and production, but also accumulated a wealth of spiritual culture of tea. This is the unique tea culture in China.

中国茶叶按照制作方法分为绿茶、白茶、黄茶、青茶、红茶、黑茶六大类，各类茶中又包括许多品种。中国茶通过不同渠道传播到海外，日本人偏爱绿茶，欧洲人偏爱红茶。

According to the preparation method, Chinese tea is divided into green tea, white tea, yellow tea, Oolong tea, black tea, and dark tea. Chinese tea spread abroad through different channels. Japanese prefer green tea while Europeans prefer black tea.

陆羽和皎然等一批文化人非常重视茶的精神享受和道德规范，讲究饮茶用具、饮茶用水和煮茶艺术，并与儒、道、佛哲学思想交融。一些士大夫和文人雅士在饮茶过程中，还创作了很多茶诗，仅在《全唐诗》中，流传至今的就有百余位诗人的四百余首，从而奠定了中国茶文化的基础。茶叶，为中国茶坛大放异彩。

Lu Yu and Jiao Ran and other intellectuals have attached great importance to the spiritual enjoyment and moral order of tea. They have paid attention to tea drinking utensils, tea drinking water and tea making art, and have blend them with Confucian, Taoist and Buddhist philosophy. Many tea poems have also been created in the process of drinking tea and more than 400 poems have been handed down from Tang Dynasty, thus laying the foundation of Chinese tea culture.

中国是文明古国，礼仪之邦，很重礼节。凡来了客人，沏茶、敬茶的礼仪是必不可少的。在外交场合，中国的领导人也多次与外国领导人一同“茶叙”，共话友好未来。

China is a country with an ancient civilization, and a country of propriety and etiquette. When guests come, the etiquette of making tea and honoring tea is essential. On diplomatic occasions, China's president has repeatedly invited foreign leaders to drink tea and talk about a friendly future.

为了满足人们对茶的需求，中国的茶馆非常多。茶馆不仅是饮茶之地，也是重要的社交、休闲、娱乐场所。在北京、成都、浙江等地有很多有名的茶馆。茶馆文化也是茶文化的重要组成部分。

In order to meet people's demand for tea, there are many tea houses in China. The tea house is not only a place to drink tea, but also an important place for social, leisure and entertainment. There are many famous tea houses in Beijing, Chengdu, Zhejiang and other places. Tea house culture is also an important part of tea culture.

地方频道
Local Channel

1. 广州的早茶

Morning Tea of Guangzhou

广州早茶是一种民间饮食风俗。广州人饮早茶，有的是当作早餐的，有的则以此消闲。今天，广州早茶中茶水已经成为配角，茶点却越发精致多样，成为广州人休闲生活中的一大特色。

In Guangzhou, many people have still kept the habit of going to a tea house early in the morning for morning tea and dim sum. Some of them take it as their breakfast, while others use it to relax. Today, the tea has already become a supporting role to dim sum, and dim sum has become more and more exquisite and diverse, which has become a major feature of Guangzhou people's leisure life.

"请早茶"也是广州人一种通常的社交方式。早茶时分可以谈生意、交换信息，也可以会朋聚友、谈天说地。生意人把茶楼当作商谈重地，普通人则在此疏解压力，换得浮生半日闲。

"Treating others with morning tea and dim sum" is a common way for Guangzhou people to socialize. During that time people can talk about business, and exchange information. Businessmen regard tea houses as the most important place for negotiation, while ordinary people relieve their pressure and enjoy a leisure day.

2. 重庆火锅
Hot Pot in Chongqing

在重庆，最有名的是火锅。重庆火锅，又称为毛肚火锅或麻辣火锅，是中国的传统饮食方式，起源于明末清初的重庆嘉陵江畔、朝天门等码头船工、纤夫的粗放餐饮方式，原料主要是牛毛肚、猪黄喉、鸭肠、毛血旺等。现在火锅成为重庆的文化符号，也是当地居民和游客必不可少的美食。

In Chongqing, the most famous food is the hot pot. Chongqing hot pot, also known as tripe hot pot or spicy hot pot, is a traditional Chinese way of eating. It originated from the extensive dining style of boatmen and boat trackers in the late Ming and early Qing Dynasties in Jialing river and Chaotianmen wharf. Raw materials are mainly cow stomach, pig artery, duck intestine, blood and so on. Now hot pot has become the cultural symbol of Chongqing, and also the essential food for local residents and tourists.

三、建筑文化
Architecture

（一）传统木结构营造技艺
Traditional Timber Construction Technology

中国传统建筑是以木结构框架为主的建筑体系，以土、木、砖、瓦、石作为主要建筑材料。

Chinese traditional architecture is a building system based on timber frames, using clay, wood, brick, tile and stone as the main materials.

中国的匠师在几千年的木结构营造过程中积累了丰富的技术工艺经验，在材料的合理选用、结构方式的确定、模数尺寸的权衡与计算、构件的加工与制作、节点及细部处理和施工安装等方面都有独特与系统的技艺，并有相关的禁忌和操作仪式。这种营造技艺以师徒之间“言传身教”的方式世代相传，延承至今。

Over the past several thousand years, Chinese craftsmen have accumulated rich experience in the construction of timber-framed structures, and developed a unique and systematic set of techniques among others: selecting materials, determining the structure and style, measuring and calculating the modular size, processing and manufacturing the component parts, handling the joints, details, and construction with related taboos and ceremonies. This architectural craftsmanship, imparted by masters to their apprentices through words and examples, has been handed down from one generation to another up to the present day.

中国传统的木结构建筑是由柱、梁、檩、枋、斗拱等大木构件形成的框架结构，来承受屋面、楼面的荷载以及风力和地震力。这种木结构体系的关键技术就是榫卯结构。也就是木质构件之间的连接不需要其他材料，而是依靠两个木质构件之间的插接。这种构件间的连接方式使木结构抗震性强，具有可以预制加工、现场装配、营造周期短的明显优势。

Chinese traditional timber-framed buildings rely on a frame constituted by big wooden components, such as: the pillar, roof, beam, square beam and corbel bracket to bear the load of the roof and floor; to resist wind and earthquakes. The key technology of the timber-framed system lies in the tenon-and-mortise structure. For example, the wooden components are connected by no materials but the joints of its own two parts. Through this way, the timber-framed buildings show a good anti-seismic capability and advantages such as prefabrication, site assembly and short construction period.

据考古发现，在中国河姆渡文化遗址建筑中，榫卯结构就已经出现了。以此推断，中国传统木结构营造技艺距今已有七千余年的历史了。

According to archaeological discoveries, the tenon-and-mortise structure has already existed in the buildings of Hemudu cultural site, which means that the traditional architectural craftsmanship of timber-framed structures can be traced back to more than 7,000 years ago.

天津市蓟州区独乐寺的观音阁是中国现存最古老的木结构楼阁，全阁有立柱两层，外檐柱 18 根，内檐柱 10 根。各层檐柱之间又有梁枋相互连接，构成内外两圈，外圈檐柱构成的外框套着内层檐柱构成的内框。内外两个框架之间又以短横梁相连。这种结构大大增强了观音阁抵御地震和大风的能力。历经千年风雨侵蚀和很多次大小地震的破坏，观音阁仍巍然屹立。

The Guanyin (Goddess of Mercy) Pavilion in Dule Temple of Jizhou District in Tianjin is China's oldest wooden structure pavilion that still exists today. The pavilion has two stories of upright posts, including 18 outer eave columns and 10 inner eave columns, which are interconnected by beams and form two frames—one outside the other. The two frames are jointed by short beams. This structure greatly enhances the pavilion's ability to resist the possible damages. Having gone through centuries of wind, and rain erosion and many earthquakes on a variety of scales, the Guanyin Pavilion is still standing there, as lofty and firm as it was before.

中国的少数民族——侗族，以建筑艺术见长。早在三国时期，侗族先民就逐渐掌握了木结构建筑营造技艺。广西三江的风雨桥、鼓楼是侗族木质建筑的代表，它们不仅造型美观，而且工艺堪称一绝。整座建筑凿榫打眼、穿梁接拱、立柱连枋不用一颗铁钉，全以榫卯连接，结构牢固，接合缜密，具有很高的工艺和艺术价值。

The Dong people, a Chinese ethnic group, are famous for their art of architecture. As early as in the Three Kingdoms Period, the ancestors of the Dong people had already mastered the craftsmanship of building timber-framed structures. As the most typical wooden buildings of the Dong ethnic group, the Shelter Bridge and the Drum Tower in Sanjiang County of Guangxi Zhuang Autonomous Region, are beautiful in appearance and excellent in art and technique. Not even one iron nail being used, the beams, the corbel brackets and the upright posts in each building are all connected by tenons and mortises, forming a firm structure with meticulous joints which shows a great technical and artistic value.

2009 年，中国传统木结构营造技艺被联合国教科文组织列入人类非物质文化遗产代表作名录。

In 2009, the traditional architectural craftsmanship for timber-framed structures was inscribed on the Representative List of the Intangible Cultural Heritage of Humanity by UNESCO.

（二）中国经典建筑
Chinese Classic Architectures

1. 故宫
The Imperial Palace

故宫是中国明清两代的皇宫，也被称为“紫禁城”。这里曾居住过24个皇帝。故宫占地面积72万平方米，有房间9 999间半，是中国现存最大、最完整的古建筑群。

The Imperial Palace was the royal palace of the Ming and Qing dynasties in Chinese history. It is also called the Forbidden City. The Imperial palace was serving as a residence for 24 emperors.

The palace complex covers an area of 720,000 square meters and consists of 9,999 and a half of room. It is the largest ancient building complex in China that remains intact.

故宫的建筑有外朝、内廷之分，内廷与外朝的建筑风格完全不同。外朝以太和殿、中和殿、保和殿为中心，是皇帝行使权力、举行盛典的地方。内廷以乾清宫、交泰殿、坤宁宫为中心，是皇帝与后妃居住的地方。

The Palace is divided into the inner and outer courts, which are completely different in their architectural styles. The outer court is centered on the Hall of Supreme

Harmony, the Hall of Central Harmony and the Hall of Preserving Harmony. It is the place where the emperors exerted their power and held grand ceremonies. The inner court is centered on the Hall of Heavenly Purity, the Hall of Union and the Hall of Earthly Tranquility. It is the place where the emperors and their concubines lived.

故宫博物院收藏有大量中国古代艺术珍品，共有 100 多万件，是中国收藏文物最丰富的博物馆。1988 年，故宫被列入《世界遗产名录》。

The Palace Museum has a collection of over a million ancient Chinese art treasures, which makes it a museum with the richest collection of cultural relics in China. In 1988, the Imperial Palace was included in the *World Heritage List*.

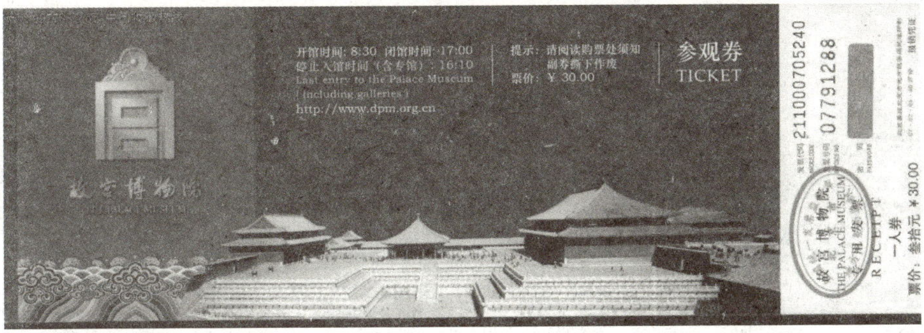

2. 兵马俑

Terracotta Warriors

兵马俑是公元前 210 年被埋到地下的，到现在已经 2 000 多年了。它们属于一个人，他就是中国第一个皇帝——秦始皇。

Terracotta warriors were buried in the year of 210 B.C., which contains a history of over 2,000 years. They belonged to one man, the first emperor of China, Qinshihuang.

秦始皇在当皇帝后不久就开始修建他的陵墓，前后用了将近 40 年的时间。墓内建有各种复杂的宫殿，工程的浩大，现代人很难想象。

As soon as Qinshihuang ascended the throne he began to build his mausoleum, which took nearly 40 years to complete. Inside the tomb, various complicated palaces were built. When visitors see the mausoleum, it is beyond what they imagined.

秦始皇的陵墓在西安附近。1974 年，当地的农民偶然发现地下有陶俑。经过考古发掘，现在已经发现了三个坑。发掘出 700 多件陶俑、100 多辆战车、400 多匹陶马、10 万多件兵器。

The mausoleum is located near Xi'an. In 1974, local farmers accidentally discovered some pottery figurines underground. The following archaeological excavations have found three vaults. Altogether over 700 pottery figurines, over 100 chariots, over 400 pottery horses and over 100 thousand weapons were unearthed.

陶俑身高在 1.75 米至 1.85 米之间，可以分为将军俑、武士俑等。坑内出土的剑、矛等青铜兵器，虽然埋在地下 2 000 多年了，但依然锋利。这是一个庞大的地下军事博物馆。1987 年，秦始皇陵及兵马俑被列入《世界遗产名录》。

These pottery figurines range from 1.75 to 1.85 meters in height, and divided into groups like generals or warriors, etc. The bronze weapons like swords and lances still have sharp blades although they had been buried underground for over 2,000 years. This is a grand underground military museum. In 1987, the Qin mausoleum and its terracotta warriors were listed on the *World Heritage List*.

3. 孔庙　孔府　孔林

Temple of Confucius, Confucius's Family Mansion and Cemetery of Confucius

孔庙，在中国山东曲阜，是为纪念孔子而建的。孔子生活在公元前 6 世纪到公元前 5 世纪之间，是中国伟大的哲学家、政治家和教育家，是儒家学说的代表。由于中国古代帝王大多推崇儒家学说，把孔子奉为圣人，因此孔庙被不断地扩建，形成了现在的规模。

The Temple of Confucius in Qufu, Shandong, was built in honor of Confucius. Confucius lived from the 6th to 5th century B.C.. He was a great Chinese philosopher, statesman and educator, and the representative of Confucian doctrine. Since most ancient Chinese emperors advocated and endorsed Confucian doctrine, they recognized and treated him as a sage. As a result, the Temple was continuously expanded, resulting in its current scale.

孔庙内种满了松树和柏树，显得庄严、肃穆。大成殿，是孔庙的正殿。大成殿内有孔子像。杏坛是孔子讲学的地方。坛旁的古树，据说是孔子亲手种植的。孔庙内还陈列着大量碑碣石刻。

The Temple of Confucius is filled with pine and cypress trees, creating a stately and solemn atmosphere. The main hall of the Temple, called Dacheng Hall contains Statue of Confucius. The Apricot Pavilion is the place where Confucius gave lectures.

The ancient trees beside the pavilion have been, supposedly, planted by Confucius himself. Many tablets and stone carvings are also displayed in the Temple.

孔庙旁边是孔府。孔府是孔子后代子孙居住的地方，它的面积仅次于明、清的皇宫。孔府中部是主体建筑，官衙在前，内宅在后，最后面是花园。

The Confucius's family mansion is located beside the Temple. It was where the descendants of Confucius lived; its area is almost as large as that of the Ming and Qing imperial palaces. The mansion's main structure is the central building; the official rooms are located in the front, followed by the residential quarters and finally the garden in the rear.

孔府附近是孔林。孔林是孔子和孔子后代的墓地，前后延续使用了约 2 500 年，一共有孔氏子孙墓十余万座。

The Cemetery of Confucius located beside the Confucius's family mansion. Confucius and his descendants are entombed in this cemetery, which has been used continuously for about 2,500 years. In total, there are over 100,000 tombs of the descendants of Confucius.

到孔子墓地，需要先经过 1 200 米的墓道，再穿过石牌坊、石桥、甬道，才能到达。埋葬在孔林的孔子子孙已经到第 76 代。作为一个家族墓地，孔林延续时间之长，墓葬数量之多，保存之完好，在世界上是独一无二的。1994 年，曲阜孔庙、孔府、孔林被列入《世界遗产名录》。

To reach the Cemetery of Confucius, you need to first pass through a 1,200-meter-long road, and then cross a stone memorial archway, a stone bridge and a paved path. There are 76 generations of Confucius' descendants buried in the Cemetery of Confucius. As a family burial ground, the Cemetery is unparalleled worldwide in terms of the length of time it has endured, the number of family members buried beneath its soil, and its degree of preservation. In 1994, the Temple, Family Mansion and Cemetery of Confucius in Qufu were listed on the *World Heritage List*.

4. 苏州园林
Gardens of Suzhou

明清时期，苏州是中国最繁华的地区之一，有许多私家园林，最多的时候有

200 多处，现在保存不错的有十几处。

During the Ming and Qing Dynasties Suzhou was one of the most prosperous areas in China, and contained many private gardens. The number of private gardens once reached over 200 at its peak, but only more than ten of them are kept in good condition now.

最有名的园林有拙政园、狮（师）子林、留园、沧浪亭等。这些私家园林，与颐和园、承德避暑山庄等皇家园林相比，规模要小得多，但它们是中国南方地区民间建筑的典型代表。

The most famous gardens include the Humble Administrator's Garden, the Lion Grove Garden, the Lingering Garden, the Surging Waves Pavilion, and so on. These private gardens are much smaller in size than the royal ones such as the Summer Palace in Beijing and the Chengde Imperial Summer Resort. But they are typical representations of folk architecture in the south of China.

苏州园林很像中国山水画，也像唐诗宋词，在有限的空间内放置了假山树木、亭台楼阁、池塘小桥。在园林中游览，好像在读诗赏画。

Gardens of Suzhou can be compared to the Chinese landscape paintings and poetry. One can see rockeries, trees, pavilions, terraces, towers, ponds and bridges, all contained in a limited space. Strolling around the gardens, one could feel as if he were reading poems and appreciating paintings.

园林中有图案精致的花窗、弯弯曲曲的小路、清澈的池塘。到处都能看出中国人在美化居住环境方面的创造力。1997 年，苏州园林被列入《世界遗产名录》。

Gardens of Suzhou contain these patterned windows with delicate designs, these zigzag paths, and these pools with clear water. The creativity of Chinese in beautifying their living environment can be seen all around. In 1997, the classical gardens of Suzhou were listed on the *World Heritage List*.

地方频道
Local Channel

重庆的吊脚楼
Featured Houses in Chongqing: Stilted Building

重庆是中国著名的“山城”，多山多水。重庆城依山而建，长江和嘉陵江穿城而过。重庆的建筑就随着山水的走向而上下起伏。吊脚楼是重庆传统的建筑，形成了重庆一道奇异的风景线。从前重庆的江边沿山坡处，到处都有几根杉杆撑着的一间间四四方方的木楼，这就是吊脚楼。吊脚楼采用的建筑材料是竹竿、泥巴和瓦片，通风而又牢固。

Chongqing, called also “mountain city”, was famous for its rich in mountain and water surroundings. The city was built along with the shape of mountains, and the Yangtze River and Jialing River pass through the city. Chongqing’s buildings fluctuate with the direction of landscape. Stilted building is a local traditional building, forming a strange scenic line in Chongqing. In the past, the whole hillside of Chongqing’s river edge was covered with stilted buildings. The building materials used in the stilted building includes bamboo poles, mud and tiles, which made it ventilated and firm.

现在，大部分吊脚楼已经成为历史。现存的吊脚楼也多为旅游景区。其中最著名的是洪崖洞。2005 年，洪崖洞景区在悬崖上建成了 9 层吊脚楼，成了人们必去的网红打卡景点。

Now, most of the stilted buildings has become a history. The existing stilted buildings are also mostly tourist attractions. One of the most famous ones is Hongyadong. In the 2005, a nine-story stilted building was established on cliff of Hongya-dong Scenic Area, which became a must-see tourist site.

四、行在中国

Traveling in China

在中国，出行十分方便。人们最常用的交通工具有飞机、高铁、私家车、共享单车等（其中高铁和共享单车还被誉为新四大发明），各种公路设施为出行提供了方便。

In China, traveling is very convenient. People’s most commonly used means of transport are airplanes, high-speed trains, private cars, shared bicycles and so on.

Among them, high-speed trains and shared cycling have also been hailed as the new four major inventions. Convenient travel is provided by various types of road facilities.

1. 港珠澳大桥
Hong Kong-Zhuhai-Macao Bridge

一方面是交通工具不断完善，另一方面是中国的公路设施也建设得越来越好。不用说贯通神州大地的中国高速公路网，就是新修建的各种桥梁，也大大便利了交通。

On the one hand, means of transportation are improving, on the other hand, road facilities are also getting better and better. China's highway network, which runs through the whole country, and a variety of new built bridges, also greatly improve traffic.

最有代表性的桥梁要数港珠澳大桥了。港珠澳大桥于 2009 年 12 月 15 日动工建设；于 2018 年 10 月 24 日上午 9 时开通运营。大桥历时 9 载，连接了香港、珠海和澳门经济带，为港珠澳出行提供方便，也为这一地区的经济腾飞奠定了基础。

The most representative bridge is the Hong Kong-Zhuhai-Macao Bridge. Construction of the Bridge commenced on December 15, 2009; it opened operations at 9 o'clock in the morning on October 24, 2018. It takes 9 years to build this bridge to connect the economic belts of Hong Kong, Zhuhai and Macao. It has facilitated travel between Hong Kong, Zhuhai and Macao, laying the foundation for economic take-off in the region.

2. 重庆的路和桥
Roads and Bridges in Chongqing

重庆是山城，出行不便，有的地方需要爬很高的楼梯，市民出行多乘坐轻轨。

重庆的轻轨很有特色，有时甚至需要穿楼而过。除轻轨外重庆还有天桥、立交桥，方便市民出行。

Chongqing is a mountain city, what makes travel quite inconvenient. Since there are places, where you have to climb a lot of high stairs, citizens prefer to travel by light rail. Chongqing's light rail is very distinctive, sometimes even passes through a building. In addition to the light rail, Chongqing also has flyovers and overpasses, making it convenient for the public to travel.

这些特别的轻轨、天桥、立交桥体现了重庆人民的智慧，成了重庆的名片。大家称呼重庆为 8D 城市。还有很多电影选在重庆拍摄，充分展示了重庆的魅力，增强了重庆的吸引力。

These distinctive light rails, flyovers and overpasses, which reflect wisdom of Chongqing's citizens, have become the business card of the city. Chongqing is said to be the 8D city. It is also selected as a shooting location for many movies, which demonstrates the charm of the city and enhances its attractiveness.

在重庆拍摄的电影有《疯狂的石头》《火锅英雄》等。电影中展示的重庆过江缆车是独一无二的，通过电影的宣传，现在也成为游客必选的体验。

The films filmed in Chongqing are *Crazy Stone*, *Hot Pot Heroes* and so on. The Chongqing cross-river cable car shown in the film is unique and because of the promotion through the film, Chongqing cross-river cable car has become a must-have experience for tourists now.

课后练习题
Practice

一、选择题
Multiple-choice

1. 下列哪项不是文中所提到的制作筷子的材料？(　　)
According to the passage, which of the following is not the material used to make chopsticks?

A. 竹子
A. Bamboo

B. 象牙
B. Ivory

C. 纸
C. Paper

D. 彩漆
D. Colored lacquer

2. 下列哪种做法是遵守筷子礼仪？（　　）
Which of the following practice is to obey chopsticks etiquette?

A. 用筷子叉取食物
A. Food be picked up in the way as with a fork.

B. 将筷子插入米饭中
B. Chopsticks be placed vertically in rice.

C. 将筷子直接放在嘴里
C. Chopsticks be sucked in the mouth.

D. 将筷子放在筷子架上
D. Chopsticks always be left on their stand when not in use.

3. 下列哪种菜系在文中没有提及？（　　）
Which one is not mentioned in this article?

A. 川菜
A. Sichuan cuisine.

B. 鲁菜
B. Shandong cuisine.

C. 粤菜
C. Guangdong cuisine.

D. 闽菜
D. Fujian cuisine.

4. (　　) 年，中国传统木结构营造技艺被联合国教科文组织列入人类非物质文化遗产代表作名录。

In (　　), Chinese traditional wood structure construction skills have been included in the UNESCO list of representative works of human intangible civilization heritage.

A. 2007　　B. 2008　　C. 2009　　D. 2010

5. 中国少数民族——(　　) 以建筑艺术见长。

Chinese ethnic group — (　　) is good at archit ecture.

A. 回族
A. Hui

B. 满族
B. Manchu

C. 侗族
C. Dong

D. 白族
D. Bai

二、填空题

Fill-in-the-blanks

1. 中国现存最古老的木结构楼阁是天津市蓟州区独乐寺的________________。

China's oldest wooden structure pavilion is ________________, in Dule Temple of Jizhou District in Tianjin city.

2. 中国菜是中国饮食文化的重要组成部分，讲究______、______、______、______、______俱全，重视选料、刀工、火候和调味四个方面。

Chinese cuisine, as part of China's food culture, values the ________,________, ________, ________ and ________ of dishes. The selection of the ingredients is considered important, along with the cutting method, the cooking temperature and the choice of condiments.

3. 一个地区，经过漫长的历史演变逐渐形成一种独特的烹饪方法和风味，这种独特的风味就形成了菜系。中国有八大菜系和四大菜系的说法。一般来说，四大菜系指的是______、______、______ 和 ______。

Chinese cuisine is divided into 8 different parts, and each has developed over a long period of history to create a special style of cooking and unique flavor. However, some people say it has four parts. Today we will talk about the four parts namely ________, ________, ________ and ________.

4. 故宫是中国______和______两代的皇宫，也被称为"______"。这里曾居住过24个皇帝。
The Imperial Palace was the royal palace of the ______ and ______ Dynasties in Chinese history. It is also called the __________. The Imperial palace was serving as a residence for 24 emperors.

5. 所谓的"汉服"，又称汉衣冠、汉装、华服，总的来说就是指______的传统服饰。它不是指 ______ 的服饰。
The so-called "Han fu", also known as Han Crown, Han dress, Chinese clothing, in general refers to the traditional costumes of the __________, and not to the __________.

三、判断题
True or False

1. 汉服不是指汉族传统的服饰，而是指汉代的服饰。
Hanfu refers to the Han Dynasty, and not to the traditional customs of the Han nationality.

2. 唐装是只能在古代穿的衣服。
Tang costume is a cloth that can just only be worn in ancient times.

3. 现在，越来越多的女性喜欢穿旗袍。
Recently, more and more women like to wear *chi-pao* (cheongsam).

4. 胶东菜分为清汤和奶汤。
The east Shandong style divides into "clear soup" and "milky soup".

5. 文人雅士很在意饮茶用具。
Intellectuals pay attention to tea drinking utensils.

四、简答题
Short-answer Questions

1. 哪个菜系在海外的影响最大？
Which style is the best known style of Chinese food outside the country?

____

____

2. 南北方小吃有什么差异？

What is the difference between north and south snacks?

3. 按照制作方法，中国茶被分为哪几种？

According to the preparation method, how many kinds can Chinese tea be divided into?

第八章

中国的节日

Chinese Festivals

课前思考
Lead-in Questions

1. 你知道哪些中国传统节日？
   What traditional Chinese festivals do you know?
2. 你们国家有哪些传统节日？它们跟中国的传统节日有相同的地方吗？
   What are the traditional festivals in your country? Do they have the similarity with Chinese traditional festivals?

一、春节

Spring Festival

春节，即农历新年，是一年之岁首，就是传统意义上的“年节”，俗称新春、新岁、新年、大年等，又称过年、过大年。在春节期间，全国各地均有举行各种庆贺新春的活动，这些活动以除旧布新、迎禧接福、拜神祭祖、祈求丰年为主要内容，形式丰富多彩，带有浓郁的地域特色，凝聚着中华传统文化精华。

The Spring Festival (the Lunar New Year) is the beginning of the year, which is the traditional “New Year’s Festival”. The festival is also known colloquially as the Spring Festival, New Age, New Year, Great Year, etc. During the Spring Festival, various activities are held throughout the country. These activities mainly focus on removing the old, greeting the new, worshiping gods and ancestors, and praying for a harvest year by rich and colorful forms with special regional characteristics and essence of

Chinese traditional culture.

（一）起源与发展 Origin and Development

春节是由岁首祈年祭祀演变而来，上古时代便有了一些过年的气氛，人们于一年农事结束后，在新一年开端的岁首，举行祭祀活动报祭天地众神、祖先的恩德，祈求丰年。中国古代民间虽然早已有过年的风俗，但那时并不叫作春节。因为那时所说的春节，指的是二十四节气中的"立春"。南北朝则把春节泛指为整个春季。据说，把农历新年正式定名为春节，是辛亥革命后的事。由于那时要改用阳历，为了区分农、阳两节，所以只好将农历正月初一改名"春节"。2006 年 5 月 20 日，"春节"民俗经国务院批准列入第一批国家级非物质文化遗产名录。

The Spring Festival evolved from praying for the New Year at the beginning of one year. At the beginning of the New Year and the end of one year's farming, Chinese people held sacrificial activities to commemorate gods and ancestors and pray for a good year. Although spring festival in Chinese ancient folk has existed for a long time, it was not named as Spring Festival at that time. The Spring Festival at that time refers to the "beginning of spring" in the 24 solar terms. The Northern and Southern Dynasties generally referred to the Spring Festival as the whole spring. It is said that the Chinese New Year was officially named as the Spring Festival after the 1911 Revolution. Because the solar calendar will be adopted at that time, the first day of lunar New Year is called "Spring Festival" in order to distinguish the two festivals of lunar New Year and solar New Year. On May 20, 2006, "Spring Festival" folklore was approved by the State Council and listed in the first batch of national intangible cultural heritage list.

（二）春节的传说 Legend of Spring Festival

有一种传说，中国古时候有一种凶猛的怪兽叫"年"，一年四季都在深海里，但逢新旧岁之交，便出来糟蹋庄稼，伤害人畜，百姓叫苦连天。有一次，它又跑到村庄里为非作歹，被一家门口晾的大红衣服吓跑了。到了另一处，又被灯光吓得抱头鼠窜。于是人们掌握了"年"怕声音、怕红色、怕火光的弱点。每至年末岁首，人们就在家门口贴红联、放鞭炮、挂红灯，院子里烧柴禾、拢旺火，用菜刀剁菜肉，发出声音把"年"吓得逃回海里，不再危害人畜。久而久之，这些便成了过年的种种习俗。

There is a legend that in ancient China there was a fierce monster called Nian, which was in the deep sea all the year round. But at the turn of New Year, it came out to spoil crops and hurt people and animals. People complained a lot. On one occasion, it ran to the village to do evil and was frightened away by the red clothes hanging in the doorway. At the other place, he was frightened by the light and ran away. So people have grasped the weakness of "Nian"—fearing voice, red and fire. At the end of each year, people put red couplets, set off firecrackers, hang red lights at their doors, burn firewood and gather fire in the yard, chop vegetable and meat with a kitchen knife, and make a loud sound to scare Nian back into the sea. Over time, these have become a variety of Customs of the New Year.

（三）习俗
Customs

我国过年历史悠久，在传承发展中已形成了一些较为固定的习俗，南北迥异，各具特色。有许多还相传至今，如办年货、扫尘、贴年红、压岁钱、拜年、舞龙舞狮、拜神祭祖、烧炮竹、看春晚等习俗。

China has a long history of celebrating the New Year, and has formed some relatively fixed customs in its inheritance and development. The north and south are quite different and have their own characteristics. Many customs still handed down to today, such as preparing New Year's Goods, cleaning dust, sticking New Year's Reds, giving lucky money, paying a New Year call, dancing dragons and lions, worshiping gods and ancestors, burning firecrackers, watching Spring Festival Gala and so on.

1. 办年货

Preparing New Year's Goods

虽然各地习俗不尽相同，但是备年货、送年礼却几乎是全国上下的“过年必备”。置办年货，包括吃的、穿的、戴的、用的、贴的（年红）、送的礼物等，统称“年货”，而把采购年货的过程称之为“办年货”。办年货是中国人过春节的一项重要活动。

Although customs vary from place to place, the preparation of New Year's Goods and the delivery of New Year's gifts are necessary in almost all parts of the country. Purchasing of New Year's Goods, including food, clothing, sticker (New Year's Red), gift and so on, is collectively known as "New Year's Goods". The process of purchasing New Year's Goods is called "preparing New Year's Goods". Holding New Year's Goods is an important activity for Chinese people to celebrate the Spring Festival.

2. 祭灶

Sacrificing Kitchen

农历十二月廿三 / 廿四日祭灶，是入夜后要把灶台刷干净，把旧的灶君神像取下烧掉，早晨把新像贴上，一送一迎，都要摆置酒肉等，烧香、点烛、放纸炮。民间祭灶，源于古人拜火习俗。灶神信仰反映了中国百姓对“衣食有余”这一梦想的追求。

On the 23rd or 24th day of the lunar calendar, it is necessary to clean the kitchen table after nightfall, remove and burn the old statues of the king of kitchen, paste the new ones in the morning, and place wine, meat and other foods, burn incense, light candles and paper cannons as soon as they are delivered and welcomed. The folk sacrificial kitchen originated from the ancient custom of worshipping fire. Kitchen God belief is a reflection of Chinese people's pursuit of "more than enough food and clothing".

3. 扫尘

Sweeping Dust

在民间，新年前有“腊月二十四，扫尘（亦称扫屋）”的习俗 。民谚称“二十四，扫房子”。民间称作“扫尘日”。扫尘就是年终大扫除，家家户户都要打扫环境。按民间的说法：因“尘”与“陈”谐音，年前扫尘有“除陈布新”的含义。扫尘的用意是要把一切穷运、晦气统统扫出门，以祈来年清吉。

In the folk, there is a custom of "sweeping the house on the 24th of December in lunar year". The folk proverb says, "Twenty-fourth, sweep the house". Chinese people call it "dust-sweeping day". Dust cleaning is year-end cleaning. According to the folklore, because of the homonym of "dust" and "old", cleaning dust before New Year has the meaning of removing the old and bringing the new. The purpose of cleaning dust is to sweep out all the bad luck in order to pray for good luck in the coming year.

4. 年夜饭

New Year's Eve Dinner

年夜饭，又称团圆饭，特指岁末除夕的阖家聚餐。年夜饭源于古代的年终祭祀仪式，拜祭神灵与祖先后团圆聚餐。年夜饭不但丰富多彩，而且很讲究意头。席上一般有鸡（寓意吉利）、鱼（寓意年年有余）、发菜（寓意发财）、生蒜（寓意会计算）、腊肠（寓意长久）等以求吉利。中国人的年夜饭是家人的团圆聚餐，这顿是年尾最丰盛、最重要的一顿晚餐。

New Year's Eve dinner, also known as reunion dinner, refers to the family dinner at New Year's Eve. It is a reunion dinner after worshipping gods and ancestors and originates from the ancient year-end ritual sacrifice. New Year's Eve dinner is not only rich and colorful, but also meaningful. There is chicken (implies luck), fish (implies surplus), vegetable (implies wealth), raw garlic (implies accounting), sausage (implies permanent) and so on for good luck. Chinese New Year's Eve dinner is a family reunion dinner, which is the most abundant and important dinner at the end of the year.

5. 压岁钱

Lucky Money

压岁钱，年俗之一，年晚饭后长辈要给晚辈压岁钱，据说压岁钱可以压住邪祟，晚辈得到压岁钱就可以平平安安度过一岁。压岁钱在民俗文化中寓意辟邪驱鬼，保佑平安。因为人们认为小孩容易受鬼祟的侵害，所以用压岁钱压祟驱邪。

Giving lucky money is one of the customs. After dinner, the elders will give the younger generation lucky money. It is said that lucky money can suppress evil spirits, and the younger generation can live safely through the whole year. New Year's money in folk culture implies to ward off evil spirits and protect peace. Because people think that children are vulnerable to sneaking, they use lucky money to drive away evil spirits.

6. 拜年

Paying a New Year Call

春节期间走访拜年是年节传统习俗之一，是人们辞旧迎新、相互表达美好祝愿的一种方式。拜年的意义所在是亲朋好友之间走访并联络感情、互贺新年，表达对亲朋间的情怀以及对新一年生活的美好祝福。古时“拜年”一词原有的含义是为长者拜贺新年，包括向长者叩头施礼、祝贺新年如意、问候生活安好等内容。遇有同辈亲友，也要施礼道贺。随着时代的发展，拜年的习俗亦不断增添新的内容和形式。除了沿袭以往的拜年方式外，又兴起了电话拜年、短信拜年、网络拜年等。

Paying a New Year call during the Spring Festival is one of the traditional customs. It is a way for people to say goodbye to the old and greet the new and express good wishes to each other. The significance of New Year's greeting lies in improving friendship between relatives and friends, congratulating to each other on the New Year, expressing feelings between relatives and friends, and wishing for the New Year's life. In ancient times, the original meaning of the word "New Year's greeting" was to celebrate the New Year for the elders, including kowtowing to the elders, congratulating them on the happy New Year and greeting them for a good life. When there are relatives and friends of the same generation, courtesy and congratulations should also be given. With the development of the times, the custom of New Year's greetings has also added new contents and forms. In addition to following the previous New Year's greetings, etiquette telephone, short message and network greetings have sprung up.

7. 春晚

Spring Festival Gala

春节联欢晚会，简称“春晚”，是中国中央电视台在每年除夕晚上为庆祝农历新年举办的综艺性文艺晚会。它起源于 1979 年，正式开办于 1983 年，2014 年被定位为国家项目。1983 年，央视举办春节联欢晚会应该说是一个偶然事件。从文化发展的角度看，中央电视台春节联欢晚会开创了电视综艺节目的先河，而且引发了中国电视传媒表达内容、表达方式等方面的重大变革。随后，全国大大小小的地方电视台频频效法并力求创新。央视春晚涵盖小品、歌曲、歌舞、杂技、魔术、戏曲、相声剧等多种艺术形式，把现场观众和电视机前的观众带入狂欢之中，打造“普天同庆，盛世欢歌”的节日景象。春晚已经成了现代人过春节的一项必不可少的娱乐项目之一。

The Spring Festival Gala is a variety of literary and artistic evening held by CCTV every year to celebrate the Lunar New Year. It was originated in 1979 and officially launched in 1983 and positioned as a national project in 2014. In 1983, the Spring Festival Gala held by CCTV should be an accidental event. From the perspective of cultural development, CCTV Spring Festival Gala pioneered TV variety shows, and triggered major changes in the content and mode of expression of Chinese television media. Subsequently, local TV stations, large and small, tried to innovate. CCTV Spring Festival Gala covers a variety of artistic forms, such as sketches, songs, dances, acrobatics, magic, operas, cross-talk dramas, etc. It brings live audiences and audiences in front of TV sets into Carnival and creates a festival scene of "universal celebration, grand age carnival". The Spring Festival Gala has become one of the indispensable entertainment items for modern people to celebrate the Spring Festival.

二、元宵节
Lantern Festival

农历正月十五日是中国传统节日元宵节。农历里正月为元月，然而古人称夜晚为宵，而正月十五日又是一年中第一个月圆之夜，所以称正月十五为元宵节。按中国传统民俗，在一元复始，大地回春的夜晚，天上明月高悬，地上彩灯万盏，人们观灯、猜灯谜、吃元宵，合家团聚，其乐融融，这充分体现了元宵节的文化内涵。

The 15th day of the first lunar month is the Lantern Festival. The first month in lunar calendar is called "Yuan month". However, the ancients called night as "*xiao*", and the fifteenth day of the first month is the night of the first full moon in a year. Therefore, the fifteenth day of the first month is called the Lantern Festival (Yuan Xiao festival). According to Chinese traditional folklore, on the evening of Lantern Festival, people watch lanterns, guess lantern riddles and eat sweet dumplings for Lantern Festival to get together at home. Its joy and harmony fully reflects the cultural connotation of Lantern Festival.

（一）起源与发展
Origin and Development

古时候，因秦始皇名嬴政，为避讳"正"字，故此"正月十五"又称"端月十五"，象征团圆与美满。正月十五在西汉已经受到重视。不过，正月十五元宵节真正作为民俗节日是在汉魏之后。从唐代起，元宵张灯即成为法定之事，并逐渐成为民间习俗。2008 年 6 月，元宵节入选第二批国家级非物质文化遗产。

In ancient times, Lantern Festival was called "Duanyue 15th" in order to avoid Emperor Ying's "Zheng". It symbolized reunion and happiness. The fifteenth day of the first lunar month has been taken seriously in the Western Han Dynasty. However, after the Han and Wei Dynasties, the Lantern Festival began to be seriously regarded as a folk festival. Since the Tang Dynasty, lantern display has become a legal matter, and gradually become a folk custom. In June 2008, Lantern Festival was selected as the second batch of national intangible cultural heritage.

（二）元宵节的传说 Legend of Lantern Festival

古人认为"太乙"天神掌管着世间人类的命运。自秦始皇始，皇帝每年都举行盛大的仪式，祈求太乙神赐予国家风调雨顺，以及他与臣民们健康长寿。到了汉武帝时代，朝廷尤其重视元宵灯会，元封七年（公元前 104 年），汉武帝将元宵节钦定为最重要的佳节之一，庆祝仪式通宵进行。因此，元宵节就是拜"太乙"神的日子。

The ancients believed that the "Tai Yi" God controlled the fate of human beings in the world. Since the beginning of Emperor Qin, emperors held grand ceremonies every year to pray that Tai Yi God would grant the country good weather, as well as his health and longevity with his people. In the period of Emperor Wu of Han Dynasty, the court paid special attention to Lantern Festival. In the seventh year of Yuanfeng (104 B.C.), Emperor Wu appointed Lantern Festival as one of the most important festivals and celebrated it all night. Therefore, Lantern Festival is the day to worship the "Tai Yi" God.

（三）习俗 Customs

元宵节主要有赏花灯、吃汤圆、猜灯谜等一系列传统民俗活动。以下是主要习俗的介绍。

Lantern Festival mainly includes a series of traditional folk activities such as watching lanterns, eating dumplings, guessing lantern riddles, and so on. The following is an introduction to the main customs.

1. 吃元宵

Eating Yuanxiao

正月十五吃元宵，“元宵”作为食品，在我国也由来已久。宋代，民间即流行一种元宵节吃的新奇食品。这种食品，最早叫“浮元子”，后称“元宵”，生意人还美其名曰“元宝”。

元宵是一种带馅儿的甜食，是由糯米粉加上甜的馅料制成。元宵节就是因此食品得名。元宵的烹制方法十分简单，将元宵倒入装满沸水的锅中煮几分钟即可。

Yuanxiao is a kind of food eaten on fifteenth day of the first lunar month. In Song Dynasty, a kind of novel food for Lantern Festival was popular among the people, and it was first called “Fuyuanzi”, which was also known as “Yuanbao” by businessmen.

Yuanxiao is a kind of sweet food with stuffing. It is made of glutinous rice flour and sweet stuffing. Lantern Festival got the name after this food. The cooking method of Yuanxiao is very simple. We only need to pour the Lantern Festival dumplings into a pot with boiling water and cook for a few minutes.

2. 赏花灯

Enjoying Beautiful Lanterns

元宵节放灯赏灯的习俗自汉代便已经形成，是由宫廷流传到民间，在唐代形成盛况空前的灯市，中唐以后更是成为全民狂欢的节日。

The custom of enjoying beautiful lanterns on Lantern Festival has been formed since Han Dynasty. It spreads from the court to common society. In the Tang Dynasty, a lantern market with unprecedented grandeur was formed. After the mid-Tang Dynasty, it became a national carnival festival.

3. 猜灯谜
Guessing Lantern Riddles

此活动起源于宋朝。灯笼的所有者将谜面写在一张纸条上，然后将纸条展示在灯笼上。假如赏灯者猜出谜语，就将纸条取出，然后找灯笼所有者确认答案。猜对的话，他们就可以领取一份小礼品。由于这种活动十分富有情趣与智慧，很快在民间流传开来。

This activity is originated in Song Dynasty. The owner of lantern wrote the riddle on a piece of paper and then displayed it on the lantern. If the lantern viewer guesses the riddle, he can take out the note and finds the lantern owner to confirm the answer. If they guess correctly, they can get a small gift. Because this activity is very interesting and wise, it soon spreads among the people.

三、清明节
Qingming Festival

清明节是传统的重大春祭节日，扫墓祭祀、缅怀祖先，是中华民族自古以来的优良传统，同时也是人们亲近自然、踏青游玩、享受春天乐趣的欢乐节日。清明节气处在公历 4 月 5 日前后，即春分后第 15 日。这一时节，大地呈现春和景明之象，正是郊外踏青春游与行清墓祭的好时节。

Qingming Festival is a traditional major festival. Tomb-sweeping and ancestor-memorizing is a fine tradition of the Chinese nation since ancient times. It is also a joyful festival for people to get close to nature, travel in the green and enjoy the joy of spring. The Qingming Festival is around the 5th of April, and is the 15th day after Spring Equinox. At this time, the Earth presents the image of spring and brightness, which is a good time for spring tours and tomb sacrifices.

（一）起源与发展
Origin and Development

清明节源自上古时代的祖先信仰与春祭活动，经历史发展，清明节在唐宋时期融汇了寒食节的习俗，兼具自然与人文两大内涵，既是自然节气点，也是传统节日。古代的青年男女，大多会在清明时节会同好友登高望远，或席地而坐，品诗会友。

Qingming Festival originated from ancestor beliefs and spring sacrifice in ancient times. With historical development, Qingming Festival integrates the customs of Cold Food Festival in Tang and Song Dynasties. It has two connotations of nature and humanity. It is both a natural solar point and a traditional festival. Ancient young men and women, mostly in Qingming Festival will climb mountains with friends, or sit on the floor to appreciate poetry.

2006 年 5 月 20 日，中华人民共和国文化部申报的清明节经国务院批准列入第一批国家级非物质文化遗产名录。

On May 20, 2006, the Qingming Festival declared by the Ministry of Culture of the People's Republic of China was listed in the first batch of national intangible cultural heritage lists with the approval of the State Council.

（二）清明节的传说
Legend of Qingming Festival

春秋时期，晋国的大臣介子推，保护晋国的大公子——重耳出逃，在饥寒交迫之际，为了不让重耳饿死，把自己的大腿肉割下来给重耳吃。后来重耳当上了晋国的国君，他重赏了当初伴随他流亡的功臣，唯独忘了介子推，然而介子推根本没有任何抱怨，和母亲隐居到大山里了。有人为了把介子推逼出来，建议从三面放火烧山，结果火烧了好多天，介子推依然没有出来。火熄后，人们才发现背着老母亲的介子推已坐在一棵老柳树下死了。重耳后悔不已。为了纪念介子推，规定这一天为寒食节。第二年晋文公率众臣登山祭奠，发现老柳树死而复活，便赐老柳树为“清明柳”，并晓谕天下，于是又把寒食节的后一天定为“清明节”。

During the Spring and Autumn Period, Jie Zitui, the Minister of Jin State, protected Chonger, the eldest son of Jin State, to flee. In the face of hunger and cold, in order to prevent Chonger from starving to death, he cut off his thigh meat and gave Chonger to eat. Later, Chonger became the king of Jin State. He rewarded the heroes who accompanied him in exile. He only forgot about Jie Zitui. However, Jie Zitui did not complain at all and lived in seclusion with his mother in the mountains. In order to push him out, some people suggested setting fire to the mountains from three sides. As a result, the fire lasted for many days, but he still did not come out. After the fire was extinguished, people found that Jie Zitui, carrying his old mother, had been sitting under an old willow tree and died. Chonger regret endlessly. In commemoration of Jie Zitui, the day was designated Cold Food Festival, which later evolved into today's Qingming Festival. In the following year, Jin Wengong led his ministers to mountaineering memorials. When he found that the old willow tree was dead and resurrected, he gave the old willow tree "Qingming willow" and spoke to the world. Therefore, he designated the day after the Cold Food Festival as "Qingming Festival".

（三）习俗
Customs

清明节的节俗丰富，扫墓祭祖与踏青郊游是清明节的两大礼俗主题，这两大传统礼俗主题在中国自古传承至今。

Qingming Festival is rich in customs. Tomb-sweeping and ancestor-sacrificing, and spring tours are two major themes of Qingming Festival. These two traditional themes have been handed down from ancient times to the present in China.

1. 扫墓祭祖

Tomb-sweeping and Ancestor-sacrificing

清明扫墓是对先人的缅怀方式，是清明节俗的中心，其习俗由来久远。清明之祭主要祭祀祖先，表达祭祀者的孝道和对先人的思念之情。按祭祀场所的不同可分为墓祭、祠堂祭。以墓祭最为普遍，墓祭又被称为扫墓。另一种形式是祠堂祭，又称庙祭。祭祖常见的做法有两种：一是整修坟墓，二是挂烧纸钱、供奉祭品。清明节祭祖，按照习俗，一般在清明节上午出发扫墓，扫墓时，人们要携带酒食果品、纸钱等物品到墓地，将食物供祭在先人墓前，再将纸钱焚化，为坟墓培上新土，或折几枝嫩绿的新枝插在坟上，然后叩头行礼拜祭。

Tomb sweeping in Qingming Festival is a way of remembering ancestors and the central custom, which has a long history. The sacrifices of Qingming Festival mainly offer sacrifices to ancestors, expressing filial piety of worshippers and their yearning for ancestors. According to the different places of sacrifice, it can be divided into tomb sacrifice and ancestral temple sacrifice. Tomb sacrifice is the most common, and is also called tomb sweeping. Another form is ancestral temple sacrifice, also known as temple sacrifice. There are two common ways to worship ancestors: one is to renovate grave, the other is to hang paper money and offer sacrifices. According to custom, Qingming Festival ancestor worship usually goes outside in the morning to start tomb sweeping. People should take wine, fruit, paper money and other items to the graveyard, and put food in front of the ancestor's grave, then burn paper money, cultivate new soil for the grave, or fold a few green branches inserted in the grave, and then kowtow worship.

2. 踏青

Having an Outing in Spring

中华民族自古就有清明踏青的习俗。踏青即为春日郊游，也称“踏春”。一般指初春时到郊外散步游玩。清明节期间到大自然去欣赏和领略春日景象，郊外远足，这种踏青也叫春游。古代叫探春、寻春，其含义就是脚踏青草，在郊野游玩，观赏春色。踏青这种节令性的民俗活动，在我国有着悠久的历史，其源泉是远古农耕祭祀的迎春习俗。这种农耕祭祀的迎春习俗对后世影响深远。

清明之时，人们扫墓之余，一家老少在山乡野间散步游玩。也有的特意于清明节期间到大自然中去欣赏和领略生机勃勃的春日景象。清明前后正是踏青的好时光，所以成为清明节俗的一项重要内容。

Since ancient times, the Chinese nation has had the custom of traveling in Qingming Festival. Ta Qing is spring outing, also known as "Ta Chun". Generally, it refers to taking a walk in the countryside in the early spring. During the Qingming

Festival, we go to nature to appreciate spring scenery, and go hiking in the countryside. This kind of outing is also called spring outing. In ancient times, it was called exploring spring and seeking spring. Its meaning was to step on grass, play in the countryside and enjoy spring. This kind of festival folk custom activity has a long history in China, and its source is the spring custom of ancient farming and sacrifice. This custom of farming and sacrificing to welcome spring has a far-reaching impact on future generations.

In the Qingming Festival, while people swept the tombs, a whole family took a walk in the countryside. There are also people who get close to nature during the Qingming Festival specially to appreciate vibrant spring scenery, which has become an important part of the Qingming Festival.

四、端午节

Dragon Boat Festival

端午节（农历五月初五）是中国民间的传统节日。端午节的名称在中国所有传统节日当中叫法最多，达二十多个。虽然名称不同，但各地人民过节的习俗还是差不多的。端午文化在世界上影响广泛，世界上一些国家和地区也有庆贺端午的活动。

Dragon Boat Festival (the fifth day of May in lunar calendar) is a traditional Chinese festival. The Dragon Boat Festival has most names among all traditional festivals in China, amounting to more than 20. Although the names are different, the customs of festivals are similar in different places. Dragon Boat Festival culture has a wide influence in the world, and some countries and regions in the world also have activities to celebrate the Dragon Boat Festival.

（一）起源与发展
Origin and Development

端午节源自天象崇拜，由上古时代龙图腾祭祀演变而来，是中国古代南方吴越民族举行图腾祭的节日。也因传说战国时期的楚国诗人屈原在五月五日跳汨罗江自尽，后来人们亦将端午节作为纪念屈原的节日。其影响最广最深，占据主流地位。时至今日，端午节仍是中国人民中一个十分盛行的隆重节日。2006 年 5 月，国务院将其列入首批国家级非物质文化遗产名录；自 2008 年起，被列为国家法定节假日。2009 年 9 月，联合国教科文组织正式批准将其列入《人类非物质文化遗产代表作名录》，端午节成为中国首个入选世界非遗的节日。

Dragon Boat Festival originated from the worship of celestial phenomena. It evolved from dragon totem sacrifice in ancient times. It is a totem sacrifice festival held by Wuyue nationality in ancient China. It is also said that Qu Yuan, a poet of the State of Chu in the Warring States Period, committed suicide by jumping the Miluo River on May 5. Later, people took the Dragon Boat Festival as a festival to commemorate Qu Yuan. This version has a widest and deepest influence, and occupied the mainstream position. Today, Dragon Boat Festival is still a very popular grand festival among the Chinese people. In May 2006, the State Council listed it in the first batch of national intangible cultural heritage list; since 2008, it has been listed as a national statutory holiday. In September 2009, UNESCO formally approved its inclusion in the List of Representatives of Human Intangible Cultural Heritage, and Dragon Boat Festival became China's first intangible cultured heritage festival.

（二）端午节的传说
Legend of Dragon Boat Festival

屈原，楚国大夫、爱国诗人。因治国主张遭反对而被罢职流放。公元前 278 年农历五月初五，屈原听到秦军攻破楚国都城的消息后，悲愤交加，心如刀割，抱石投入汨罗江，以身殉国。沿江百姓纷纷引舟竞渡前去打捞，并将粽子投入江中，以免鱼虾蚕食他的身体。以后，在每年的农历五月初五，就有了龙舟竞渡、吃粽子的风俗，以此来纪念爱国诗人屈原。

Qu Yuan is a minister and patriotic poet of the State of Chu. His idea of governing country was opposed and exiled. On the fifth day of May of lunar month in 278 B.C., Qu Yuan heard the news that Qin army had broken the capital of State of Chu. He was filled with grief and indignation, and plunged into the Miluo River to martyr his country. People along the river raced to pull him up and put rice dumplings into the river to avoid fish and shrimp eating his body. Later, on the fifth day of May of lunar month every year, there was the custom of dragon boat racing, eating rice dumplings to commemorate the patriotic poet Qu Yuan.

（三）习俗
Customs

端午节是集祈福消灾、欢庆娱乐和饮食为一体的民俗大节，在传承发展中杂糅了多地多种民俗为一体，节俗内容丰富。赛龙舟与食粽是端午节的两大礼俗主题，这两大传统礼俗主题在中国传承至今。

Dragon Boat Festival is a folk festival that integrates praying for good fortune and disaster relief, celebrating and entertaining, and eating. In the process of inheritance and development, many kinds of folk customs are mixed together, thus the content of festival is rich. Dragon boat racing and eating rice dumplings are two main themes of Dragon Boat Festival. These two traditional themes have been handed down from ancient times to the present in China.

1. 赛龙舟
Dragon Boat Racing

赛龙舟是端午节的一项重要活动，至今在我国南方沿海一带仍十分流行。传出国外后，深受多国人民的喜爱并形成了国际比赛。龙舟竞渡前一般都要举行隆重的祭祀仪式，先要请龙、祭神。在过去，人们祭祀龙神时气氛很严肃，多祈求福佑、风调雨顺、去邪祟、事事如意。

Dragon boat racing is an important activity of Dragon Boat Festival, which is still very popular in the southern coastal areas of China. After being spread abroad, it has been deeply loved by the people of many countries and formed an international competition. Before the Dragon Boat race, a solemn sacrificial ceremony should be held. First, dragons and gods should be invited and worshipped. In the past, people sacrificed dragon gods in the serious atmosphere. They prayed for blessings, good weather, evil spirits and good luck.

2. 吃粽子

Eating Traditional Chinese Rice Dumplings

端午食粽，是中国民间的传统习俗。粽子由来久远，花样繁多，古往今来，中国各地都一样。粽子最初是用来祭祀祖先和神灵；到了晋代，成为端午的节庆食物。每年五月初，中国百姓浸糯米、洗粽叶、包粽子，其花色品种繁多。从馅料看，北方多包枣粽；南方则有豆沙、鲜肉、火腿、蛋黄等多种馅料。吃粽子的风俗，千百年来，在中国各地盛行不衰，而且流传到朝鲜、日本及东南亚诸国。

Eating rice dumplings in Dragon Boat Festival is a traditional Chinese custom. Rice dumpling has a long history and various patterns. It has been the same in all parts of China since ancient times. Rice dumpling was originally used to sacrifice ancestors and gods; in the Jin Dynasty, it became the festival food of the Dragon Boat Festival. At the beginning of May, Chinese people soak glutinous rice, wash leaves and wrap dumplings. There are many varieties of rice dumplings. As for the stuffing, rice dumpling in north is packed with jujube dumplings, while the south is packed with bean paste, fresh meat, ham, egg yolk and other stuffing. The custom of eating rice dumplings has been prevalent throughout China for thousands of years and has spread to the Democratic People's Republic of Korea, Japan and Southeast Asian countries.

五、中秋节
Mid-Autumn Festival

中秋节，又称团圆节等，是中国民间的传统节日。根据我国的历法，农历八月在秋季中间，为秋季的第二个月，称为“仲秋”，而八月十五又在“仲秋”之中，所以称“中秋”。因中秋节的主要活动都是围绕“月”进行的，所以又俗称“月节”；中秋节月亮圆满，象征团圆，因而又叫“团圆节”。中秋节以月之圆兆人之团圆，以寄托思念故乡、思念亲人之情，祈盼丰收和幸福，已成为丰富多彩、弥足珍贵的文化遗产。

Mid-Autumn Festival, also known as the reunion festival, is a traditional Chinese festival. According to Chinese calendar, August is in the middle of autumn, the second month of autumn and 15th is in the middle of August, so it is called “Mid-Autumn”. Because the main activities of Mid-Autumn Festival are around the “moon”, it is also known as the “Moon Festival”. The Moon of the Mid-Autumn Festival is full and symbolizes reunion, so it is also called the “reunion festival”. The Mid-Autumn Festival, with reunion of the full moon as a symbol of people’s longing for their homeland and their relatives, wishes for a bumper harvest and happiness, and becomes a rich and precious cultural heritage.

（一）起源与发展
Origin and Development

中秋节源自天象崇拜，由上古时代秋夕祭月演变而来，唐朝初年更加受到重视，盛行于宋朝，至明清时，已成为与春节齐名的中国传统节日之一。受中华文化的影响，中秋节也是东亚和东南亚一些国家尤其是当地的华人华侨的传统节日。2006 年 5 月 20 日，被国务院列入首批国家级非物质文化遗产名录。

The Mid-Autumn Festival originated from the worship of celestial phenomena. It evolved from the worship of the moon on the autumn evening in ancient times. In the early Tang Dynasty, more attention was paid to it. It was prevalent in the Song Dynasty. By the Ming and Qing Dynasties, it had become a famous traditional Chinese festival with Spring festival. Influenced by Chinese culture, Mid-Autumn Festival is also a traditional festival for overseas Chinese in East and Southeast Asia. On May 20,

2006, the State Council listed the Mid-Autumn Festival in the first batch of national intangible cultural heritage lists.

（二）中秋节的传说
Legend of Mid-Autumn Festival

后羿射日有功，王母奖励两颗长生不老仙丹，由后羿的妻子嫦娥保管。后羿的徒弟蓬蒙在八月十五去抢仙丹，嫦娥为保仙丹，全部吞下，立刻就飞升到月宫之中却下不来了。后羿因为思念嫦娥就照八月十五月亮的样子做成食物，等待嫦娥归来，这就是中秋节。

The Queen Mother rewarded two immortals to Hou Yi for his success in shooting the sun. They were kept by Chang'e, his wife. Peng Meng, his apprentice, went to rob immortals on August 15, and Chang'e swallowed all of them in order to protect immortals. After that, she immediately flew up to the Moon Palace, but could not come down. Hou Yi made food like the moon expressing his miss to Chang'e on August 15 and waited Chang'e to return. This is the legend of Mid-Autumn Festival.

（三）习俗
Customs

中秋节自古便有祭月、赏月、拜月、吃月饼、赏桂花、饮桂花酒等习俗，流传至今，经久不息。

Since ancient times, the Mid-Autumn Festival has the customs of offering sacrifices to the moon, enjoying the moon, worshipping the moon, eating moon cakes, appreciating osmanthus fragrances, drinking osmanthus wine and so on. It has been handed down for a long time.

1. 吃月饼
Eating Moon Cakes

中秋节赏月和吃月饼是中国各地过中秋节的必备习俗，俗话说，“八月十五月正圆，中秋月饼香又甜”。月饼一词，源于南宋，那时仅是一种点心食品。到后来人们逐渐把赏月与月饼结合在一起，寓意家人团圆，寄托思念。同时，月饼也是中秋时节朋友间用来联络感情的重要礼物。

Moon appreciation and eating moon cakes are the necessary customs of Mid-Autumn Festival in China. As the saying goes, the moon in August 15th is the most full and Mid-Autumn moon cakes are sweet and fragrant. The term "moon cake" originated in the Southern Song Dynasty, when it was only a snack food. Later, people gradually combined moon appreciation with moon cakes, which means family reunion and longing. At the same time, moon cakes are also important gifts for friends to connect with each other during Mid-Autumn Festival.

2. 赏桂花、饮桂花酒

Appreciating Osmanthus Fragrance and Drinking Osmanthus Fragrance Wine

人们经常在中秋时吃月饼赏桂花，食用桂花制作的各种食品，以糕点、糖果最为多见。

中秋之夜，仰望着明月，闻着阵阵桂香，喝一杯桂花蜜酒，欢庆合家甜甜蜜蜜，已成为节日一种美的享受。到了现代，人们多是拿红酒代替。

People often eat moon cakes and sweet-scented Osmanthus wine in the Mid-Autumn Festival. They eat all kinds of food made of sweet-scented Osmanthus, especially cakes and candies.

On the night of Mid-Autumn Festival, looking up the Mid-Moon, smelling the fragrance of sweet Osmanthus, drinking a cup of sweet Osmanthus wine, celebrating the sweetness of the family, has become a beautiful festival enjoyment. In modern times, people mostly drink red wine instead of Osmanthus wine.

六、重阳节

Double Ninth Festival

重阳节，为每年的农历九月初九日，是中国民间的传统节日。"九"为阳数，"九九"两阳数相重，故曰"重阳"，古人认为九九重阳是吉祥的日子。古时民间在重阳节有登高祈福、秋游赏菊、佩插茱萸、拜神祭祖及饮宴求寿等习俗。传承至今，又添加了敬老等内涵，于重阳之日享宴高会，感恩和敬老。

Double Ninth Festival, the ninth day of September in the lunar calendar, is a traditional Chinese festival. "Nine" is defined as the number of Yang, and double Nine is the number of two Yangs, so it is called "Chongyang". The ancients believed that

"Nine-Nine Chongyang" is an auspicious day. In ancient times, there were customs of climbing high to pray for blessings, visiting chrysanthemums in autumn, wearing dogwood, worshipping gods to ancestors, and feasting for longevity. Up to now, it has added the connotation of respecting elderly, feasting on the day of Chongyang, and thanking and respecting the elderly.

（一）起源与发展
Origin and Development

重阳节的源头，可追溯到上古时代。古人在九月农作物丰收之时祭天帝、祭祖，以谢天帝、祖先恩德的活动。这是重阳节作为秋季丰收祭祀活动而存在的原始形式。重阳节起始于上古，成型于春秋战国，普及于西汉，鼎盛于唐代以后。唐代是传统节日习俗糅合定型的重要时期，其主体部分传承至今。

1989年，农历九月九日被定为"敬老节"，倡导全社会树立尊老、敬老、爱老、助老的风气。2006年5月20日，重阳节被国务院列入首批国家级非物质文化遗产名录。

The origin of Double Ninth Festival can be traced back to ancient times. The ancients offered sacrifices to the Emperor of Heaven and ancestors in September when crops were harvested, in order to thank the Emperor of Heaven and ancestors for their kindness. This is the original form of Double Ninth Festival as a harvest festival in autumn. The Double Ninth Festival began in ancient times, formed in the Spring and Autumn Period and the Warring States Period, popularized in the Western Han Dynasty, and flourished after the Tang Dynasty. Tang Dynasty is an important period in which traditional festival customs are combined and finalized. Its main part has been inherited to this day.

In 1989, September 9 of the lunar calendar was designated as "Respect for the Elderly Day", advocating the whole society to establish a culture of respecting, loving and helping the elderly. On May 20, 2006, Chongyang Festival was listed in the first national intangible cultural heritage list by the State Council.

（二）重阳节的传说
Legend of Double Ninth Festival

相传东汉时汝河有个瘟魔，每年九月初九出来，它一出现，家家都有人病倒、丧命。青年恒景的父母因此丧命。恒景决心出去访仙学艺，为民除掉瘟魔。恒景在一仙长那里学到一身非凡武艺。仙长送给他一包茱萸叶，一盅菊花酒，并且密授避邪用法，让恒景九月初九回家为民除害。九月九日早晨，恒景按仙长的叮嘱把乡亲们领到了附近的一座山上，发给每人一片茱萸叶，一盅菊花酒，按仙人传授之道，成功杀死瘟魔。从此九月初九登高避疫的说法年复一年地流传下来。

It is said that there was a plague in the Ru River in Eastern Han Dynasty, which came out on the ninth day of September every year. As soon as it appeared, some people fell ill and died. Heng Jing's parents died for it. Heng Jing was determined to go out to visit immortals and learn art so as to rid people of the plague. Heng Jing learned an extraordinary martial art from a immortal. The immortal gave him a pack of cornel leaves, a cup of chrysanthemum wine, and secret usage of evasion, so that Heng Jing returned home on the ninth day of September to eliminate harmful effects for the people. On the morning of September 9, Heng Jing took villagers to a nearby mountain at the advice of the immortal, and gave everyone a piece of dogwood leaf and a cup of chrysanthemum wine, which succeeded in killing the demon according to the way imparted by the immortal. From then on, the idea of climbing high to avoid epidemics has been passed down year after year.

（三）习俗
Customs

1. 登高
Mountain Climbing

登高源于古人对山岳的崇拜。 九月九日，正是秋高气爽、山青云淡的时节，此时登高远眺，使人心旷神怡，有益于人们的身心健康。如今有许多地方都在这期间举行登山会。

Mountain climbing originated from ancient people's worship of mountains. September 9th is the time when autumn is comfortable and mountains are green and cloudy. At this time, climbing high and overlooking can make people relaxed and happy, which is beneficial to people's physical and mental health. Nowadays many places hold mountaineering meetings during this period.

2. 敬老

Respecting the Old

在国家的大力推动下，重阳节越来越受到全社会的关注。每到这一日，外出的儿女们会购买重阳糕，带回家探望父母，送糕点寄托了儿女们对老人健康长寿的祝福。没有时间回家陪伴父母的儿女们，都会打电话问候老人。各地也都组织老年人登山秋游，开阔视野，交流感情，锻炼身体。

With the vigorous promotion of the country, Double Ninth Festival has attracted more and more attention from the whole society. On this day, children working outside will buy Double Ninth Cake to visit their parents, and send cakes to express their wishes for the health and longevity of the elderly. If there is no time to go home to accompany their parents, they will call to greet the elder. There are activities of organizing the elder people's mountain climbing and autumn outing to broaden their horizons, exchange feelings and take exercise.

课后练习题
Practice

一、选择题
Multiple-choice

1. 在中秋节人们常常吃（　　）。
People often eat (　　) on Mid-Autumn Festival.

A. 月饼　B. 粽子　C. 米饭　D. 元宵
A. moon cakes　B. zongzi　C. rice　D. dumpling

2. 端午节最重要的活动是（　　）。
The most important activity of Dragon Boat Festival is (　　).

A. 登山　B. 赏月
A. climbing　B. observing the moon
C. 赛龙舟　D. 唱歌
C. dragon boat racing　D. singing

3. 清明节气处在公历 4 月 5 日前后，即春分后（　　）。
The Qingming Festival is around the 5th of April, and is (　　) after Spring Equinox.

A. 第 2 天　B. 第 12 天　C. 第 5 天　D. 第 15 天
A. the 2nd　B. the 12th　C. the 5th　D. the 15th

4. 在元宵节人们一般吃一种传统食品（　　）。
People usually eat a traditional food (　　) on the Lantern Festival.

A. 元宵　B. 月饼　C. 粽子　D. 米饭
A. dumplings　B. moon cakes　C. zongzi　D. rice

5. 春节的时候小孩子一般都会收到父母给的（　　）。
During the Spring Festival, children usually receive (　　) from their parents.

A. 书　B. 玩具　C. 新衣服　D. 压岁钱
A. books　B. toys　C. new clothes　D. lucky money

二、填空题

Fill-in-the-blanks

1. 春节传说中的怪兽叫__________。

   There is a legend that in ancient China there was a fierce monster called __________.

2. 元宵节的主要习俗____________________。（不少于两个）

   Lantern Festival mainly includes a series of traditional folk activities such as ______________________________。(more than 2)

3. 清明节最重要的习俗是____________________。

   ____________________ is the central custom in Qingming Festival.

4. 端午节是纪念__________的节日。

   Dragon Boat Festival is a festival to commemorate __________.

5. 中秋节的习俗有____________________。（不少于两个）

   The Mid-Autumn Festival has the customs of __________________. (more than 2)

三、判断题

True or False

1. 春节，即农历新年，是一年之岁首。

   The Spring Festival, also named the Lunar New Year, is the beginning of the year.

2. 正月十五一般都要吃元宵。

   Yuanxiao as a kind of food which is eaten on the fifteenth day of the first lunar month has a long history in China.

3. 清明节人们要吃粽子。

   Eating rice dumpling in Qingming Festival is a traditional Chinese custom.

4. 端午节是为了纪念中国古代著名的爱国诗人李白。

   People took the Dragon Boat Festival as a festival to commemorate Li Bai.

5. 在重阳节这天人们表达对老人的关心。

   People show their concern for the old men on the Double Ninth Festival.

四、简答题
Short-answer Questions

1. 清明节有哪两大礼俗主题？
   What are the two major themes of Qingming Festival?

2. 什么是春晚？
   What is Spring Festival Gala?

3. 端午节有什么纪念活动？
   What kinds of activities are held on the Dragon Boat Festival?

第九章

中国的国粹

Chinese Quintessence

课前思考

Lead-in Questions

1. 我们知道英文书写体中有哥特体、意大利体等书写样式，你能数出中国书法的多少种字体呢？
   As we know, there are Gothic and Italian styles in English writing. How many writing styles can you count in the Chinese calligraphy?
2. 你能分辨京剧脸谱和相关人物吗？
   Can you match the Peking Opera facial makeup to related characters?

一、书法

Chinese Calligraphy

（一）书法简介

Brief Introduction of Chinese Calligraphy

书法是文字的书写艺术，也可以说是用毛笔写汉字的艺术。对于中国和一些受中国文化影响的国家来说，书法独有其妙。在中国艺术史上，书法和绘画具有同等重要的地位。自古以来汉字书法都因其美学价值而获得欣赏，现在它被视为一种艺术形式。书法不仅仅注重于书写的方法，在书写的过程中也注重怡养性情和旷达胸怀。

In China, calligraphy is the art of writing and it can also be said to be the art of writing Chinese characters with a brush. For China and some countries influenced by Chinese culture, calligraphy holds a unique charm. In the history of Chinese art, calligraphy has always been held in equal importance to painting. From ancient times to the present, Chinese calligraphy has been appreciated for its aesthetic quality, and today it is regarded as one form of art. Chinese calligraphy focuses not only on methods of writing but also on cultivating one's character and is taught as a pursuit of lofty spiritual realm.

中国的汉字，经历了从图画到符号再到创造最后统一定型的过程。而中国书法也经历了由古文字篆体，再到隶、行、草、楷体等书体的演变。在书写应用汉字的过程中，汉字书法逐渐成了世界各民族文字中唯一的、可以独立门类的艺术。汉字书法被誉为：无言的诗，无形的舞，无声的乐。

With the development of Chinese characters, Chinese calligraphy developed into various styles from ancient seal script to clerical script, semi-cursive script, cursive script and regular script. In the process of writing and applying Chinese characters, Chinese calligraphy has gradually become the unique and independent art in the world. Chinese calligraphy is known as speechless poetry, intangible dance and silent music.

（二）主要书体介绍
Introduction to the Main Styles of Calligraphy

1. 甲骨文
Oracle Bone Script

甲骨指的是用来刻写占卜文字的龟甲兽骨。甲骨文指的是刻写在动物骨头上的汉字。甲骨文是迄今为止人类所知最早的文字雏形。人们明确所指的甲骨文，即刻在牛的肩胛骨和龟壳上的文字，在如今河南北部的安阳首次发现。绝大多数的甲骨文都出土于河南安阳的殷墟。这些甲骨文记录了商代从武丁开始的最后九位皇帝的卜辞。虽然不同学者有不同的看法，但大致认为武丁在位的时间是在公元前1250年至公元前1192年。

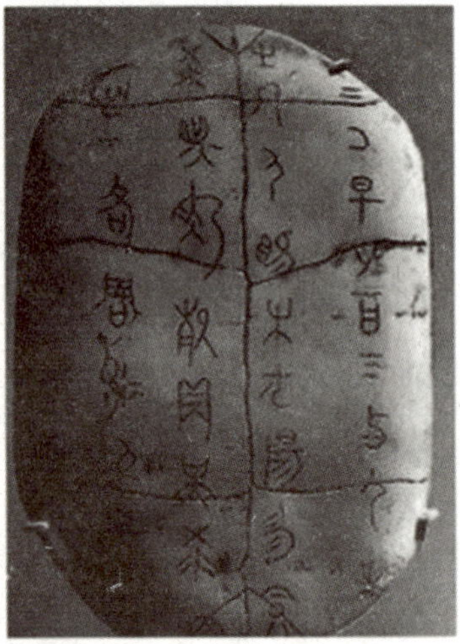
刻在龟甲上的甲骨文

Oracle bone script was one of the forms of Chinese character written on animals bones. Written on oracle bones—animal bones, it is the earliest known form of Chinese writing. The first appearance of what we recognize unequivocally to refer as "oracle bone inscriptions" comes in the form of inscribed ox scapula and turtle plastrons from sites near modern Anyang on the northern border of Henan province. The vast majority were found at the Yinxu site (in modern Anyang, Henan Province). They record inscriptions of the last nine kings of the Shang Dynasty, beginning with Wu Ding, whose reign time is approximatly 1250 B.C.–1192 B.C., assumed by different scholars.

2. 青铜器铭文
Bronze Inscription

铭文指古人在青铜器上浇铸的文字以记录铸造该铜器的缘由、所纪念或祭祀的人物。不同的历史时期有不同方法来题刻铭文。商朝的青铜器铭文是在青铜器浇铸时一同铸成的。后来西周春秋时期的铭文是在青铜工具浇铸成型以后印刻上去的。铜器铭文是书写型体中最古老的一种，是在甲骨文基础上发展起来的文字。

Bronze inscription refers to the characters cast by the ancients on the bronzes to record the reason for casting the bronzes, the figures who are commemorated or sacrificed. There are different ways to inscribe inscriptions in different historical periods. The bronze inscriptions of the Shang Dynasty were cast together when the bronze was cast. Later, the inscriptions of the Western Zhou Dynasty and the Spring and Autumn Period were printed after the bronze tools were cast and formed. Bronze inscription is the oldest type of writing, which is developed on the basis of oracle bone inscriptions.

3. 篆书
Seal Script

篆书是公元前一世纪后半叶通行的一种古老的汉字书体。它从周朝的字体演变而来。当时，篆书缺乏统一性，同一个字有很多种写法。公元前221年，秦始皇统一了中国，建立了中央集权制国家，他命令李斯采集当时民间流行的字体风格以便统一书写系统。李斯奉命执行了任务，于是创造了小篆书写体。此后，秦代的篆书变体逐渐成了标准篆体，在整个秦朝时期被用作正式的书体。今天，最有价值的小篆遗迹记录在山东泰山神殿的一块石碑上，石碑上刻有小篆创造者李斯的亲笔手记。经历了2 200多年的风霜雨雪，这块石碑上仅有九个半字留存了下来。

Seal script is an ancient style of writing Chinese characters that was common throughout the latter half of the 1st millennium B.C. It evolved organically out of the Zhou Dynasty script. At the beginning, seal script lacked uniformity and many characters were written in invariant forms. In 221 B.C., the first emperor of Qin unified the whole of China under one central government, and he ordered Li Si to collect and sort all the different systems of writing hitherto prevalent in different parts of the country in a great effort to unify the written language under one system. Li Si successfully completed the task and created the ancient zhuan (small seal) script. From then on, the Qin variant of seal script eventually became the standard, and was adopted as the formal script for all of China during the Qin dynasty. Today we have a most valuable relic of this ancient writing in the creator Li Si's own hand engraved on a stone standing in the Temple to the God of Mount Tai in Shandong Province. The 2200-year-old stone, worn by age and weather, has only nine and a half characters left on it.

4. 隶书

Clerical Script

隶书也是一种古老的汉字书体，盛行于东汉时期，尽管很早以前它的地位被楷书取代，但它仍然被视为一种正式的书写体，因为用标准的隶书写出的字与用楷书写的字非常相像。标准的隶书呈方形，没有连笔，具有建筑的样式。

The clerical script is an archaic style of Chinese calligraphy and it is popular in East Han Dynasty. The clerical script is considered as a form of modern script because the graphic forms written in mature clerical script closely resemble those written in standard (regular) script. The standard writing today is square in form, non-cursive and architectural in style.

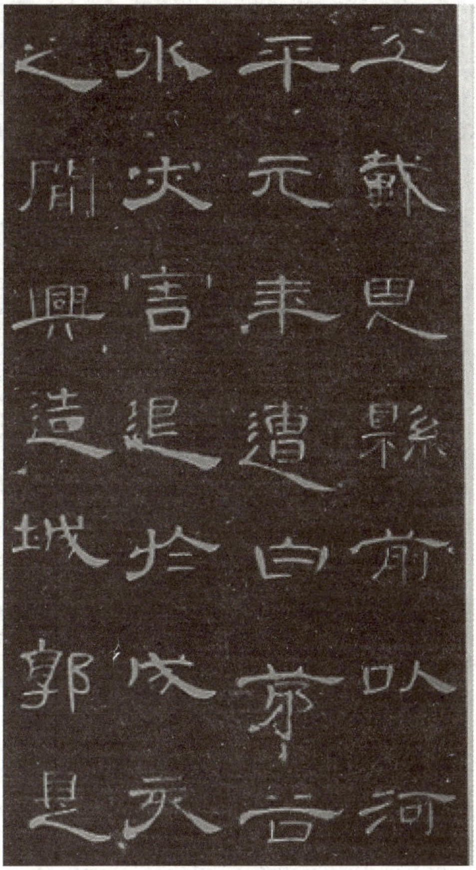

5. 楷书

Regular Script

楷书是书法字体中最新的成员。它首次出现于汉魏年间，然而当时楷书并不受欢迎。楷书在 7 世纪的时候以其独特的风格发展成熟。第一个写楷书的人叫钟繇，他用楷书写了一些诸如皇帝祭文的公文。他被誉为是楷书之父。

Regular script (or standard script) is the newest of the Chinese script styles. The regular script first came into existence between the Han and Wei Dynasties, even though it is not popular. The regular script became mature stylistically around the 7th century. The first master of regular script is Zhong Yao. Zhong Yao first used regular script to write some very serious pieces such as memorials to the emperor. He is known as "father of regular script".

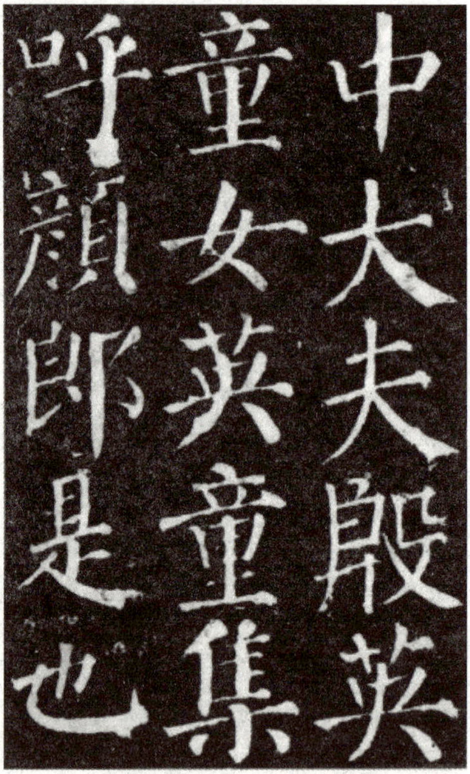

6. 行书

Semi-cursive Script

行书是一种偏向于草书形态的字体。因为它不像真正的草书那样简略，大部分认得楷书的人都能认得行书。行书兼具很高的实用性和艺术性。

Semi-cursive script is a cursive style of Chinese characters. Because it is not as abbreviated as cursive, most people who can read regular script can read semi-cursive. It is highly useful and also artistic.

中国所有的书法家都认为，东晋时期的书法家王羲之的《兰亭集序》是行书的典范之作。想要写好书法，必须长期刻苦训练，这一点是中国很多书法名家达成的共识。历史上众多书法家和学者都受到王羲之的影响并对他高度敬仰。据说他小时候因为每天练习书法后清洗工具，把家门前的一池子水都染黑了。

The best example and model for semi-cursive script, all Chinese calligraphers will agree, is the inscription *Preface to the Lanting Pavilion Collection* in the hand of Wang Xizhi (321–379) of the Eastern Jin Dynasty. To learn to write a nice hand in Chinese calligraphy, assiduous and persevering practice is necessary. This has been borne out by the many great masters China has produced. Wang Xizhi, the great artist just mentioned, who has exerted a profound influence on, and has been held in high esteem by, calligraphers and scholars throughout history, is said to have blackened all the water of a pond in front of his house by washing the writing implements in it after his daily exercise.

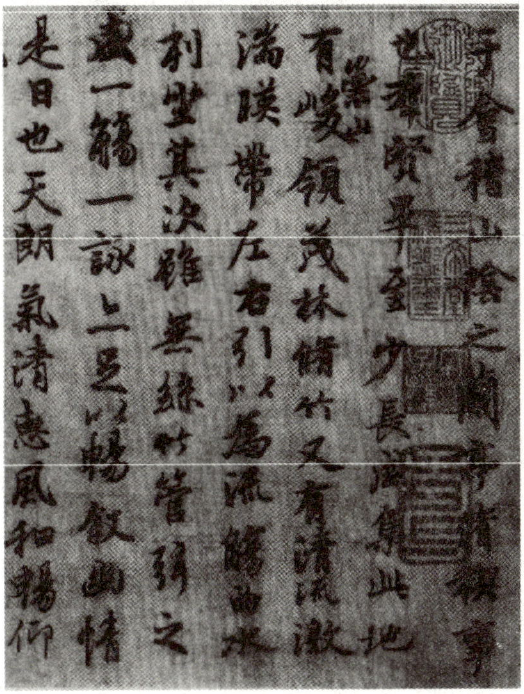

7. 草书

Cursive Script

草书，起源于汉代至晋朝过渡的时期。草书比其他字体写起来更快，但对于那些不熟悉它的人来说难以辨认。汉语中的“草”也有“粗野、简单、粗略”的意思，“草书”这个词中的“草”使用了同样意义上的“草”。术语“草书”具有广义和狭义之分。从广义上讲，它是非时间性的，可以指任何匆匆书写的汉字。

从狭义上讲，它指的是汉代的特定笔迹风格。草书又分为章草和今草两种风格。用章草书写的汉字，虽然写得很快、很流畅，但是每个字都是分开独立的，点画也没有附着在其他笔画上。今草于东汉时期兴起，在晋朝和唐朝兴盛，至今广受欢迎。今草的精髓是笔画行云流水，汉字很快就写成了。字与字通常连在一起写，上一个字的最后一笔和下一个字的第一笔连在一起。同一幅作品中的汉字大小不一，这看起来就像创作者即兴发挥出来的。

Cursive script originated in China during the Han Dynasty through the Jin period. The cursive script is faster to write than other styles, but difficult to read for those unfamiliar with it. The "grass" in Chinese was also used in the sense of "coarse, rough; simple and crude." It would appear that 草 in the term 草 书 (literally grass script) was used in this same sense. Cursive script has broad and narrow meanings. In the broad sense, it is non-temporal and can refer to any characters which have been hastily written. In the narrow sense, it refers to the specific handwriting style in Han Dynasty. This style is subdivided into two schools: Zhangcao and Jincao (modern cursive). The characters written in Zhangcao, though written rapidly, still stand separate one from another and the dots are not linked up with other strokes. Jincao is said to have been developed from Eastern Han Dynasty, flourished in the Jin and Tang dynasties and is still widely popular today. It is the essence of Jincao, that the characters are executed swiftly with the strokes running together. The characters are often joined up, with the last stroke of the first merging into the initial stroke of the next. They also vary in size in the same piece of writing, all seemingly dictated by the whims of the writer.

著名的唐代草书书法家张旭，他因为不按章法随性发挥而著名。据说，他不喝得酩酊大醉不会执笔写字，这就是他的风格。刷子在纸上驰骋，一个个连续的笔画弯曲伸展、蜿蜒回环，由此形成了他的首创风格。现在我们还能看到刻有他字迹的碑石，该碑石保存于陕西省博物馆。

A great master at cursive script was Zhang Xu of the Tang Dynastry, noted for the complete abandon with which he applied the brush. It is said that he would not set about writing until he had got drunk. His original writing style is to utilize the brush to gallop across the paper, twisting or meandering in one unbroken stroke. Today one may still see fragments of a stele carved with character in his handwriting, kept in the Provincial Museum of Shaanxi.

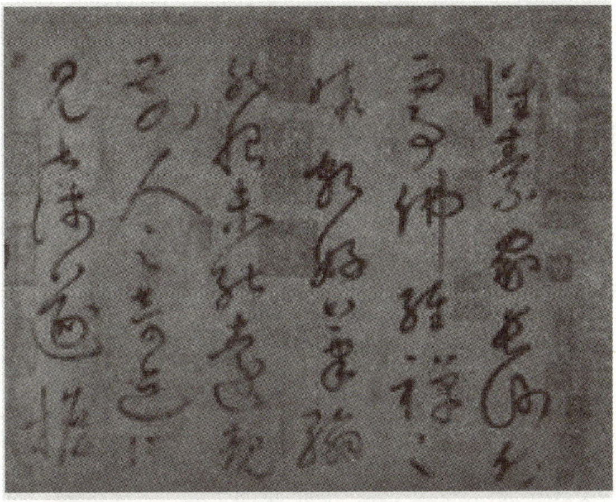

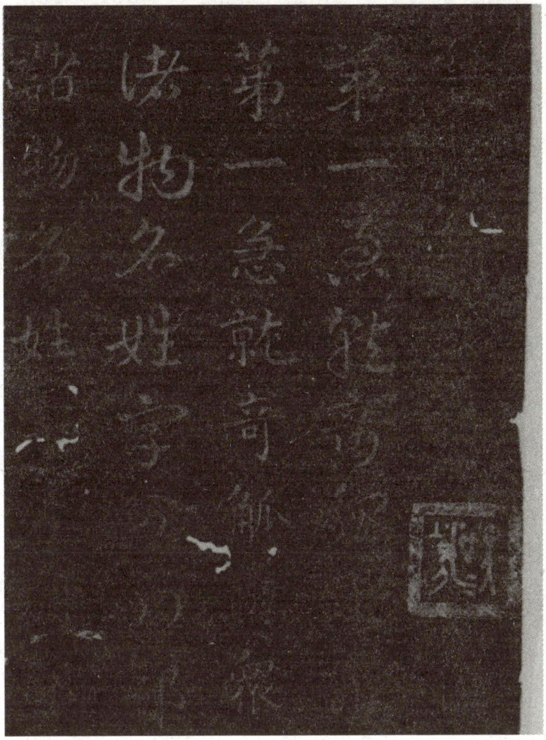

（三）书写材料和工具
Materials and Tools of Chinese Calligraphy Writing

毛笔、墨水、宣纸和砚台是中国书法的必备工具。他们被称为“文房四宝”。除了这四种工具之外，书法家还使用滴壶、桌垫和镇纸。

The ink brush, ink, paper, and ink stone are essential tools of Chinese calligraphy. They are known together as the Four Treasures of the Study. In addition to these four tools, a water-dropper, desk pads and paperweights are also used by calligraphers.

1. 笔

Brush

毛笔是中国书法的传统书写工具。毛笔的笔杆通常由竹子或木头、瓷器、牛角等其他材料制成。毛笔的笔头部通常由动物毛发制成，例如黄鼠狼、兔子、鹿、山羊、猪、老虎、狼等。按照功能区分，笔又分为三个类别：软、硬、适中。

A brush is the traditional writing instrument for Chinese calligraphy. The body of the brush is commonly made from bamboo or other materials such as wood, porcelain, or horn. The head of the brush is typically made from animal hair, such as weasel, rabbit, deer, goat, pig, tiger, wolf, etc. On the basis of function, brushes are classified into three groups: hard, soft and both.

2. 墨和墨棒

Ink and Inkstick

墨是由炭黑和黏合剂制成的，做成墨棒的样子是为了方便与水一同在砚台中研磨达到适宜的浓度。对绘画和书法来说，墨是一种特殊的颜料。最有名的墨棒是由长在安徽黄山上的松树制成的徽墨（安徽墨棒）。学会磨墨是书法学习的基本功。

Ink is made from lampblack (soot) and binders, and comes in inksticks which must be rubbed with water on an ink stone until the right consistency is achieved. The ink stick is a unique pigment used for Chinese traditional painting and calligraphy. The most famous ink stick is Hui mo (Anhui ink stick), made of pines that grow on Huangshan Mountain in Anhui Province. Learning to rub the ink is an essential part of calligraphy study.

3. 纸

Paper

东汉年间蔡伦发明了纸。虽然纸的种类繁多，但是宣州京城（今安徽省）生产的宣纸是中国书法最好的书写材料。这种纸是由青檀做主料，配合稻草、竹子、大麻等辅料制作而成的纸张。它质地柔软细腻，用来书法和绘画，有很好的艺术表现力。这种纸张有很好的伸展性和防止虫蛀的特性，因此可以长效保存。

Paper was invented by Cai Lun in the Eastern Han Dynasty. While paper comes in many varieties, Xuan paper, produced in the Jing Prefecture of Xuanzhou (today's Anhui Province), is considered the best for Chinese calligraphy. It is made from the Tatar wingceltis, as well as other materials including rice, bamboo, hemp, etc. The paper is soft and fine textured, suitable for conveying the artistic expression of both Chinese calligraphy and painting. With a good tensile strength and mothproof quality, the paper can be preserved for a long time.

4. 砚台

Ink Stone

端砚、歙砚和洮砚是三种著名的砚台。三种砚台的共同特征是石头都很坚硬，而且材质细腻。尽管有这样的特质，但是砚台并不十分干燥和光滑。墨棒在坚硬而具有光泽的石头上研磨，很容易就能磨出墨汁来。砚台既是将墨棒磨成液体的工具也是盛装墨汁的容器。砚台作为艺术品受到高度重视，而且有大量的文献专门研究它的历史，鉴赏它的艺术性。

Duan, She and Tao are three famous ink stones. Features common to all three in slabs are the stone's hardness and fineness. Although the stone is hard and fine, it is not dry or slippery. Using a hard, smooth stone, liquid ink can be produced easily by rubbing the ink stick against the stone. Ink stone is used to grind the solid ink stick into liquid ink and to contain the ink once it is liquid. Chinese ink stones are highly prized as art objects and an extensive bibliography is dedicated to their history and appreciation.

Chinese Inkstone and Inkstick

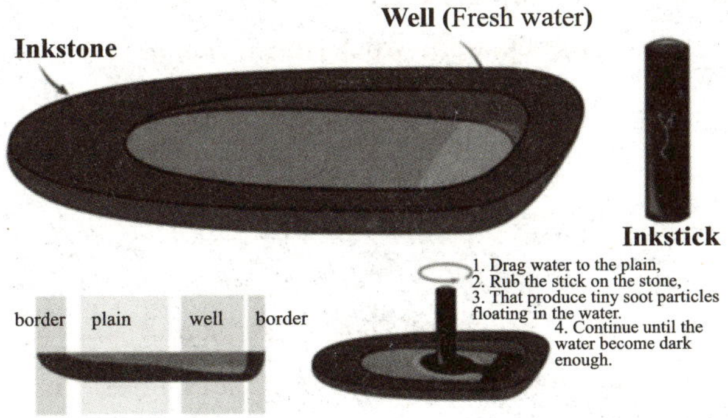

地方频道 Local Channel

西安频道：西安碑林
Xi'an Chanel: The Stele Forest in Xi'an

西安碑林是我国收藏古代碑石墓志时间最早、名碑最多的一座艺术宝库，它不仅是中国古代文化典籍刻石的集中地点之一，也是历代著名书法艺术珍品的荟萃之地，有着巨大的历史和艺术价值。

The Stele Forest (Beilin Museum) in Xi'an is the first artistic museum that houses the maximum number of famous steles and stone sculptures in China. The museum displays not merely the stone sculptures of Chinese classics and historical records, but the precious works of painting and calligraphy by masters in history with tremendous historical and artistic values.

西安碑林位于三学街北侧。“碑林”一名始于清代，有“碑石丛立如林”之意。今日之西安碑林，收藏了汉代至民国（公元前 206—1949 年）的碑石、墓志 4 000 余通（方），共有大型陈列室、展览廊各 7 座，以及碑亭 8 座。罗马城不是一天建成的，作为我国收藏碑石较早和古代碑石最多的一座宏伟艺术殿堂，它已经历了 900 余年历史。

Located on the north side of Sanxue Street, Xi'an Stele Forest earned its name dating back to Qing Dynasty for a widespread saying “The vast number of steles stand like the lush forest”. Nowadays, the museum, with respective seven large-scale showrooms and exhibition galleries and eight pavilions housing the stone rubbings, has collected 4,000 stone steles and epitaphs from Han Dynasty to the Republic of China (206 B.C.–1949). As Rome is not built in one day, the Stele Forest has weathered over 900 years.

大家非常熟悉的《九成宫》《圣教序》的碑刻实物都在西安碑林，所以，西安碑林是书法家非常向往的一个书法圣地。

The well-known authentic works of *Stele of Jiucheng Gong* and *Stele of Sheng Jiao Xu* are housed in the museum, which makes the Stele Forest the Holy Land for the calligraphers.

二、京剧
Peking Opera

（一）概述
Overview

中国传统戏剧连同古希腊悲剧、喜剧和印度梵语戏剧被称为世界三大古代戏剧。中国古代戏种超过 360 种，京剧的历史虽然不足 200 年，但是这个年轻的戏种却成了中华民族戏剧的代表。京剧是一种集音乐、声乐表演、哑剧表演、舞蹈和杂技于一体讲述历史故事或民间传说的中国戏曲。它起源于 18 世纪后期，并在 19 世纪中期得到了充分发展和认可。京剧在清朝的宫廷中广受欢迎，并被认为是中国的文化宝藏之一。2010 年 11 月 16 日，京剧被列入人类非物质文化遗产代表作名录。京剧的主要表演团体分布在北京、天津和上海。我国台湾地区也保存了京剧的艺术形式。除此以外，京剧还扩散到世界其他地区，如美国和日本。

Chinese traditional opera is considered one of the world's three ancient operas, together with Greek tragedy and comedy, and Indian Sanskrit opera. Among the more than 360 ancient local operas in China, Peking Opera is known as Chinese national opera, despite its comparatively young 200-year history. Peking opera or Beijing opera is a form of Chinese opera which combines music, vocal performance, mime, dance and acrobatics to tell stories from Chinese history and folklore. It arose in the late 18th century and became fully developed and recognized by the mid-19th century. The form was extremely popular in the Qing Dynasty court and has come to be regarded as one of the cultural treasures of China. On November 16, 2010, Peking Opera was included in the List of Representatives of the Intangible Cultural Heritage of Mankind. Major performance troupes are based in Beijing, Tianjin and Shanghai. The art form is also preserved in Taiwan. It has also spread to other regions such as the United States and Japan.

（二）京剧的起源
Origin of Peking Opera

徽班在 1790 年的时候从安徽带来徽剧为乾隆皇帝庆祝 80 岁生日，此后京剧由此演变创生。京剧最初只在宫廷中演出，随后才为普通市民所接触。1828 年，几个著名的湖北戏班子来到北京，和徽剧戏班子同台表演，两个戏种合璧渐渐形成了京剧的唱腔。所以京剧虽然被称为北京戏剧，但是它的起源要追溯到安徽南部和湖北东部地区。京剧一般被认为是在 1845 年完全形成，其主要的两种唱腔：西皮和二黄大约在 1750 年后衍生于汉剧。京剧的曲调与汉剧极为相似，因此汉剧被普遍称为京剧之母。"西皮"作为京剧主要的唱腔，其字面意思为"动物皮木偶秀"，指的是源于陕西的一种木偶表演。一些学者认为西皮的音乐形式源于秦腔，同时大量的演出套路、表演元素和审美原则来自昆曲。因此，京剧不是一种整体单一的形式，而是多种戏剧形式的融合。

Peking opera was born when the "Four Great Anhui Troupes" brought Anhui opera, or what is now called Huiju, in 1790 to Beijing, for the eightieth birthday of the Qianlong Emperor. It was originally staged for the court and only made available to the public later. In 1828, several famous Hubei troupes arrived in Beijing and performed jointly with Anhui troupes. The combination gradually formed Peking opera's melodies. Although it is called Peking opera (Beijing theater style), its origins are in the southern Anhui and eastern Hubei. Peking opera is generally regarded as having fully formed by 1845. Peking opera's two main melodies, Xipi and Erhuang, were derived from Han opera after about 1750. The tune of Peking opera is extremely similar to that of Han opera, therefore Han opera is widely known as the Mother of Peking opera. Xipi as the main melody of Peking opera, literally means "Skin Puppet Show", referring to the puppet show that originated in Shaanxi province. Some scholars believe that the Xipi musical form was derived from the historic Qinqiang, while many conventions of staging, performance elements, and aesthetic principles were retained from Kunqu.

Thus, Peking opera is not a monolithic form, but rather a coalescence of many older forms.

（三）京剧的四种表演形式
Four Means of Peking Opera

唱、念、坐、打是京剧的四种表演形式，也是京剧的四项基本技能。京剧通常是通过模仿的手势和动作来重现场景和道具。舞台上没有真实的门、马车、船、山或马，因此手势、步法和一些其他动作就表示了开门、进门、上车、划船、登山、骑马的动作。每一个动作都具有高度的象征性。这些具有象征意义的动作传达出了思想和感受。这种独特的艺术手法在表演中已经运用多年。

Singing, recitation, acting, and acrobatic fighting are the four artistic means and the four basic skills of Peking opera. Peking opera recreates settings and props through the use of mimed gestures and actions. The stage has no real door, carriage, boat, mountain or horse; hence gestures, footwork and other movements express the action of opening the door, entering through the door, getting on a carriage, rowing a boat, climbing up a mountain and riding a horse. Each action of performer is highly symbolic. Feelings and ideas are often expressed through these symbolic motions and the unique format has developed over years of performance.

（四）角色分类
Classifications of Roles

京剧人物通常按照性别、年龄、性格、职业和社会地位进行分类。现代京剧主要有四种角色：生（男性）、旦（女性）、净（画花脸的男性）、丑（小丑）。

The characters of Peking opera are classified according to sex, age, disposition, profession, and social status. There are four major roles in Peking opera in modern time: Sheng (male), Dan (female), Jing (male with a painted face) and Chou (clown).

生角一般是由男性扮演。这个角色又可以细分为老生、武生、小生和娃娃生。老生指的是中年或上了岁数的男性，一般具有忠诚和睿智的特点。老生也叫须生，因为他们总是戴着假的胡须登台。武生是有武艺技能的将才。小生通常长得眉清目秀，一表人才。小生在表演中最显著的特征是用真声和假声结合进行说唱。假声发出来又尖又细又高，是为了让声音听起来年轻，为了将老生和小生做区分。

Sheng are generally positive and can be divided into laosheng (elderly men), wusheng (military men), xiaosheng (young men), and wawasheng (children). Laosheng are middle-aged or elderly men who are decisive and honest. They are also called xusheng (beard men), because they wear artificial beards. Wusheng are young generals skilled in martial arts. Xiaosheng are clean-shaven and handsome. The most distinctive feature of the performances by xiaosheng is the combination of real and falsetto voices in singing and speaking. The falsetto voice is sharp, thin, and high-pitched in order to sound young and to distinguish the young men from elderly. Wawasheng are performed by children.

旦角指的是各种各样的女性角色，包括老旦、青衣、花旦、武旦和彩旦。老旦是老年女性。老旦表演者用自然的声音演唱，听起来饱满、洪亮、高昂，富有旋律感。青衣大体指的是那些个性刚强或心思细腻的中青年女性。她们大多数是忠诚的妻子、慈爱的母亲，还有来自封建社会的纯洁女性。花旦是聪颖伶俐的女孩，她们性格直爽开朗。她们的人物原型通常来自贫苦家庭或者艺术作品，其中包括了女将、绿林好汉和仙女。彩旦指的是滑稽表演和喜剧中的小丑。

Dan refers to various female roles, including laodan, qingyi, huadan, wudan and caidan. Laodan are elderly women. Laodan performers use their natural voices, which are rich, loud, high-pitched and melodious. Qingyi are generally young or middle aged women of strong character and fined disposition. Most of them are faithful wives, loving mothers, and pure women from feudal society. Huadan are agile young women with frank and open personalities. They are most from humble families or arts, including generals, heroic forest outlaws and fairies. Caidan are clowns in farces and comedies.

梅兰芳、尚小云、程砚秋和荀慧生是著名的四大旦角表演艺术家，他们为旦角的艺术表演和京剧的发展做出了重要的贡献。

Mei Lanfang, Shang Xiaoyun, Cheng Yanqiu, and Xun Huisheng are the famous "Four Great Dan Actors" who made significant contribution to the performance of dan roles and the development of Peking opera.

净角通常用彩色颜料修饰面部，因此也叫花脸。净可分为正净、副净和武净。正净又叫大花脸。正净主要表演唱功，大多数正净都是严厉忠诚、主持正义的官员和将领。副净主要表演来回走动、说话和做动作。武净表演杂技和翻跟斗，极少有说和唱的表演。

Jing wear colorful paints on their faces, so they are known as hualian. They can be classified into zhengjing (primary face-painted role), fujing (secondary face-painted role) and wujing (military face-painted role). Zhengjing is also known as dahualian. A zhengjing performer mainly sings. Most zhengjing are serious, loyal officials and generals who firmly uphold justice. Fujing performers mainly move about, speaking and making postures. Wujing roles involve acrobatic fighting and tumbling with minimal singing and speaking.

丑角扮演的都是聪明伶俐、诚实善良的人。文丑（滑稽的平民角色）表演说和一般动作，武丑（杂耍打斗的喜剧角色），既要表演说也要表演杂耍打斗。

Chou are sharp-witted, clever, humorous, honest, and kind men. There are wenchou (comic civilian role) who speak, act, and wuchou (acrobatic-fighting comic role) whose performance involves both speaking and acrobatic fighting.

Role 角色	Alternative name 别名	Definition 定义	Face design 面部特征	Major subtypes 主要子类型
Sheng (生)		Gentlemen 绅士	Slight make-up 面部淡妆	Laosheng (老生 middle-aged or elderly men) (also referred to as Mo [末]), Xiaosheng (小生 , young men), Wusheng (武生 , men with martial skills), Wawa-sheng (娃娃生 , children)
Dan (旦)		Women 女士	Slight make-up 面部淡妆	Qingyi (青衣 , women with strict moral code), Laodan (老旦 , elderly women), Huadan (花旦, young girls) , Caidan (彩旦 , clowns)
Jing (净)	Hualian (花脸)	Men with distinctive features 品格或相貌有突出特点的男性	Painted 面部涂画	Zhengjing (正净 , primary face-painted role), Fujing (副净 , secondary face-painted role), Wujing (武净 , military face-painted role)
Chou (丑)	Xiaohualian (小花脸)	Male clowns 男性小丑	Painted 面部涂画	Wenchou (文丑 , civilian clown), Wuchou (武丑 , clown with martial skills)

生

旦

净

丑

脸谱

Facial Makeup

脸谱是运用色彩和线条构成各种图案，以象征人物的性格和品质。脸谱的作用可归纳成四点：暗示性格、介绍特点、褒贬善恶、明辨美丑。它基本可分为六类：红、白、黑、黄、蓝和绿、金和银。其中，红表示忠义、耿直、有血性，如：“三国戏”里的关羽；白表示奸诈多疑，含贬义，代表凶诈，如：“三国戏”里的曹操；黑表示性格严肃、不苟言笑，为中性，代表猛智，如“包公戏”里的包拯；黄表示凶猛阴险，如典韦；蓝和绿表示中性，如草莽英雄；金和银表示神秘，代表妖神一类，如美猴王和白骨精。

Facial makeup indicates that colors and lines are used to form various patterns to symbolize the personality and morality of the characters. The function of facial makeup can be summarized into four points: suggesting personality, introducing features, praising virtue or punishing vice and identifying beauty and ugliness.

Basically the facial makeup can be divided into six categories: red, white, black, yellow, blue and green, gold and silver. Red means the character is loyalty, straightness, and bloodiness, such as Guan Yu in the "Three Kingdoms". White means the character is treacherous and suspicious, representing murder, such as: Cao Cao in the "Three Kingdoms". Black means that the character is serious, not frivolous, neutral, and represents wise, such as Bao Zheng in the "Bao Gong Opera". Huang means that the character is fierce and insidious, such as Dian Wei. Blue and Green represent neutral character of rebellious heroes. Gold and silver express mystery, representing the demons and ghosts, such as the Monkey King and White Bones Demon in *Journey to the West*.

（五）京剧走向世界
Peking Opera around the World

京剧除了在中国生存和发展以外，还传播到许多其他地方，比如在海外华人社区中也能找到京剧的身影。

In addition to its presence in China, Peking opera has spread to many other places. It also can be found in overseas Chinese communities elsewhere.

梅兰芳是著名的旦角表演艺术家，在海外也是最伟大的京剧推广者之一。

19世纪20年代他在日本表演京剧，这为他1930年2月在美国的巡游演出埋下了伏笔。虽然有些人认为京剧在美国永远不可能取得成功，但是梅兰芳和他在纽约的剧团用获得的好评反击了这一言论。他们演出的地点从第49街剧院搬迁到更大的国家剧院，巡演时间从两周延长到五周。梅兰芳在美国各地巡演，还获得了加州大学和波莫纳学院的荣誉学位。之后他于1935年继续在苏联巡回演出。

Mei Lanfang, one of the most famous Dan performers of all time, was also one of the greatest popularizers of Peking opera abroad. During the 1920s, he performed Peking opera in Japan. This inspired an American tour in February 1930. Although some believed that Peking opera could never be a success in the United States, the favorable reception of Mei and his troupe in New York City disproved this notion. The performances had to be relocated from the 49th Street Theater to the larger National Theater, and the duration of the tour extended from two weeks to five. Mei traveled across the United States, receiving honorary degrees from the University of California and Pomona College. He followed this tour with a tour in the Soviet Union in 1935.

夏威夷大学马诺阿分校的戏剧系作为英语京剧的故乡已有超过25年的历史。该学校开设亚洲戏剧专业，并定期举办京剧表演，经常公演的剧目是《穆桂英和杨家将》。

The theatre department at the University of Hawaii at Manoa has been home to English language of Peking opera for more than twenty-five years. The school offers Asian Theatre as a major and has regular Peking opera performances, with *Lady Mu and the Yang Family Generals* being the most regular plays.

三、武术
Martial Art

（一）概况
Overview

“武术”字面意思就是“搏斗的艺术”。这个词由两个字组成，“武”是“搏斗的”“军事的”，而“术”可理解为“艺术”、“规则”或“技巧”。“拳法”是中国武术的另一个术语，它指的是“用拳的方法”或“行拳的规则”。

"Martial art" is literally formed from the two Chinese characters 武 and 术 : 武 , meaning "martial" or "military" and 术 which translates into "art", "discipline", "skill" or "method". Quanfa is another Chinese term for Chinese martial arts. It means "fist method" or "the law of the fist". Although as a compound term it usually translates as "boxing" or "fighting technique".

中国武术又叫中国功夫，它是一种具有数千年发展历史，包含数百种武打形式的搏斗艺术。由于历史发展和地域分布的关系，武术衍生出不同流派。中华武术主要内容包括搏击技巧、格斗手法、攻防策略和武器使用等技术。当中又分为理论和实践两个范畴。实践部分主要指有关体育、健身和中国武术独有之气功及养生等重要功能，理论部分则是来自前人之武术经验和拳谱的记录。因此，它体现了中华民族对攻防技击及策略的理解。武术以内外结合、协调统一为原则，有软有硬，有松有紧，有上有下，有收有放，有思想也有动作。武术不仅以外在形体美著称，如架势、动作以及技巧，而且其内在美更为独特，被称为"生活之本，力量之源"。现代不同派别的武术融合了各民族的智慧和文化。

Chinese martial arts, often named Kung Fu are the several hundred fighting styles that have developed over the centuries in China. Due to historical development and geographical distribution, martial arts have derived different sects. The main contents of Chinese martial arts include fighting techniques, combating skills, offensive and defensive strategies, and weapons use. It is mainly divided into two categories: theory and practice. The practice part mainly refers to the important functions related to sports, fitness, Qigong and health preservation. The theoretical part is the experience of martial arts and boxing record from the predecessors. Therefore, martial arts reflects the Chinese nation's understanding of attack and defense strategies. Martial arts requires a balanced combination of the inseparable internal and external principles: hard and soft, relaxed and tense, up and down, opening and closing, thought and action. Martial arts is characterized not only by exterior beauty, impostures, movements and techniques, but also deep interior beauty, emphasizing "life essence, vital energy and spirit." The present different schools and styles of martial arts embody the wisdom and culture of all the ethnic groups in China.

（二）中国武术的起源和发展
Origin and Development of Chinese Martial Art

有神话传说是这样描述的，在半神话时期，黄帝最早在中国推行武术。他在成为君主以前是一位著名的将领并写下了许多关于医学、占卜术和武术的著作。而他的主要对手蚩尤是角抵术的发明者，蚩尤被誉为现代中国武术的先驱。从春秋战国开始，中国历朝历代的史书都有对武术的记载。唐朝女皇帝武则天于公元 702 年制定出武举制度，用武术选举军将人才，这大大促进了武术的发展。

According to legend, Chinese martial arts originated during the semi-mythical period more than 4,000 years ago. It is said the Yellow Emperor introduced the earliest fighting systems to China. The Yellow Emperor is described as a famous general who, before becoming China's leader, wrote lengthy treatises on medicine, astrology and the martial arts. One of his main opponents was Chiyou who was credited as the creator of Jiaodi, a forerunner to the modern art of China. Since the Spring and Autumn Period and the Warring States Period, the history books of all dynasties recorded the martial arts. Wu Zetian, the emperor of the Tang Dynasty, set up military official selecting institution in 702 A.D., which used martial arts to elect military personnel and greatly promoted the development of martial arts.

（三）中国武术的分类
Types of Chinese Martial art

中国武术有悠久的历史渊源，有数百种拳法。过去两千年，许多独具特色的拳法在技巧和思想上都得到了发展。虽然拳法之间有差异，但是依据共性它们可以被归类为不同的“家”“派”“门”。其中有模仿动物的拳法，也有受中国哲学神话传说启发而创造的拳法。一些拳法强调用“气”，然而另一些注重竞技。

China has a long history of martial arts traditions. Martial arts have hundreds of different styles. Over the past two thousand years, many distinctive styles have been developed, each with its own set of techniques and ideas. There are also common themes to the different styles, which are often classified by “families” (家; jia), “sects” (派; pai) or “schools” (门; men). There are styles that mimic movements from animals and others that gather inspiration from various Chinese philosophies, myths and legends. Some styles put most of their focus into the harnessing of qi, while others concentrate on competition.

中国武术可以按照用“气”来进行分类，注重运气的拳叫内家拳，那些注重肌肉训练和血管保健的拳叫外家拳。也可以按照地域来归类，分为北拳和南拳。

黄河是中国南北方的分界线，起源于南方的叫南拳，起源于北方的叫北拳。从认知上来说，南拳和北拳的差异在于北拳强调快而有力的踢腿动作、高跳动作和流畅而快速地移动，而南拳重视强壮的手臂、手上动作、稳健的姿势和快速的步伐。长拳和形意拳属于北拳，白眉派、五祖拳、蔡李佛拳、咏春拳属于南拳。中华武术还按照宗教命名，例如象形拳，还可以以家族命名，例如洪家拳。中国的武术甚至还可以以省份和城市来命名。

Chinese martial arts can be split into external and internal according to the manipulation of "qi". Some styles focus on the harnessing of qi and are labeled internal, while others concentrate on improving muscle and cardiovascular fitness and are labeled external. Chinese martial arts can also be categorized by location, as in northern and southern as well, referring to what part of China the styles originated from, separated by the Yellow River; The main perceived difference between northern and southern styles is that the northern styles tend to emphasize fast and powerful kicks, high jumps and generally fluid and rapid movement, while the southern styles focus more on strong arm and hand techniques, and stable, immovable stances and fast footwork. Examples of the northern styles include Changquan and Xingyiquan. Examples of the southern styles include Bak Mei, Wuzuquan, Choy Li Fut, and Wing Chun. Chinese martial arts can also be divided according to religion, imitative-styles, and family styles such as Hung Gar. Chinese martial arts may even be classified according to their province or city.

（四）现代武术的五大类别
Five Categories of Modern Martial Art

用拳:拳法的种类包括长拳、太极拳、南拳、形拳、八卦拳、少林拳、醉拳等。

Boxing: Boxing includes long boxing 长拳, shadow boxing 太极拳, southern boxing 南拳, form boxing 形拳, Eight-Trigram boxing 八卦拳, Shaolin boxing 少林拳, and drunkard boxing 醉拳, etc.

武器训练：武器训练包括练习长矛、手杖等长兵器，剑和军刀等短兵器，还包括双剑、双钩等的双兵器以及九节鞭、三节棍等软兵器。

Weapon exercises: Weapon exercises include exercises with long weapons such as spears and staffs, short weapons such as swords and sabers, double weapons such as double-swords, double-hooks, and soft weapons such as nine-section whips and three-section sticks.

对打练习：对打练习包括徒手对练、器械对练和徒手对器械练习。

Sparring exercises: Sparring exercises include sparring exercises barehanded, with weapons, and barehanded against weapons.

实战：实战包括散打、推手和使用长短兵器的武打。

Actual combat: Actual combat includes free sparring, hand-pushing and fighting with long or short weapons.

团体练习：团体练习包括六人或六人以上组成团队一起习武。他们可以使用武器，也可以不使用武器。

Teamwork: Teamwork includes exercises or performances by six or more people working together with or without weapons.

你知道吗？ Do you know?

少林功夫 Shaolin Kung Fu

少林功夫也叫少林拳，是中国武界各大流派中历史最悠久、种类最繁多、体系最庞大的门派。它结合了禅宗佛教和武术，起源于中国河南省少林寺，至今已有 1 500 多年的历史。民间流传了这样两句话：天下武功出少林，少林功夫甲天下。可见少林功夫对武术的影响不可小觑。

Shaolin Kung Fu (Chinese: 少林功夫; pinyin: Shaolingongfu), also called Shaolin Wushu (少林武术; Shaolinwushu) or Shaolin quan (少林拳; Shaolinquan), is one of the oldest, largest, and most famous styles of Wǔshù. It combines Zen Buddhism and martial arts and originated and was developed in the Shaolin temple in Henan province, China during its 1500-year history. Popular sayings in Chinese folklore related to this practice include "All martial arts under heaven originated from Shaolin" and "Shaolin Kung Fu is the best under heaven," indicating the influence of Shaolin Kung Fu among martial arts.

太极拳
Taijiquan (Tai Chi)

太极拳是内家拳，练习太极拳不仅可以防御他人进攻还对自己的身体有好处。太极指的是哲学中的“阴”“阳”概念。这是两股与运动相关的力量。太极拳讲究意、气、形、神的统一。它要求注意力集中和身心宁静。“头脑是指挥官，身体是士兵。”“一动则全动，一静则全静。”简单的力量并不是首要的，太极拳中的力量如同车的轮，而腰部就像轮的轴，太极拳的动作就像是在连续的画圆。呼吸要深，不动的时候要站得像山一样稳，动起来要像河流一样连贯。太极拳动作强调圆润、轻柔、缓慢、稳健、均匀。它讲究伸展和协调，所有的动作都来自阴阳对立的统一体。

Taijiquan is an internal Chinese martial art practiced for both its defense training and its health benefits. The term taiji refers to a philosophy of the forces of Yin and Yang, related to the moves. Taiji quan is characterized by the unification of mind, breath and motions. It requires concentration of mind and calmness of motions. “Mind works as a commander and body a soldier.” “When in motion all of the body moves. When at rest, all of the body rests.” Simple force is not preferred. Force is like a wheel and waist is its axis. The motions are continuous as a circle. The breath is deep. Be concentrated, gentle and natural. Be stable as a mountain when not moving, and be flowing as a river when moving. The moves are characterized by roundness softness, slowness, stability and evenness. They are extended but very well coordinated, and all are antithetical unity of Yin and Yang.

香港功夫电影
Hong Kong Kung Fu films

在华语圈，武打片分为两种，一种是武侠片，另一种是功夫片。在武侠小说盛行了几千年之后武侠片开始受到欢迎。金庸和古龙的武侠小说被改编成电影，让武侠片占据了电影市场的半壁江山。在华语圈外，最出名的武侠片是由李安执导的《卧虎藏龙》。该部影片获得了四项奥斯卡奖，其中一项为最佳外语片奖。

In the Chinese-speaking world, martial arts films are commonly divided into two subcategories: the wuxia period films, and the more modern Kung Fu films. The wuxia period films came into vogue due to the thousands of years' popularity of wuxia novels. For example, the wuxia novels of Jin Yong and Gu Long directly led to the prevalence of wuxia period films. Outside of the Chinese speaking world the most famous wuxia film made was the Lee Ang film *Crouching Tiger, Hidden Dragon*, which earned four Academy Awards, including one for Best Foreign Film.

20 世纪 70 年代，李小龙带领香港功夫片开始异军突起。李小龙去世以后，成龙在功夫片中融合喜剧、危险特技和现代都市背景，让功夫片大卖热卖。而另一个人李连杰，则用他真真正正的武艺技术吸引了海内外众多观众。以下是一些功夫片代表作:《精武门》《黄飞鸿》《龙争虎斗》《少林寺》。

In the 1970s, Bruce Lee led the Hong Kong Kung Fu films to a sudden emergence. After his death, Jackie Chan used comedy, dangerous stunts, and modern urban settings in action films to make Kung Fu films sell well. Another person is Jet Li, whose authentic marshal arts skills appealed to both eastern and western audiences. Some representatives of Kung Fu films are as follows: *Fist of Fury; Once Upon a Time; Enter the Dragon; Shaolin Temple.*

四、中医
Chinese Medicine

中医是具有 2 500 多年历史的传统医学。中医涵盖多种形式，包括中药、针灸、推拿、拔罐、气功、食疗和刮痧。中医将健康看作是人体和外部世界互动产生的一种和谐状态，而疾病则是互动中不和谐的表现。不同医疗手段有一个共同点就是它们都帮助人体功能恢复平衡。中医的四诊：望、闻、问、切是诊断疾病的四个基本步骤，也是疾病正确归类和治疗的前提。

Traditional Chinese medicine is a style of traditional medicine based on more than 2,500 years of Chinese medical practice that includes various forms of Chinese herb medicine, acupuncture, Chinese medical massage, cupping, qigong, food therapy, and skin scraping. Traditional Chinese medicine describes health as the harmonious interaction of these entities and the outside world, and disease as a disharmony in interaction. The common thread among diverse practices is to help the body restore the balancing of various functions. The four diagnostic methods of Chinese medicine, namely inspection, auscultation and olfaction, inquiry, pulse taking and palpation, are the four basic procedures used in diagnosing a disease. They are the presuppositions of correct differentiation and effective treatment in traditional Chinese medicine.

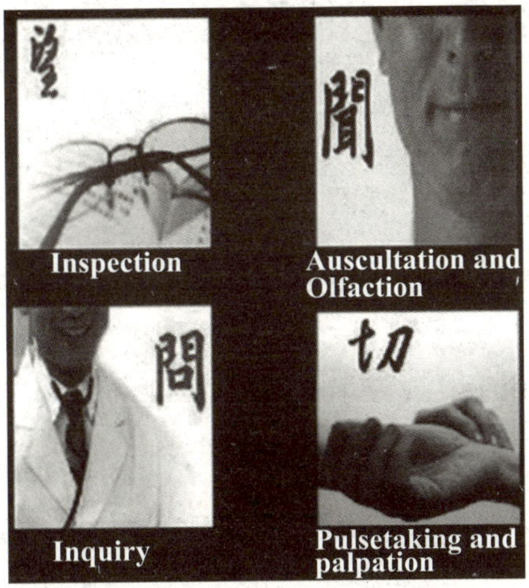

中药是中医治疗的核心部分。不同的中药成分都有独特的功效，互相协调帮助人体保持健康，具有提气和保持阴阳平衡的作用。

Chinese herb medicine is a vital part of Chinese healing. Each ingredient has unique characteristics. The ingredients work in harmony to help a person's body. Herbs can help boost "qi" and balance Yin and Yang.

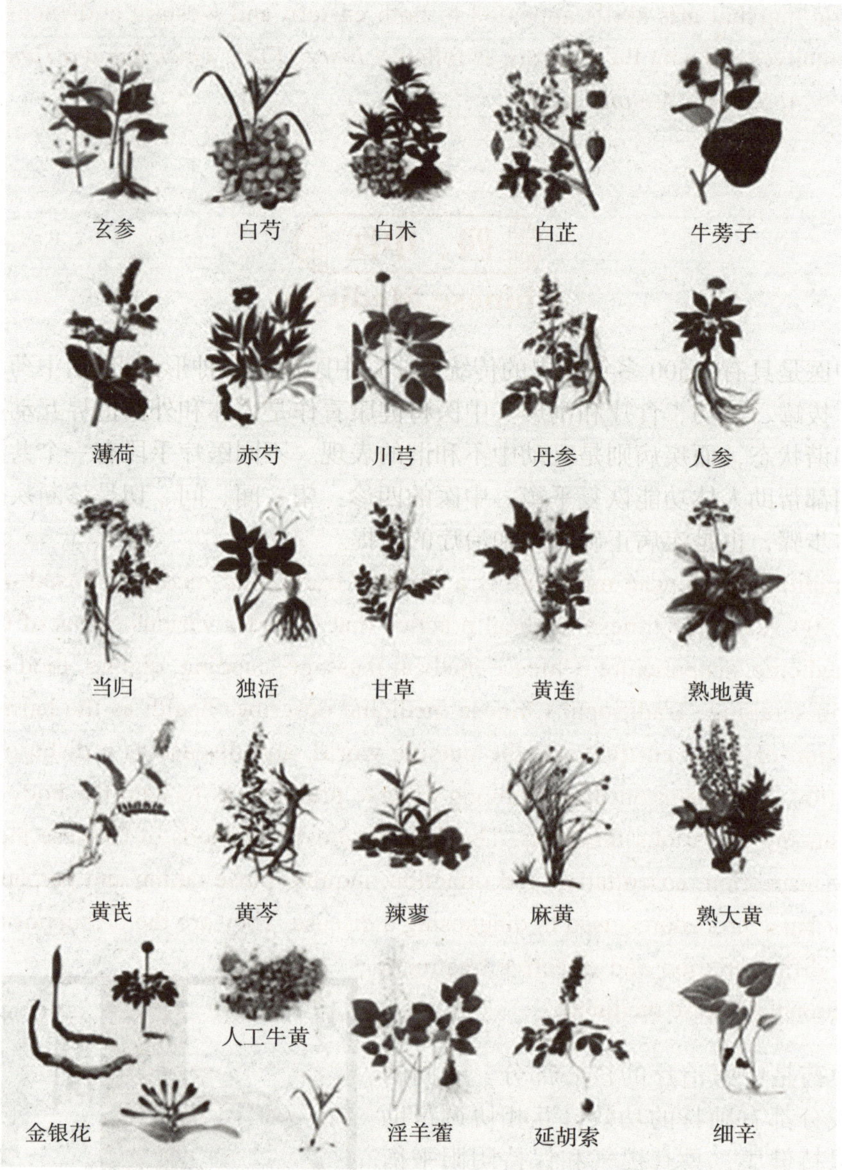

针灸是用细针刺激人体穴位。与你的想象恰好相反的是，病人在针灸时通常极少感觉到疼痛或者几乎感觉不到疼痛。针灸用的银针像头发丝那么细，常常是用手扎或者用电刺激。这些针都必须扎在阴阳经络点上。

Acupuncture involves the stimulation of anatomical points on the body with thin needles. Contrary to what you might think, acupuncture patients usually feel from little to no pain. Acupuncture needles are hair-thin and are manipulated either by hand or electricity. Needles are placed at "Yin/Yang Meridian points"

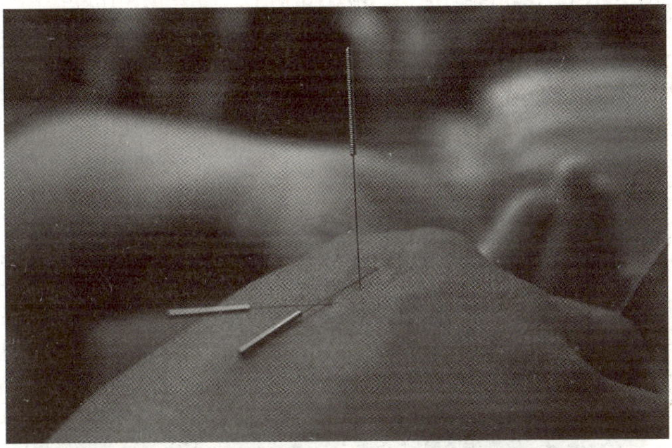

艾灸是用艾蒿进行治疗的传统疗法。艾蒿长成以后会分化出艾绒，将艾绒进一步加工成类似于雪茄的棒状，点燃艾条，用燃烧的热量加热身体或者针灸部位。

Moxibustion is a traditional therapy by using moxa (艾蒿) or mugwort. Mugwort is aged and grouped up to a fluff. Then the fluff is further processed into a stick that resembles a cigar and it is used to warm areas of the body and acupuncture points.

拔罐疗法是中医非药物治疗的重要组成部分，已有数千年的历史。通过拔和按的机械操作，在负压的作用下，这种疗法可以疏通经络，促进血液循环，去除血淤，解毒输氧。 它被认为在全身性疾病、呼吸系统疾病、循环系统疾病、消化系统疾病等方面的治疗具有显著功效。

Cupping therapy is an important part of non-drug therapy in traditional Chinese medicine, with a history of thousands of years. Under the action of negative pressure, this therapy dredges meridians, promotes blood circulation, removes blood stasis, detoxifies and oxygenates by mechanical effects of dragging and pressing. It is thought to have the ability to offer significant effects on systemic disease, respiratory system disease, circulation system disease, digestive system disease, and others.

推拿也是一种治疗手段，推拿师用手接触患者体表，在患者受伤部位运用推、握、按、搓、揉、点击和拍打等一系列技术手段让患者疏通经络、减轻疼痛。

Chinese medical massage is a treatment method, by which the physician apply his hands to the body surface, in proximity to the patients' injuries using multiple techniques (pushing, holding, pressing, friction, rubbing, kneading, dotting and patting), in order to "dredge meridians" and relieve pain.

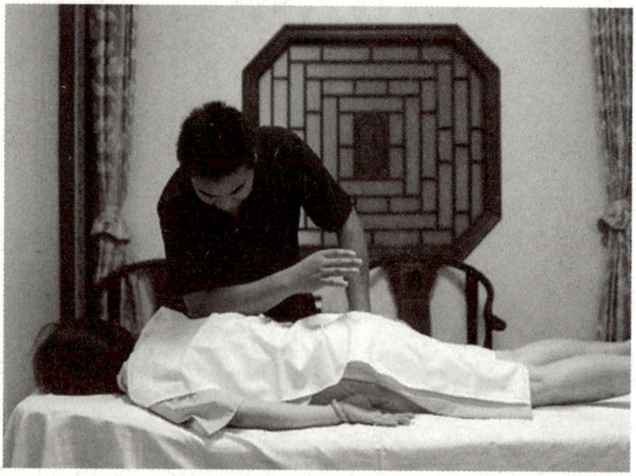

刮痧疗法是以经络和穴位理论为指导，使用特殊的器具和方法在人体表面一次次地刮擦。这种疗法可以调节肌肉的张弛，从而调节软组织压力，改善血液流动。该方法具有治愈的理论和实践基础。

Scraping therapy is guided by the theory of meridians and acu-points, and in-so-doing scrapes and rubs the body surface again and again using special instruments and methods. This therapy can adjust the contraction and tension of muscle, which may adjust the pressure between tissues and improve blood flow. This method has both practical and theoretical foundations for healing.

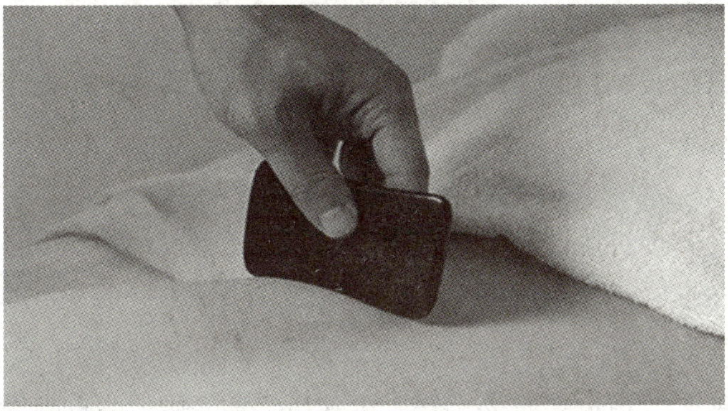

气功可以调节呼吸、沉淀思想，提升体内气的流动。气功可以用来治病。外气功指的是气功大师作用于某个人身上的功力，而内气功是一个人独自修炼的功法。

Qigong regulates the mind and breathing to promote the flow of Qi. Qigong is often used to treat diseases. External Qigong is performed on a person by a Qigong master, while Internal Qigong is practiced by oneself.

课后练习题

Practice

一、选择题

Multiple-choice

1. 在京剧中，那些聪明伶俐、性格直爽开朗的女孩叫作（　　）。
   In Peking opera, (　　) is played by clever and extroverted girls.

   A. 花旦　　B. 武生

   A. Huadan　　B. wusheng (military men)

C. 正净　　D. 丑

C. zhengjing (primary face-painted role)　　D. chou (clown)

2. (　　) 是用细针刺激人体穴位。

(　　) involves the stimulation of anatomical points on the body with thin needles.

A. 针灸　　B. 推拿

A. acupuncture　　B. Chinese medical massage

C. 拔罐　　D. 气功

C. cupping　　D. qigong

3. 有神话传说是这样描述的，在半神话时期，(　　) 最早在中国推行武术。

According to legend, Chinese martial arts originated during the semi-mythical period more than 4,000 years ago. It is said (　　) introduced the earliest fighting systems to China.

A. 炎帝　　B. 黄帝　　C. 蚩尤　　D. 武则天

A. Yan Emperor　　B. Yellow Emperor　　C. Chiyou　　D. Wu Zetian

4. (　　) 是著名的旦角表演艺术家，在海外也是最伟大的京剧推广者之一。他在美国各地巡演，还获得了加州大学和波莫纳学院的荣誉学位。

(　　), one of the most famous Dan performers of all time, was also one of the greatest popularizers of Peking opera abroad. He traveled across the United States, receiving honorary degrees from the University of California and Pomona College.

A. 荀慧生　　B. 尚小云

A. Xun Huisheng　　B. Shang Xiaoyun

C. 程砚秋　　D. 梅兰芳

C. Cheng Yanqiu　　D. Mei Lanfang

5. (　　) 指的是刻写在动物骨头上的汉字。

(　　) was one of the forms of Chinese character written on animals bones.

A. 青铜器铭文　　B. 篆书

A. Bronze inscription　　B. Seal script

C. 甲骨文　　D. 楷书

C. Oracle bone script　　D. Regular script

二、填空题

Fill-in-the-blanks

1. 中国书法也经历了由__________，再到隶、行、草、楷体等书体的演变。

   Chinese calligraphy developed into various styles from __________ to clerical script, semi-cursive script, cursive script and regular script.

2. __________连同古希腊悲剧、喜剧和印度梵语戏剧被称为世界三大古代戏剧。

   __________ is considered one of the world's three ancient operas, together with Greek tragedy and comedy, and Indian Sanskrit opera.

3. ______是一种集音乐、声乐表演、哑剧表演、舞蹈和杂技于一体讲述历史故事或民间传说的中国戏曲。

   ______ is a form of Chinese opera which combines music, vocal performance, mime, dance and acrobatics to tell stories from Chinese history and folklore.

4. 中国武术又叫_________，是一种具有数千年发展历史，包含数百种武打形式的搏斗艺术。

   Chinese martial arts, often named _________, are the several hundred fighting styles that have developed over the centuries in China.

5. 文房四宝指的是______、______、______、______。

   So-called "scholar's four jewels" are ______, ______, ______ and ______.

三、判断题

True or False

1. 铭文指古人在青铜器上浇铸的文字以记录铸造该铜器的缘由、所纪念或祭祀的人物。

   Inscription refers to the characters cast by the ancients on the bronzes to record the reason for casting the bronzes, the figures who are commemorated or sacrificed.

2. 京剧连同古希腊悲剧、喜剧和印度梵语戏剧被称为世界三大古代戏剧。

   Peking opera is considered one of the world's three ancient operas, together with Greek tragedy and comedy, and Indian Sanskrit opera.

3. 中医的四诊：望、闻、问、切是诊断疾病的四个基本步骤，也是疾病正确归类和治疗的前提。

   The four diagnostic methods of traditional Chinese medicine, namely inspection, auscultation and olfaction, inquiry, pulse taking and palpation, are the four basic procedures used in diagnosing a disease. They are the presuppositions of correct differentiation and effective treatment in traditional Chinese medicine.

4. 书法是汉字的书写艺术，也可以说是用钢笔写汉字的艺术。
In China, calligraphy is referred to the art of writing Chinese characters with a pen.

5. 中国武术又叫中国功夫，是一种具有数千年发展历史，包含数百种武打形式的搏斗艺术。
Chinese martial arts, often named Kung Fu, are the several hundred fighting styles that have developed over the centuries in China.

四、简答题
Short-answer Questions

1. 京剧的四种表演形式（四项基本技能）是什么？
What are the four artistic means or the four basic skills of Peking opera?

____

____

2. 什么是京剧脸谱？
What is facial makeup of Peking opera?

____

____

3. 气功的作用是什么？
What is the function of Qigong?

____

____

第十章

中国的少数民族

Ethnic Minority Group in China

课前思考
Lead-in Questions

1. 你知道中国有多少个少数民族吗？他们住在中国的哪些地方？
   Do you know how many ethnic minority groups there are and where they live in China?
2. 很多国家都有少数民族，在你们国家有少数民族吗？他们的地位怎么样？
   Many countries have their own ethnic minority groups. Are there ethnic minority groups in your country? What about their status?

一、中国民族概述
Overview of the Chinese Ethnic Groups

民族，指在文化、语言、历史方面与其他人群不一样的一群人。一个国家可以有不同民族，一个民族可以生活在不同的国家里。你们国家有几个民族？

An ethnic group refers to a group of people who are different from the rest of the population in terms of culture, language and history. One country can have different ethnic groups, and one ethnic group can live in different countries. How many ethnic groups are there in your country?

中国是一个多民族的国家。一共有 56 个民族。这些民族组成一个大的民族，叫作中华民族。其中汉族是人数最多的民族，大约有 13 亿，约占全国人口总数的 92%，其他 55 个民族总人口很少，约占全国总人口的 8%，这些民族称作少数民族。

China is a multi-ethnic country. There are 56 ethnic groups in total, and all of them form one big Chinese nation. Among them the Han ethnic group is the largest, with about 1.3 billion people, approximately taking about 92% of the total Chinese population. The total population of other 55 ethnic groups is very small, occupying about 8% of total Chinese population. Those ethnic groups are called ethnic minority group.

少数民族分布范围广，但主要集中于中国西部及边疆地区。人口主要集中在西南、西北和东北各省、自治区，包括内蒙古、新疆、西藏、广西、宁夏等。云南和新疆是少数民族最多的省份。

Those ethnic minority groups are widely spread, but the main concentration of them is in the west and the border area of China. They live in southwest, northwest, all provinces of northeast and the Autonomous Regions including inner Mongolia, Xinjiang, Xizang, Guangxi, Ningxia and so on. Yunnan Province and Xinjiang Autonomous Region have the largest number of ethnic minority groups.

中华人民共和国成立后，中国政府的民族政策是：少数民族和汉族有平等的地位；团结少数民族；少数民族区域自治；各民族共同发展。多年来，少数民族人口增长比汉族快，就是一个证明。

After the founding of the People's Republic of China, the policy towards ethnic groups of the Chinese government is that the ethnic minority groups and the Han ethnic group have equal status; uniting ethnic groups; also giving them regional autonomy; common development and prosperity of all ethnic groups. The fact that the population of ethnic minority group has grown faster than Han ethnic group over the years is a testament to this.

下面我们主要介绍人口超过一百万的以及与国外关系密切的民族。

Below are mainly introduced the ethnic groups with a population of over one million and those closely related to foreign countries.

二、朝鲜族

Korean Ethnic Group

朝鲜族，是东亚主要民族之一。“朝鲜族”的称呼特指中国少数民族朝鲜族，是拥有中华人民共和国国籍的中国人，在非中国地区生活的朝鲜民族人不自称“朝鲜族”。朝鲜族主要分布在中国东北吉林、辽宁和黑龙江三省。少数散居在内蒙古和内陆一些城市。朝鲜族有自己的语言文字，语言一般认为属阿尔泰语系。朝鲜族的价值观具有明显的儒家特点，受到中原汉族古文化的影响较大。据 2010 年人口普查统计，朝鲜族人口为 1 830 929 人。

Korean ethnic group is one of the main ethnic groups in East Asia. The term “Korean ethnic group” refers specifically to the Korean ethnic minority group in China, a Chinese national with the nationality of the People’s Republic of China, and a non-Chinese ethnic Korean living in a non-Chinese area does not claim to be a “Korean ethnic”. The Korean ethnic group is mainly distributed in Jilin, Liaoning and Heilongjiang Provinces in northeastern China. A few scattered in Inner Mongolia and some cities in the interior. The Korean ethnic group has their own written and spoken language, which is generally considered to belong to the Altaic family. The values of the Korean ethnic group have obvious Confucian characteristics and are greatly influenced by the Han ancient culture in the central plains. According to the 2010 census, the ethnic Korean population was 1,830,929.

（一）服饰

Apparel

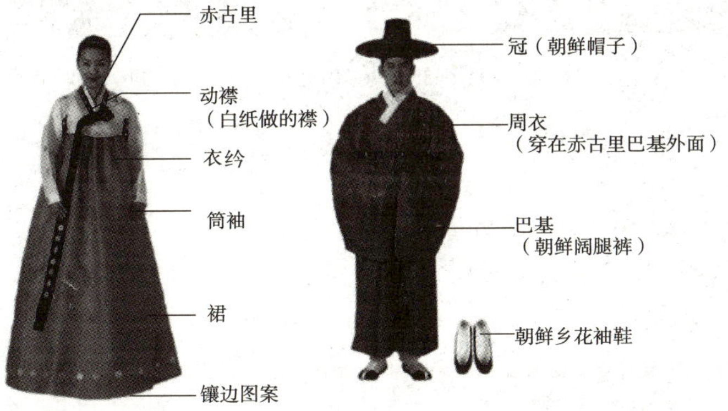

朝鲜族比较喜爱素白色服装，故有“白衣民族”之称。朝鲜族服装的特点是斜襟，无纽扣，以长布带打结。妇女传统日常服装为短衣（“则高利”）、长裙（“契码”）、斜襟，以长布带在右肩下方打蝴蝶结。男子服装为短上衣，外加坎肩，下身穿裤腿宽大的长裤，外出时多穿斜襟以布带打结的长袍。现在改穿制服或西服了。

Korean ethnic group preferred plain white clothing, so they're known as the “white people”. Their clothing is characterized by a slanted skirt, without buttons, and long cloth tied with a belt. Women traditionally wear short garments, long skirts, and slanted skirts, bowing with a long cloth strap below the right shoulder. Men's clothing consists of short jacket, extra waistcoat, baggy trousers, and they wear a long robe with a ribbon knot when going out. Nowadays it has changed to Western style uniforms or suits.

（二）饮食
Food and Drink

朝鲜族主要分布在中国东北三省，主食一般是大米和小米，喜欢吃“辣白菜”、打糕、冷面、大酱汤、辣椒等。其中最有名的是打糕、冷面、泡菜，他们经常吃羊肉串和五花肉。

The Korean ethnic group mainly lives in the three provinces of northeastern China. The staple food is rice and millet. They like to eat “spicy cabbage”, rice cake, cold noodles, big sauce soup, chilli and so on. The most famous ones are rice cake, cold noodles and pickles. They often eat mutton shashlik and pork belly.

（三）传统节日 Traditional Festivals

朝鲜族节日与汉族基本相同。“岁首节”即朝鲜族的春节，这是朝鲜族一年中最喜庆的节日之一。春节是朝鲜族最盛大的节日。正月初一先祭祖，而后儿童们穿着华丽的衣裳给老人和长辈们拜年。正月十五，朝鲜族不论男女老幼都吃“五谷饭”，喝“开耳酒”。

The Korean ethnic group's festivals are basically the same as the Han ones. The first day of the year is the Spring Festival for Koreans, one of the most festive days of the year for the Korean ethnic group. Spring Festival is the biggest festival for the Korean ethnic group. On the first day of the first month of the first lunar month, they worshipped ancestors first, then children wore gorgeous clothes to pay a New Year to the olders. On the 15th day of the first lunar month, all ethnic Koreans, men and women, young and old, eat "rice with five grains" and drink "appetizing wine".

（四）禁忌 Taboos

1. 晚辈不能在长辈面前喝酒、吸烟；吸烟时，年轻人不得向老人借火，更不能接火，否则便被认为是一种不敬的行为。

The younger generation cannot drink or smoke in front of their elders. When smoking, young people should not borrow fire from old people. They should also not give fire. Otherwise, it's considered disrespectful to do so.

2. 与长者同路时，年轻者必须走在长者后面，若有急事非超前不可，须向长者恭敬地说明理由；途中遇有长者迎面走来，年轻人应恭敬地站立路旁问好并让路。

When walking with the elderly, the young must walk behind the elderly. If something urgent needs to be done, he should respectfully explain his reasons to the elderly. When an elder comes to you on the way, the young man should stand respectfully by the roadside and give way.

3. 婚丧、佳节期间不宰狗、不食狗肉。

Not killing dogs or eating dog meat during weddings and funerals.

4. 吃饭要先给老人盛，并为其摆单桌，待老人举匙开始就餐了，全家人才开始吃饭。

The food should be given to the oldest man first, and the table shall be set for him, and the family shall not eat until the old man has raised his spoon and started to eat.

（五）汉族与朝鲜族的关系
Relationship between the Han and the Korean Ethnic Group

虽然从种族的概念上分析，两个族群差异很大，但从文化思维的角度上看，汉族与朝鲜族都深受儒家文化的影响，两个民族有很多共同点。

Although from the concept of race, the two ethnic groups are very different, but from the perspective of cultural influence, the two ethnic groups have a lot in common. Both Han and Korean people are deeply influenced by Confucian culture.

朝鲜族与汉族同属于一个文化圈，尤其是在儒家思想观念的影响下，逐渐形成的是朝鲜族的传统民俗。朝鲜族十分重视人生仪礼中的冠、婚、丧、葬四大仪礼。

Korean ethnic group and Han ethnic group belong to the same cultural circle. Especially because of being under the influence of Confucianism, what gradually formed is the traditional Korean folk custom. The Koreans attach great importance to the four rites of life: crown, marriage, funeral and interment.

三、满族
Manchu Ethnic Group

满族主要住在辽宁、吉林、黑龙江三个省，其中辽宁省最多。满族人口约 1 038.7 万，在中国 55 个少数民族中仅次于壮族、回族，居第三位。满族有自己的语言、文字。满语属阿尔泰语系，目前使用满语的人很少。满族的历史有 2 000 多年，他们在中国的历史上建立了中国最后一个王朝——清朝（1616—1911 年），为中华民族留下了非常丰富的文化遗产。

Manchu people mainly live in Liaoning, Jilin and Heilongjiang Provinces, among which most of them live in Liaoning. The population of Manchu is about 10.387 million, ranking in the third place in China's 55 ethnic minorities and after Zhuang and Hui. Manchu has its' own written and spoken language. The Manchu language belongs to the Altaic family of languages but few people speak Manchu at present. The history of the Manchus has more than two thousand years. They established the last Chinese dynasty in the history of China, the Qing Dynasty (1616–1911), which left a very rich cultural heritage for the Chinese nation.

（一）服饰
Apparel

满族的传统衣服是旗袍。满族无论男女都穿旗袍。旗袍发展到现在，已经成为中国和世界华人女性的传统服装，它被称为中国国粹和女性的国服。

Manchu's traditional clothes are cheongsam. Both Manchu men and women wear cheongsam. The cheongsam has become a traditional dress for Chinese women in China and around the world. It is called the quintessence of Chinese culture and women's national dress.

除了旗袍，满族的传统服饰还有马褂和千层底鞋等。

In addition to the cheongsam, the traditional clothes of the Manchus include mandarin jacket and thousand-floor shoes.

马褂是男子常着服装，是一种短褂衣衫。千层底鞋是旗人男女在家时常穿的鞋。

A mandarin jacket is a man's clothing, a type of short bottomed jacket. The thousand-floor shoes were often worn at home by both Manchu men and women.

（二）饮食
Food and Drink

满族传统主食有饽饽、煮饽饽（饺子）、米饭、高粱米（休米）豆干饭、豆糕、酸汤子等。他们尤其喜欢吃黏食和甜味食品，如饽饽、年糕等。今天我们见到的“驴打滚”“萨其玛”都是满族的传统点心。火锅、全羊席、酱肉也是满族人的传统吃肉方法。酸菜是他们喜欢的素食，或炒，或炖，或凉拌。

The traditional staple food of the Manchus includes: stop palpitation, cooking cakes (dumplings), rice, sorghum rice (Humi), dried rice with bean card, bean cake, sour soup, etc. They especially like to eat sticky food and sweet food, such as cakes, rice cakes and so on. Nowadays we consider the “donkey rolling” “Sakima” as Manchu traditional snacks. Chafing dish, whole lamb mat and sauced meat are also traditional ways of preparing meat for the Manchus. Sauerkraut is one of their favorite vegetarian dish, or stir-fried, or stewed, or salad.

（三）传统节日
Traditional Festivals

满族的许多节日受到汉族人的影响，在今天也过一些汉文化的传统节日，主要有春节、元宵节、二月二、端午节和中秋节。节日期间一般都要举行珍珠球、跳马、跳骆驼和滑冰等传统体育活动。满族比较有特色的传统节日是颁金节。

颁金节是满族“族庆”之日。1635 年农历十月十三日，清朝第一个皇帝——皇太极发布谕旨，正式改族名“女真”为“满洲”，这标志着一个新的民族共同体形成。各地满族同胞在农历十月十三日满族命名日自发地举行纪念活动，以纪念满族的诞生。但活动时使用的名称不尽相同，或称“命名日”，或称“诞生日”，或称“纪念日”等。

Many Manchu festivals are influenced by the Han people, and today they celebrate some traditional festivals of Han culture, such as the Spring Festival, the Lantern Festival, the February 2nd, the Dragon Boat Festival and the Mid-Autumn Festival. During the festivals, traditional sports activities such as pearl ball, vaulting horse, jumping camel and skating are usually held. The traditional festival of Manchu is the Golden Festival.

Golden Festival is the day of Manchu's "National Festival". On the 13th day of the 1635 lunar calendar, the first emperor of the Qing Dynasty, Huang Tai Chi, issued an edict to officially change the name of "Nvzhen" to "Manchuria", which marked the formation of a new national community. On the 13th day of October, the naming day of the Manchus was held spontaneously to commemorate the birth of the Manchus. But the ways of calling the event are not the same; "named day", or "birth day", or "anniversary", and so on.

（四）宗教 Religions

满族人信仰萨满教和佛教。

Manchus believe in Shamanism and Buddhism.

萨满教是满族人最终信仰的宗教，萨满教主张万物有灵，以萨满作为人灵交通的使者。崇拜的神灵包括自然神（如山神）、动物神（如马王）、祖先神以及人间神（如关帝）。后来满族虽崇信佛教，然而萨满祭祀并未废除。

Shamanism is the ultimate religion of the Manchus. Shamanism holds that all things have spirit, and Shaman is the emissary of spiritual communication. The gods of worship include natural god (such as mountain god), animal god (such as horse king), ancestor god and human god (such as Guan Di). Although the Manchus believed in Buddhism, the sacrifice of Shaman was not abandoned.

满族信仰佛教。由于历史的原因，蒙古族在清朝的地位仅次于满族，而且满蒙允许通婚，所以蒙古族信仰的藏传佛教（喇嘛教）很快传入满族。另外汉传佛教对满族也产生了影响。满族信仰佛教出家为僧者少，信徒多居家念佛。

Manchu believed in Buddhism. Due to historical reasons, in the Qing Dynasty the Mongolians were only inferior to the Manchus, and the Manchus were allowed to intermarry with Mongolian. Therefore, the Tibetan Buddhism (Lamaism) of the Mongolian faith soon spread to Manchu. In addition, the Han Buddhism also had an effect on the Manchu. Most Manchus believers practiced Buddhism at home rather than being monks in temples.

（五）禁忌
Taboos

满族人不吃狗肉，也不穿用狗皮做的衣服。满族将西墙作为供奉祖先的神圣部位，不准在此挂衣物，张贴年画；西炕俗称“佛爷炕”，供有“祖宗板子”。通常客人也不得在西炕休息，更不许将狗皮帽子或鞭子放在里面。

Manchu people do not eat dog meat or wear clothes made of dog skin. The Manchus took the western wall as the sacred, holy place to worship their ancestors Where clothes and New Year pictures are not allowed to post. Bed in the west was popularly known as the “Buddha Bed”, for placing memorial tablet (for ancestral worship). Usually guests are not allowed to rest on the bed in the west, let alone put a dog skin hat or whip here.

四、蒙古族
Mongolian Ethnic Group

蒙古族是一个有很长历史的民族，他们分布很广，世界各地都有蒙古族。他们对世界历史产生过非常重要的影响，这个民族曾经建立了横跨欧亚大陆的大蒙古帝国。他们的民族英雄是世界的征服者成吉思汗。现在在蒙古高原上仍然有一个以蒙古族为主体的国家叫作蒙古国。中国的蒙古族人口约为650万，主要分布在中国内蒙古和东北地区，在新疆、河北、青海也都有分布，其余散布于河南、四川、贵州、北京和云南等地。这个民族曾经在中国建立了一个强大的中央王朝——元朝。

Mongolian ethnic group is a nation with long history. Mongolians are widely spread all over the world. They had a very important influence on the history of the world, a nation that once founded the Great Mongol Empire across Eurasia. Their national hero is the conqueror of the world, Genghis Khan. There is still a country on the Mongolian Plateau that is dominated by Mongolians called Mongolia. The population of Mongolian ethnic group in China is about 6.5 million. Mongolian ethnic group mainly scattered in Inner Mongolian Autonomous Region and northeast China, and in Xinjiang, Hebei and Qinghai Provinces. The rest scattered in Henan, Sichuan, Guizhou, Beijing and Yunnan Provinces. Mongolians once established a strong central dynasty in China, the Yuan Dynasty.

蒙古族是从草原来的民族，他们的传统生活习惯总是跟草原与畜牧有关。

Mongolians are ethnic group people from the grassland; their traditional lifestyle was always related to grassland and animal husbandry.

（一）服饰
Apparel

蒙古族的传统服饰是蒙古袍，主要包括长袍、腰带、靴子、首饰等。但因地区不同在式样上有所差异。蒙古族服饰具有浓郁的草原风格特色，以袍服为主，便于鞍马骑乘。

The traditional Mongolian costumes are the Mongolian robes, which mainly include robes, belts, boots, jewelry, etc. But there are differences in style from one area to another. Mongolian costumes are characterized by rich grassland style, mainly robes that are easy to ride on pommel horse.

（二）饮食
Food and Drink

蒙古族传统饮食分为红食、白食两种。以奶为原料制成的食品，蒙古语

称“查干伊得”，意为圣洁、纯净的食品，即“白食”；以肉类为原料制成的食品，蒙古语称“乌兰伊德”，意为“红食”。有名的蒙古族传统食物有手抓羊肉、烤全羊、蒙古馅饼。

The Mongolian traditional diet is divided into two kinds: red food and white food. The food made from milk is called “Chagan Yide” in Mongolian, which means holy and pure food, namely “white food”. The food made from meat is called “Wulan Yide” in Mongolian, which means “red food”. The famous Mongolian traditional dishes are: hand-held mutton (mutton pieces on the bone, eaten with fingers), the whole roasted sheep, and the Mongolian pie.

此外，蒙古族喜欢喝马奶酒。每年七八月份是酿制马奶酒的季节。勤劳的蒙古族妇女将马奶收贮于皮囊中，加以搅拌，数日后便乳脂分离，发酵成酒。马奶酒性温，有驱寒、舒筋、活血、健胃等功效。

In addition, the Mongolians like to drink Kumis (horse milk wine). July and August is season to brew Kumis. The hard-working Mongolian women put mare’s milk into the leather bag and stir it. After a few days, the milk separates and ferments into wine. Horse milk alcoholic can dispel cold, relax sinew, invigorate blood, invigorate the stomach and has other effects.

（三）传统节日 Traditional Festivals

每年七八月牲畜肥壮的季节举行“那达慕”大会是蒙古族历史悠久的传统节日，这是人们为了庆祝丰收而举行的文体娱乐大会。“那达慕”大会上有赛马、摔跤、射箭三项传统比赛。

In July and August of each year, there is a "Nadam Conference". It's a traditional festival with a long Mongolians history, which is held to celebrate the harvest, and have cultural and recreational activities. The Nadam Conference has three traditional competitions: horse racing, wrestling and archery.

（四）宗教 Religions

蒙古族的宗教跟满族的宗教很相似，都信奉萨满教与佛教。

The Mongolian religion is very similar to that of Manchu, both of which believe in Shamanism and Buddhism.

（五）禁忌 Taboos

在生活和交往中蒙古族有许多禁忌，下面是需要注意的地方：

There are many taboos in life and social intercourse of the Mongolian people. The following are the points that should be mentioned:

1. 吃肉时须用刀，给人递刀时忌刀尖冲接刀者。

When eating meat by a knife, avoid tip punches when handing the knife to others.

2. 蒙古族认为水是纯洁的神灵。忌讳在河流中洗手或沐浴，更不许洗脏衣物，或者将不干净的东西投入河中。

Mongolians believe that water is a pure spirit. They do not wash hands, bathe or wash clothes in rivers, and they do not throw unclean things into the river.

3. 蒙古族将“9”视为吉数，9为永恒的意思。

The Mongolians regard “9” as an auspicious number and 9 as an eternal meaning.

4. 敖包是蒙古语，意即“堆子”。蒙古族生活在大草原上，人们用石头堆成堆子，作为道路和境界的标志，起指路、辨别方向和划分行政区域的作用，后来逐步演变成祭山神、路神和祈祷丰收、家人幸福平安的象征。

Aobao is a Mongolian word meaning “heap”. Mongolians live on the prairie, and people pile up stones as a sign of the road and boundary, and act as a guide, direction and administrative division. Later, it gradually became a symbol of sacrifice to mountain god, the road god, and a pray for a good harvest, happiness and peace of family.

五、藏族

Tibetan Ethnic Group

早在 4 000 多年前，藏族的祖先就在雅鲁藏布江流域繁衍生息了。藏族主要分布在中国、尼泊尔、印度、不丹等。在中国境内主要分布在西藏自治区、青海省和四川省西部，人口为约 650 万。藏族人信奉藏传佛教。藏传佛教对藏族人民的影响深入到日常生活的各个方面。

More than 4,000 years ago, the ancestors of the Tibetans began to breed in the Yarlung Zangbo River. Tibetans are mainly spread in China, Nepal, India, Bhutan, etc. In China they're mainly spread in the Xizang Autonomous Region, Qinghai Province and the western part of Sichuan Province, and the population of about 6.5 millions. Tibetans believe in Tibetan Buddhism. The influence of Tibetan Buddhism on the Tibetan people has penetrated into every aspect of daily life.

（一）服饰

Apparel

藏族服饰的基本特征是长袖、宽腰、长裙、长靴以及藏帽。服饰多姿多彩，其特点还突出地表现在色彩的搭配和构图上。藏族同胞特别重视“哈达”，把它看作最珍贵的礼物。

The basic features of Tibetan costumes are long sleeves, wide waist, long skirts, boots and Tibetan hats. Costumes are colorful. Their major characteristics are represented in the combination of colors and pictures. Tibetans attach great importance to Hada (a piece of silk, usu. in white color) as the most precious gift.

（二）饮食 Food and Drink

藏餐分为主食、菜肴、汤三大类。酥油、茶叶、糌粑、牛羊肉被称为西藏饮食的“四宝”，此外，还有青稞酒和各式奶制品。藏餐的口味讲究清淡、平和，很多菜，除了盐巴和葱蒜，一般不放辛辣的调料。糌粑是藏族的一种重要食品。藏族人一般只吃牛羊肉，不吃马、驴、骡，尤忌吃狗肉。

Tibetan food is divided into three categories: staple food, dishes, and soup. Ghee, tea, zanba, beef and mutton are called the “four treasures” of the Tibetan diet, as well as barley wine and various dairy products. The taste of Tibetan food is light and calm, and many dishes, except salt and leek, usually do not put spicy condiments. Zanba is an important food for the Tibetans. Generally they eat only beef and mutton, not horses, donkeys, mules, especially not dog meat.

（三）传统节日与宗教 Traditional Festivals and Religion

藏族节日繁多，基本上每个月都会有节日。藏历元月，是节日最多也最隆重的月份，在这个月里，几乎天天都在过节。藏族节日是藏族文化最主要的表现。藏传佛教在中国西藏已有 1 300 多年的历史，成为藏族人民生活的一部分，西藏的节日由于受其深刻影响，而具有浓厚的宗教色彩，有的已演化成纯粹的宗教节日。

Tibetan festivals are numerous and almost every month has its own festival. Tibetan January has the most festivals and is the most solemn month. In this month, almost every day has the festival. Tibetan festival is the most important expression of Tibetan culture. Tibetan Buddhism has a history of more than 1,300 years in Xizang, China, and has become a part of the life of the Tibetan people. As a result of its profound influence, Tibetan festivals have become very religious and some of them have evolved into pure religious festivals.

雪顿节，是西藏藏族人民的重要节日之一，每年藏庆七月一日举行，为期三至五天。雪顿的意思是“酸奶宴”，于是雪顿节便被解释为喝酸奶的节日。按藏传佛教格鲁派（黄教）的规定，每年藏历六月十五至三十日为禁期，大小寺庙的喇嘛不许外出，以免踩死小虫，待六月三十日解禁之后方可下山。喇嘛下山时，农牧民拿出酸奶敬献，形成雪顿节。

Xue dun Festival is one of the important festivals of the Tibetan people in Xizang. It is held on 1st of July each year for three to five days. Xue dun means “yogurt feast” in Tibetan language, so Xue dun Festival is interpreted as the festival of drinking yoghurt. According to the regulations of the Gelug Sect of Tibetan Buddhism (Huang Sect), the Tibetan Calendar is banned from June 15th to 30th each year. Lamas of all sizes of temples are not allowed to go out to avoid trampling on small insects until the ban is lifted on June 30th. As the lama descended from the mountain, the farmers and herdsmen took out yoghurt and offered it as a Xue dun Festival.

（四）民族习俗与禁忌
Tibetan Ethnic Customs and Taboos

见到长者或尊敬的人，要脱帽，弯腰45度，帽子拿在手上，接近于地面。见到平辈，头稍稍低下即可，帽子可以拿在胸前，这时的鞠躬只表示一种礼貌。献哈达是藏族待客规格最高的一种礼仪，表示对客人热烈的欢迎和诚挚的敬意。

If you see an elder or a respected person, take off your hat and bend it down 45 degrees. Hold the hat in your hand, close to the ground. If you see a person close to your age, lower your head slightly and hold your hat in front of your chest. The bow at this point is only a courtesy. Presenting a Hada is the highest standard of Tibetan hospitality, expressing warm welcome and sincere respect to the guests.

见面称呼时，忌直呼其名，要加敬称，以示尊敬和亲切。

You should avoid calling other's names directly when meeting, and you should add complimentary modifier before their names to show respect and kindness.

（五）满族、蒙古族、藏族之间的关系
The Relationship among Manchu, Mongolian and Tibetan Ethnic Groups

满族、蒙古族、藏族都曾经深度参与过中国的历史进程，蒙古族和满族先后在中国建立了王朝，藏族从唐朝开始融入中国的大家庭。历史上满族与蒙古族有密切的关系。满族在明朝后期长期与蒙古族通婚，通过很多方式建立了强大的联盟，在蒙古族大力支持下灭亡了明朝，建立清朝。蒙古贵族的女儿大多数都与满族贵族男子通婚，清朝皇后都是蒙古族女子，所以有“满蒙一家亲”的说法。经过长期的友好交流，两个民族在宗教信仰、文化习俗等方面都有很多共同点。比如满语的文字就是借用了蒙古语的文字系统改造而成的；满族人的佛教信仰也是深受蒙古族喇嘛教的影响。

Manchu, Mongolian and Tibetan ethnic groups have been deeply involved in the historical processes in China. Mongolian and Manchu established dynasties in China one after another, and the Tibetans began to integrate into the Chinese extended family in the Tang Dynasty. Manchu had a close relationship with Mongolian in history. The Manchus intermarried with the Mongols for a long period of time in the late Ming Dynasty and established a strong alliance by many means, and destroyed the Ming Dynasty and established the Qing Dynasty under the strong support of the Mongolians. Most of the daughters of Mongolian nobles were intermarried with Manchu noble men, and the Qing Dynasty queens were Mongolian women, so there was the saying of “Manchu Mongolian family”. After a long period of friendly exchanges, the two nations have a lot in common in religious belief, cultural practice and so on. For example, the Manchu letter is borrowed from the Mongolian script system transformation and the Buddhist faith of Manchu was also deeply influenced by Mongolian Lamaism.

六、回族与维吾尔族
Hui and Uygur Ethnic Group

（一）回族
Hui Ethnic Group

13世纪，大批穆斯林从西辽迁入黄河流域，并同当地的汉族、维吾尔族、蒙古族等融合，在长期历史过程中通过通婚等多种形式，逐渐形成了回族。回族现在主要居住在宁夏回族自治区。回族人口在20万以上的地区还有：北京、河北、内蒙古、辽宁、安徽、山东、河南、云南、甘肃和新疆等。据2010年人口普查，目前回族人口有10 586 087人。

In the 13th century, a large number of Muslims moved into the Yellow River valley from the Western Liao Dynasty and merged with the local Han, Uygur and Mongolian nationalities. In the long-term historical process, they gradually formed the Hui ethnic group through intermarriage and other factors. Hui people now mainly live in Ningxia Hui Autonomous Region. Other areas with a population of more than 200,000 are Beijing, Hebei, Inner Mongolia, Liaoning, Anhui, Shandong, Henan, Yunnan, Gansu, Xinjiang Autonomous Region, Provinces and so on. According to the 2010 census, there are currently 10,586,087 Hui people.

当代回族通用汉语，不同地区持不同方言。在回族先民东迁初期，是阿拉伯语、波斯语和汉语同时使用的。由于长期和汉族杂居，特别是汉人在回族中日渐增多，在长期发展过程中，就逐渐习惯了以汉语作为本民族的共同语言，并保留了一些阿拉伯语和波斯语的词汇。

Contemporary Hui people commonly use Chinese and have different dialects in different regions. At the beginning of the migration of Hui ancestors to the east, Arabic, Persian and Chinese were used at the same time. Due to the long-term mixed residence with the Han nationality, especially the increasing number of Han ethnic groups in the Hui ethnic group, in the long-term development process, they gradually became accustomed to using Chinese as the common language of their own ethnic group and retained some Arabic and Persian vocabulary.

伊斯兰教在回族的形成和发展中始终起着不可忽视的作用，在回族形成后，各地回族一直延续着这一信仰。

Islam has always played an important role in the formation and development of the Hui people. After the formation of the Hui people, the Hui people all over the country have continued this belief.

1. 服饰

Apparel

回族服饰的主要标志在头部。男子们都喜爱戴白色的圆帽。回族妇女常戴盖头。无论是在江南水乡，还是在北方的黄土地、黑土地上，凡是回族聚居的地方，头饰的习俗都是很明显的。这一习俗与中国汉族的服饰习俗形成了鲜明的对比。

The main symbol of Hui ethnic group's clothing is on the head. Men all like to wear white round hats. Hui women often wear caps. No matter in the south of the Yangtze River, or in the yellow and black lands in the north, the custom of headdress is obvious in places where Hui people live in compact communities. This custom is in sharp contrast with the dress custom of the Han ethnic group in China.

2. 传统饮食

Traditional Diet

回族人的主要饮食是面食和牛羊肉。

The main diet of the Hui people is pasta and beef and mutton.

羊杂汤是回族人最具代表性的传统美食之一，羊杂汤是用羊下水（羊下水就是羊肠、羊肝、羊肚等）以及羊肉制作而成。

Mutton soup is one of the most representative traditional delicacies of the Hui people, and it is made of sheep offal (sheep intestines and liver), sheep belly, and mutton.

羊肉泡馍是比较有名的回族特色美食。羊肉泡馍在西安是非常有名的，由羊肉作为主要原料，后加入葱末、粉丝等。在西安，很多人都把羊肉泡馍当作早餐来吃，因为羊肉泡里有汤有饭，肉烂汤浓，营养丰富，让人食后回味无穷。

Mutton and Bread Pieces in Soup is a very famous Hui people's characteristic. It is very famous in Xi'an. Mutton is considered as the main ingredient in the food, followed by chopped green onion, and vermicelli. In Xi'an, many people eat Mutton and Bread Pieces in Soups as breakfast. Because it contains soup and rice, and meat rotten soup, it is thick and nutritious, which makes people full-satisfied after eating it.

3. 传统节日

Traditional Festivals

回族有三大节日：开斋节（大尔迪）、宰牲节（小尔迪）、圣纪节，最重要的是开斋节。

开斋节是回族穆斯林的斋月，是伊斯兰教历九月（莱麦丹月）。回族穆斯林为什么要封斋呢？据《古兰经》记载，伊斯兰教先知穆罕默德 40 岁那年（伊斯兰教历九月），安拉开始把《古兰经》的启示给他。因此，回族视斋月为最尊贵、最吉庆、最快乐的月份。

The Hui people have three major festivals: Eid al-fitr, Eid al-adha, and a holy day, and the most important is Eid al-fitr. Eid al-Fitr is the Muslim holy month of Ramadan and it's the month of September in the Islamic calendar. According to the *Quran* (Muslims holy book), when the Islamic prophet Muhammad was 40 years old, Allah began to give him the revelation of the *Quran*. Therefore, the Hui people regard Ramadan as the most honorable, auspicious and happiest month.

4. 禁忌
Taboos

（1）回族穆斯林忌食猪肉、狗肉、马肉、驴肉和骡肉，不吃未经信仰伊斯兰教者屠宰的和自死的畜禽肉，不吃动物的血等。回族不吃自死的、也不吃外族人屠宰的肉，必须吃清真寺四掌教（刀师傅）或阿訇屠宰的。

Hui Muslims avoid eating pork, dog, horse, donkey and mule meat. They do not eat livestock and poultry slaughtered or killed by non-Islamist, or animal blood. The Hui people do not eat meat dead or slaughtered by foreigners. They eat the meat that must be slaughtered by master knife or imam.

（2）回族禁用食物开玩笑，也不能用禁食的东西做比喻，如不得形容辣椒的颜色像血一样红等。

The Hui people are banned to make joke on food, and they could not use it as a metaphor. For example, they could not describe the color of hot pepper as red as blood.

（二）维吾尔族
Uygur Ethnic Group

维吾尔族是一个多源民族，最主要的来源有两支：一支是来自蒙古草原的回纥人，另一支是南疆绿洲上的土著居民。这两部分人于公元 840 年大规模汇合，至 16 世纪初完全融合完成。维吾尔族的民族语言为维吾尔语，属阿尔泰语系突厥语族，他们普遍信仰伊斯兰教。“维吾尔”意为“联合”。维吾尔族主要聚居在新疆维吾尔自治区，少量居住在湖南桃源、常德以及河南开封、郑州等地。据 2010 年人口普查，维吾尔族人口总数为 10 069 346 人。

Uygur is a multi-source ethnic group. The main sources are: one is the Huihe people from Mongolian grassland, the other is the indigenous people in the oasis of southern Xinjiang. The two groups converged on a large scale in 840 A.D. and were fully integrated in the early 16th century. Uygur people's mother tongue is Uygur language, belonging to the Turkic language family of Altaic language family, and they widely believe in Islam. "Uygur" means "united". Uygur people mainly live in Xinjiang Uygur Autonomous Region, and a small number live in Taoyuan and Changde of Hunan Province, Kaifeng and Zhengzhou of Henan province and other places. According to the 2010 census, the total Uygur population was 10,069,346.

在漫长的历史发展过程中，维吾尔族人民用勤劳和智慧创造了优秀的文化，有着独特的民族风情，是中华民族大家庭中重要的一员。

In the long process of historical development, the Uygur people have created excellent culture with diligence and wisdom, and have unique national customs. The Uygur ethnic group is an important member of the big family of the Chinese nation.

1. 服饰

Apparel

维吾尔族不论男女老幼都喜欢戴“尕巴”（四楞花帽），用黑白两色或彩色丝线绣出各种民族形式的花纹图案。

Uygur people, both men and women, old and young, like to wear “Gaba” (four-corrugated cap), embroidering various national patterns with black and white or color silk thread.

维吾尔族男性的衣服讲究黑白效果，粗犷且奔放。 维吾尔族妇女喜用对比色彩，使红得更亮，绿得更翠。 维吾尔族是个爱花的民族，人们戴的是绣花帽，着的是绣花衣，穿的是绣花鞋，扎的是绣花巾，背的是绣花袋，衣着服饰无不与鲜花息息相关。

Uygur men generally wear black and white color clothes, bold and unrestrained. Uygur women prefer to use contrasting colors to make the red brighter and the green darker. Uygur is a flower-loving nation. Uygur people wear embroidered hats, embroidered clothes, embroidered shoes, embroidered towels and embroidered bags. The styles of clothes are closely similar to flowers.

2. 传统饮食

Traditional Diet

维吾尔族的传统饮食以面食为主，喜食牛羊肉，蔬菜吃得相对较少。主食的种类很多，最常吃的有馕、抓饭、包子、拉面等。

Uygur traditional diet meal is mainly pasta. They like beef and mutton, but vegetables are relatively less eaten. There are many kinds of staple foods; the most common ones are steamed bread, grabbed rice, ramen, etc.

馕，是用小麦面或玉米面制成的，在特制的火坑内烤熟，为形状大小和厚薄不一的圆形饼。

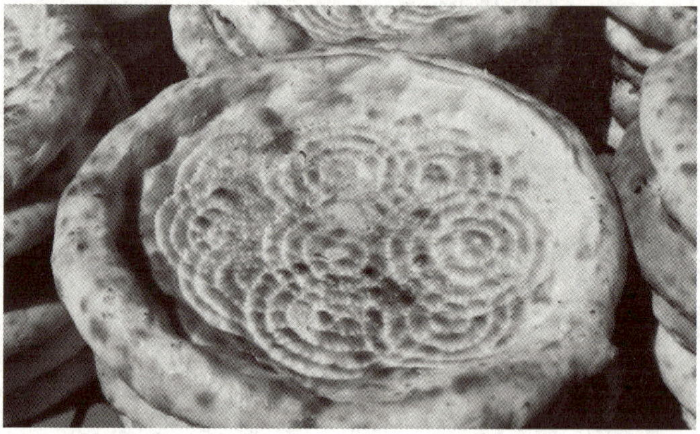

抓饭，维吾尔语称"颇罗"，是用大米、羊肉、羊油、食油、胡萝卜焖成的一种饭食，味道鲜美。

Steamed bread, called Nang in Chinese, made of wheat or corn flour, is roasted in a special fire pit. It is a round cake of different shapes, sizes and thicknesses.

Grab rice is called "Po Luo" in Uygur language, is stewed with rice, mutton, lamb oil. Carrots can also be added to provide spectacular taste to the meal.

3. 习俗与禁忌

Customs and Taboos

（1）维吾尔族人路遇尊长或朋友，要把右手放在胸口，男子相见要握手，妇女相见要互相拥抱，贴一下右脸，都以"撒拉木"问安，最后，双手抚膝躬身道别。晚辈要先向长辈施礼，现在多以握手作为见面礼。

Uygur people should put their right hand on their chest when they meet elderly people or friends. Men shake hands when they meet men, while women hug each other when they meet women, and stick their face right to each other. They all greet each other with "Salam". Finally, they touch their knees and bow to say goodbye. The younger people should give gifts to elders; nowadays they usually shake hands instead.

（2）维吾尔族在人际关系中不直接称呼别人的名字，在族内长幼辈之间、师徒长幼辈之间也忌讳相互直呼对方的名字。

Uygur people do not call other people's names directly. In addition, they are not allowed to call each other's names directly between the elders and younger members, and between the elders and younger members of the teachers and apprentices.

（三）回族与维吾尔族的关系
The Relationship between Hui and Uygur Ethnic Group

回族和维吾尔族都信奉伊斯兰教，所以在饮食、传统节日以及禁忌方面都有某些相似之处。

The Hui and Uygur ethnic groups believe in Islam. Therefore, there are some similarities in diet, traditional festivals and taboos.

从人种属性来看，维吾尔族比较接近白色人种，而回族人几乎和汉族人长相无异。

From the perspective of ethnicity, Uygurs are close to the white race, while Hui people are almost the same as Han people.

回族历史很悠久，但因祖先分属于中亚、西亚的各个民族，而且长期处于分散状态，所以无法形成自己的民族语言。为了方便生活，汉语是回民的主要语言。回族在遵守伊斯兰教教义的前提下，为中国美食做出了巨大贡献，改良了大量穆斯林食品，比如市面上常见的各种油炸糕点、面点等。

Hui people have a long history. Their ancestors belong to different nationalities in Central Asia and West Asia, and they have been dispersed for a long time, so they can't form their own national language. For the convenience of life and frequent use, Chinese is the main language of Hui people. On the premise of abiding by the Islamic doctrine, the Hui people have made great contributions to Chinese cuisine and improved a large number of Muslim cuisines, such as various kinds of fried cakes and pastries, which are very common.

课后练习题
Practice

一、选择题
Multiple-choice

1. 中国一共有多少个民族？（　　）

How many ethnic minority groups are there in China? (　　)

A. 56　　B. 55　　C. 54　　D. 53

A. Fifty-six　　B. Fifty-five　　C. Fifty-four　　D. Fifty- three

2. 中国哪个民族人数最多？(　　)

Which ethnic group has the largest population in China?

A. 土家族　　B. 汉族

A. Tujia ethnic group　　B. Han ethnic group

C. 苗族　　D. 蒙古族

C. Miao ethnic group　　D. Mongolian

3. 朝鲜族的春节是(　　)。

The Spring Festival of Korean ethnic group is (　　).

A. 泼水节　　B. 岁首节

A. the Water-Sprinkling　　B. the Beginning of the Year

C. 端午节　　D. 万圣节

C. the Dragon Boat Festival　　D. Halloween

4. 满族在历史上建立的最后一个王朝是(　　)。

The last dynasty of Manchu in history is (　　).

A. 清朝

A. Qing Dynasty

B. 唐朝

B. Tang Dynasty

C. 商朝

C. Shang Dynasty

D. 魏晋南北朝

D. Wei, Jin, Southern and Northern Dynasties

5. 回族穆斯林忌食什么？（　　）

What do Hui Muslims avoid eating?

A. 鸡肉

A. Chicken

B. 羊肉

B. Mutton

C. 猪肉

C. Pork

D. 牛肉

D. Beef

二、填空题

Fill-in-the-blanks

1. 请列举 3 个中国的少数民族：______、______、______。

Please list three ethnic groups in China __________, __________ and __________.

2. 中国是一个多民族的国家。中国的______个少数民族分布范围广，但主要集中于中国______及______地区。

China is a multi-ethnic country. China's ______ ethnic groups are widely spread, but the main concentration of them is in the __________ and ________.

3. 朝鲜族主要分布在______、______、______三省。

Korean people are mainly distributed in __________, __________ and ________Provinces.

4. 藏族在中国境内主要分布在__________、__________和__________。

Tibetan in China are mainly distributed in __________, __________ and __________.

5. ______被称为中国国粹和女性的国服。

______ is known as the quintessence of Chinese culture and woman's national uniform.

三、判断题

True or False

1. 汉族是人数最多的民族，大约有 12.8 亿，约占全国人口总数的 91%。

Han is the most populous ethnic group, about 1.28 billion, accounting for about 91% of the total population of the country.

2. 蒙古族是一个有很长历史的民族，他们分布很广，世界各地都有蒙古族。
Mongolian has a long history, their distribution is very wide, and all parts of the world have Mongolian.

3. 蒙古族将“8”视为吉数，8 为永恒的意思。
The Mongolians regard “8” as an auspicious number and 8 as an eternal meaning.

4. 雪顿节，是西藏藏族人民的重要节日之一，每年藏历五月一日举行，为期四五天。
Xue dun Festival is one of the important festivals for the Tibetan people in Xizang. It is held every year on May 1 in Tibetan calendar and last for four or five days.

5. 维吾尔族是一个多源民族，最主要的来源有两支：一支是来自蒙古草原的回纥人，另一支是南疆绿洲上的土著居民。
Uygur ethnic group is a multi-source ethnic group. The main sources are: one is the Huihe people from Mongolian grassland, the other is the indigenous people in the oasis of southern Xinjiang.

四、简答题
Short-answer Questions

1. 蒙古族的“那达慕”大会上举办什么传统比赛？
What are the traditional competitions in the “Nadam” conference of the Mongolian ethnic group?

____

____

2. 维吾尔族喜欢穿什么衣服？
What clothes do Uygurs like to wear?

____

____

3. 回族是怎么形成的？
How did Hui ethnic group form?

____

____

第十一章

中国的创造

Chinese Creation

课前思考

Lead-in Questions

1. 你知道中国古代的四大发明是什么吗？

   Do you know what the four great inventions are in ancient China?

2. 你们国家有哪些重要的发明？

   What are the important inventions in your country?

一、四大发明

Four Great Inventions

中国古代的四大发明是中国古代人民为世界留下的一串光耀的足迹，为人类文明进步做出了巨大的贡献。其中，造纸术的发明为人类提供了经济、便利的书写材料，掀起文字载体革命；印刷术的发明大大推动了文化的传播；指南针的发明为早期欧洲航海家的航海活动提供了条件；火药的发明则直接改变了作战的方式，加速了人类的历史进程。

The four great inventions of ancient China were a series of glorious footprints left by the ancient Chinese ancestors for the world, and made great contributions to the progress of human civilization. Among them, the invention of paper-making provided humans with economical and convenient writing materials, and set off a revolution in text carriers; the invention of printing greatly promoted the spread of culture; the invention of compass provided conditions for the navigation activities of early European navigators; the invention of gunpowder directly changed the way of combat and accelerated the historical process of mankind.

（一）造纸术
Paper-making

纸是与人类日常生活息息相关的必需品。不论我们做笔记、画画，还是看报纸，都需要用纸。在纸发明之前，中国人曾把贝壳、兽骨、竹片、木片以及丝绸等作为记录文字的载体。

Paper is a daily necessity. Whether we take notes, draw or read newspapers, we need paper. Before paper was invented, ancient Chinese used shells, animal bones, bamboo chips, wood chips and silk as carriers for recording text.

在商朝，中国就有了刻在龟甲和兽骨上的文字，称为甲骨文。在春秋时期，用竹片和木片替代龟甲和兽骨刻录文字，称为竹简和木牍。由于甲骨和简牍很厚重，不方便携带，西汉时在宫廷贵族中又出现了在轻薄的缣帛或绵纸上书写文字的做法。缣帛的优点是便于书写，能比简牍写的多，而且可以在上面作画，缺点则是价格昂贵，只能供少量贵族使用。

In the Shang Dynasty (1600–1046 B.C.), text engraved on tortoise shell and animal bone, called oracle, firstly appeared in China. When the history developed to the Spring and Autumn Period (770–476 B.C.), bamboo and wood chips, lighter and easier to get, were used instead of tortoise shells and animal bones to engrave text, and they are named bamboo strips and wood strips. No matter the oracle bones or shackles, both are very heavy and inconvenient to carry. Then in the Western Han Dynasty (206 B.C. –25 A.D.), there appeared characters written on the thin plaque or tissue paper among court nobles. The advantage of thin plaque and tissue paper is that it is easy to write, more words can be written on, and it can also be painted. But the disadvantage is that it is expensive and can only be used by a small number of nobles.

西汉时期，中国便出现了纸。在东汉时，蔡伦改进了造纸术，他用树皮、麻头、破布、渔网，经过挫、捣、抄、烘等一系列的工艺加工制成植物纤维纸，并得到皇帝的称赞。公元 3 至 4 世纪，纸基本取代了帛、简，成为中国最主要的书写材料。公元 6 至 10 世纪，纸的种类不断增多，材质不断提高，印刷术的流行大大刺激了书籍印刷业的发展。

In the Western Han Dynasty, paper started its journey in China. In the Eastern Han Dynasty (25 A.D.–200 A.D.), Cai Lun (62 A.D.–121 A.D.) improved the paper-making technique. He used bark, hemp, rags and fish nets to make plant fiber paper through a series of processes such as pressing, smashing, filtering and baking, and was praised by the emperor. From the 3rd to the 4th century, paper basically replaced silk and wood or bamboo strips, and became the most important writing material in China. From the 6th to the 10th centuries, varieties of papers continued to increase, and the materials continued to improve. With the popularity of printing, the development of the book printing industry was greatly stimulated.

从 6 世纪开始，造纸术逐渐传往朝鲜、日本，以后又经阿拉伯、埃及、西班牙传到欧洲的希腊、意大利等地。1150 年，西班牙开始造纸，建立了欧洲第一家造纸厂。此后，法国、意大利、德国、英国等都先后建厂造纸。到 16 世纪，纸张已流行欧洲。中世纪的欧洲，据说抄一本《圣经》要用 300 多张羊皮，文化信息的传播因材料的限制，范围极其狭小，纸的发明则为当时欧洲教育、政治、商业等的蓬勃发展提供了便利。

Since the 6th century, paper-making has gradually spread to the Demacratic People's Republic of Korea and Japan, and later to Europe including Greece, Italy and other places via Arabia, Egypt and Spain. In 1150, Spain began to make paper and established the first paper mill in Europe. Since then, France, Italy, Germany, the United Kingdom, etc. have successively set up factories to make paper. By the

16th century, paper had become popular in Europe. In medieval Europe, it is said that more than 300 pieces of sheepskin were used to copy a Bible. The spread of cultural information was extremely limited due to material limitations. The invention of paper provided convenience for the vigorous development of education, politics and commerce in Europe at that time.

（二）印刷术 Printing

中国古代印刷术分为雕版印刷与活字印刷两个阶段。早期的印刷是把图文刻在木板上用水墨印刷，统称雕版印刷术。雕版印刷的前身是公元前流行的印章捺印和后来出现的拓印碑石等。造纸和制墨等生产技术也促进了雕版印刷术的发明。

The ancient Chinese printing can be divided into two stages: block printing and movable type printing. In the early stage, the way pictures or characters were engraved on the wood boards printed with ink, was collectively called block printing. It can be rooted from the making of seals before the common era and the later stone rubbing. The development of paper-making and ink-making techniques has also facilitated the invention of block printing.

雕版印刷术发明于唐朝，在唐朝中后期开始普遍使用。世界上现存最早的印刷物是唐咸通九年（公元 868 年）印制的《金刚经》（全长 4 877 毫米，高 244 毫米）。雕版印刷比手工抄写更快捷，但是也很费时间，成本较高。到了 11 世纪中期的宋代，毕昇发明了活字印刷术，主要使用胶泥活字，比雕版印刷省时且省钱，让印刷术得到普遍推广。

Block printing was invented in the Tang Dynasty (618–907 A.D.) and began to be widely used in the middle and late Tang Dynasty. The earliest extant print in the world is the *Diamond Sutra* (length 4877 mm, height 244 mm), which was printed in the nine years of Tang Xiantong (868 A.D.). Block printing is more efficient than manual transcription, but it is also time consuming and costly. In the Song Dynasty in the middle of the 11th century, Bi Sheng invented the movable type printing technique. He mainly used clay type, which saved much time and money compared with block printing. After that the printing was widely promoted.

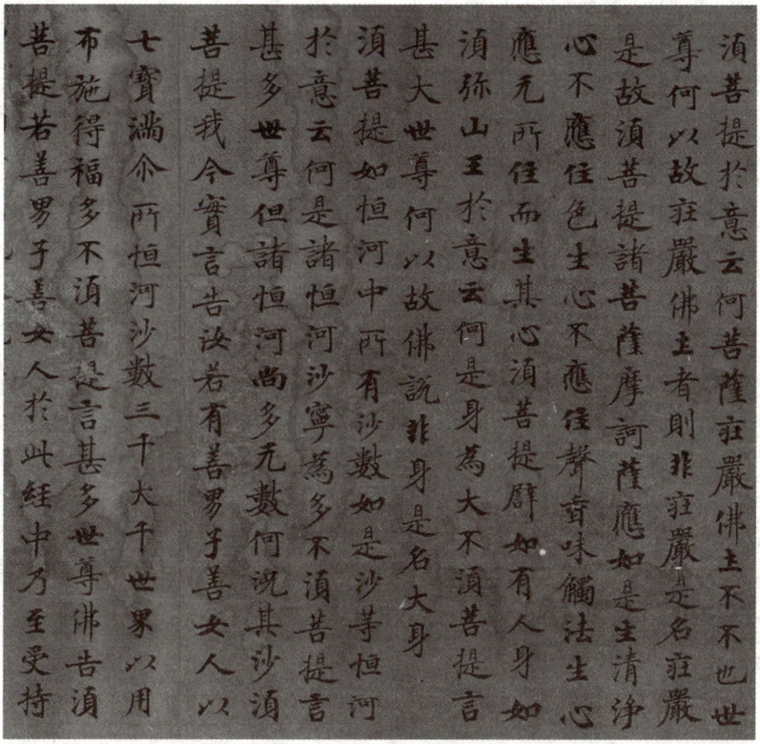
須菩提於意云何菩薩莊嚴佛土不不也世
尊何以故莊嚴佛土者則非莊嚴是名莊嚴
是故須菩提諸菩薩摩訶薩應如是生清淨
心不應住色生心不應住聲香味觸法生心
應无所住而生其心須菩提譬如有人身如
須彌山王於意云何是身為大不須菩提言
甚大世尊何以故佛說非身是名大身
須菩提如恒河中所有沙數如是沙等恒河
於意云何是諸恒河沙寧為多不須菩提言
甚多世尊但諸恒河尚多无數何況其沙須
菩提我今實言告汝若有善男子善女人以
七寶滿尒所恒河沙數三千大千世界以用
布施得福多不須菩提言甚多世尊佛告須
菩提若善男子善女人於此經中乃至受持

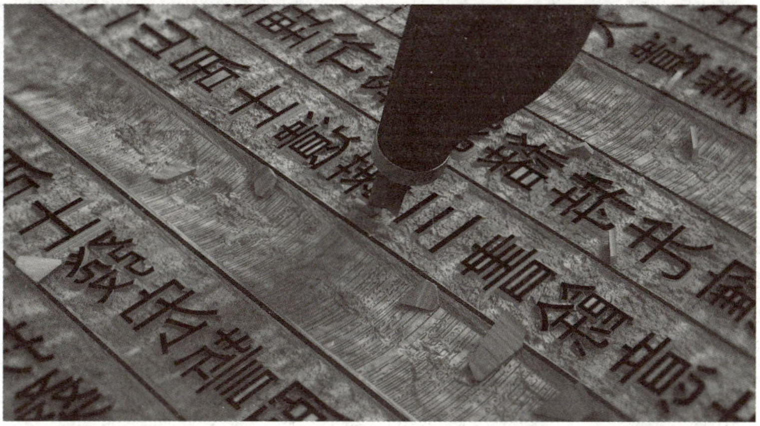

中国的雕版印刷在元朝时传到了阿拉伯地区，随后又传到非洲和欧洲。印刷术传到欧洲后，改变了原来只有修道士才能读书和接受较高教育的状况，为欧洲的科学从中世纪漫长黑夜之后的突飞猛进发展以及文艺复兴运动的出现提供了重要的物质条件。

China's block printing technique was spread to the Arabic region during the Yuan Dynasty (1206–1368 A.D.) and then to Africa and Europe. When Europeans acquired skills of printing, it changed the situation of literacy that in the past only monks could read and receive higher education. Printing provided an important material condition for the European science to develop rapidly after the long night in the medieval time and the emergence of the Renaissance.

（三）火药 Gunpowder

隋唐时期，中国古代炼丹家发明了火药。火药是一种黑色或棕色的炸药，由硝酸钾、木炭和硫黄直接混合而成。最初，一般把火药制成粉末状，随后才制成大小不同的颗粒状用于不同的用途。在人类采用无烟火药之前，火药一直都是唯一的军用发射药。

During the Sui (581–618) and Tang Dynasties, ancient Chinese alchemists invented gunpowder. Gunpowder is a black or brown explosive that is made by directly mixing potassium nitrate, charcoal and sulfur. Initially, it was generally made into the shape of powder, and then be made into pellets of different sizes for different uses. In history, gunpowder has been the only military propellant before smokeless gunpowder was invented.

欧洲人约在 13 世纪时才懂得黑火药的作用，在经过数个世纪的发展与改良后，尤其是在粒状火药和火帽出现后，黑火药兵器逐步取代了冷兵器，在陆地战争战术、攻城筑城技术以及海军战列舰的发展和战术等各方面，产生了革命性的影响。黑火药作为爆炸药和推进剂，一直到 19 世纪中后期才逐渐被无烟火药、三硝基甲苯、苦味酸、季戊炸药、旋风炸药等新发明的炸药所取代。

Till the 13th century Europeans started to use black gunpowder after it was spread from China. After centuries of development and improvement, especially after the appearance of granular gunpowder and fire caps, weapons with black gunpowder gradually replaced cold weapons. It had great influences on land warfare tactics, siege of the city and the development of naval battleships. As an explosive drug and propellant, black gunpowder was gradually replaced by newly invented explosives such as smokeless gunpowder, trinitrotoluene, picric acid, penta explosive, and cyclone explosive until the mid-nineteenth century.

中国最早把火药用于军事。唐代末年，出现了火炮、火箭等新式武器。在宋朝时期，火器普遍用于战争。蒙古人在与宋、金作战时学会了制造火药和火器的方法，阿拉伯人又从与蒙古人作战中学会了制造火器。13 世纪后期，欧洲人从阿拉伯人的书籍中获得了火药知识，到 14 世纪前期，又从伊斯兰教国家战争中学到了制造火药、使用火器的方法。火器在欧洲城市市民反对君主专制的过程中发挥了巨大作用，推进了历史发展的进程，是欧洲文艺复兴的重要支柱之一。

China firstly used gunpowder for military purposes. In the late Tang Dynasty, new weapons such as artillery and rockets appeared. In the Song Dynasty, firearms were commonly used in war. When the Mongols fought against Song (960–1279) and Jin (1115–1234) Dynasties, they learned how to make gunpowder and firearms. Then Arabs learned to make firearms from the battle with the Mongols. In the late 13th century, Europeans gained knowledge of gunpowder from books of Arabs. In the early 14th century, they learned the methods of making gunpowder and using firearms from the Islamic national war. Firearms played an important role in opposing the monarchy for European citizens and promoted the process of historical development. It was one of the important pillars of the European Renaissance.

（四）指南针 Compass

指南针是用以判别方位的一种简单仪器。前身是战国时期出现的司南，主要组成部分是一根装在轴上可以自由转动的磁针。磁针在地磁场作用下能保持在磁子午线的切线方向上。磁针的北极指向地理的北极，利用这一性能可以辨别方向。指南针常用于航海、大地测量、旅行及军事等方面。

The compass is a simple instrument used to determine the position. The predecessor was Sinan, which appeared in the Warring States Period (475 B.C.–221

B.C.). The main component was a magnetic needle that was mounted on the shaft and was free to rotate. The magnetic needle can maintain the tangential direction of the magnetic meridian under the action of the earth magnetic field. The north pole of the magnetic needle points to the geographical north pole, and this performance can be used to distinguish the direction. Compass has been commonly used in navigation, geodetic, travel and military.

中国是世界上公认的发明指南针的国家，指南针的始祖大约出现在战国时期。据古书记载，远在春秋战国时期，由于正处在奴隶制社会向封建社会过渡的大变革时期，生产力有了很大的发展，特别是农业生产更是兴盛发达，因而促进了采矿业、冶炼业的发展。在长期的生产实践中，人们从铁矿石中认识了磁石，开始了对磁性质的了解。人们首先发现了磁石吸引铁的性质，后来又发现了磁石的指向性。经过多方面的实验和研究，终于发明了实用的指南针。

China is recognized as the inventor of compass in the world. The predecessor of compass appeared in the Warring States Period. According to ancient records, due to the great transformation period of the transition from slavery society to feudal society during the Spring and Autumn Period and the Warring States Period, productivity has developed greatly. In particular, the agricultural production has prospered and developed, thus it promoted mining and smelting. In the long-term production practice, people have known magnets from iron ore and began to understand the magnetic properties. People firstly discovered the nature of magnet attraction to iron, and later discovered the directionality of magnets. After many experiments and researches, a practical compass was finally invented.

北宋时期，人们发明了用人工磁化铁针制成指南针的方法，并开始应用于航海。南宋时，指南针普遍应用于航海，同时传到阿拉伯。13 世纪初指南针传入了欧洲。指南针在航海中的应用意义重大，它帮助哥伦布发现了美洲新大陆，麦哲伦完成了环球航行，加速了世界经济发展。

During the Northern Song Dynasty, people invented the method of artificial magnetization of iron needles to make compasses, and began to apply to navigation. In the Southern Song Dynasty, the compass was generally used in navigation and at the same time spread to Arabia. The compass was introduced to Europe in the early 13th century. The application of the compass in navigation was of great significance, helping Columbus discover the new world of the Americas, and Magellan complete the voyage around the world, accelerating the development of the world economy.

二、大国重器
The Pillars of a Great Power

从 1978 年改革开放至今，中国的装备制造业创新发展，取得了令人瞩目的成就。中国制造了水面大型舰艇——航母，建成了世界最大单口径、最灵敏的射电望远镜——“天眼”，完成了蛟龙号载人潜水器深潜科学研究，实施了嫦娥探月工程，中国为人类的共同福祉贡献出了自己的智慧与创造力。

Since the Reform and Opening-up Policy was started in China in 1978, China's equipment manufacturing industry has made remarkable achievements. China has built aircraft carrier, the world's largest single-caliber and the most sensitive radio telescope-FAST (Five-hundred-meter Aperture Spherical Telescope), completed the deep dive scientific research of the Jiaolong manned submersible, and implemented the Chang'e Lunar Exploration Projects. China has been making contributions for the common well-being of human beings with its own wisdom and creativity.

（一）航母
Aircraft Carrier

2012 年 9 月，中国第一艘服役的航空母舰——辽宁号正式入列中国海军，该舰搭载了中国第一代舰载战斗机歼十五，这标志着中国海军防御力量的实质得到提升。辽宁号航空母舰的前身是苏联海军的库兹涅佐夫元帅级航空母舰次舰瓦良格号。20 世纪 80 年代中后期，瓦良格号于乌克兰建造时遭逢苏联解体，建造工程中断，完成度为 68%。1999 年，中国购买了瓦良格号，并于 2002 年抵达中国大连港。2005 年，中国海军继续对其建造改进，直至 2012 年交付使用。在航母甲板上，当歼 15 起飞时，两名身穿背部印有“起飞”字样黄色马甲的起飞助理同时指挥，该动作姿势迅速引起网友围观并被大量模仿，被称为“航母 Style”。

In September 2012, China's first aircraft carrier Liaoning officially joined in the service of People's Liberation Army's Navy. The ship was equipped with China's first-generation carrier-based fighter jets—J 15, which marked the real improvement of the Chinese navy's defense forces. The aircraft carrier Liaoning was formerly the Vladimir of the Soviet Navy's Marshal-class aircraft carrier Kuznetsov. In the mid-to-late 1980s, the Soviet Union was disintegrated, and the construction of Varyag was suspended with 68% completion in Ukraine. In 1999, China purchased the Varyag and dragged back to Dalian Port of China in 2002. In 2005, the Chinese Navy continues to build and equip it until 2012. When the J 15 took off on the deck of the aircraft carrier, two take-off assistants wearing yellow vests with the words "TAKE OFF" on the back simultaneously commanded. That action posture quickly gets popular on internet and was imitated the most very often, which is called the Aircraft Carrier Style.

辽宁舰飞行甲板以下有十余层，航母内部感觉类似迷宫，到处都是通道、舱室，整个航母内部的通道加起来的总长度达到数十千米。航母内设施设备齐

全，有现代化的餐厅、超市、邮局、洗衣房、健身房、垃圾处理站等，全舰有3 000多个舱室，有1 000多人生活在辽宁舰上。

目前，中国001A型航空母舰，也就是首艘自主建造的国产航母已经交付海军，中国将在未来拥有多个航空母舰战斗群，以保卫中国漫长的海岸线。

There are more than ten layers below the flight deck of the Liaoning. The interior of the aircraft carrier feels like a labyrinth. There are passages and cabins everywhere. The total length of the passage inside the aircraft carrier is over tens of kilometers. The aircraft carrier is fully equipped with modern restaurants, supermarkets, post office, laundry room, gymnasium, garbage disposal station, etc. The whole ship has more than 3,000 cabins and more than 1,000 people live on it.

At present, China's 001A aircraft carrier, the first self-built aircraft carrier, has been launched. In future, China will have multiple aircraft carrier battle groups to defend its long coastline.

（二）天眼
FAST (Five-hundred-meter Aperture Spherical Telescope)

中国“天眼”工程，即500米口径球面射电望远镜（Five-hundred-meter Aperture Spherical Telescope），简称FAST，位于贵州省黔南布依族苗族自治州平塘县克度镇大窝凼的喀斯特洼坑中，该工程为国家重大科技基础设施，由我国天文学家南仁东在1994年提出构想，历时22年建成，于2016年9月25日落成启用。天眼是由中国科学院国家天文台主导建设，具有我国自主知识产权，是世界上最大单口径、最灵敏的射电望远镜。其综合性能是著名的射电望远镜阿雷西博的十倍。

Tianyan, the Five-hundred-meter Aperture Spherical Telescope (FAST), is located in the karst crater of Guizhou province in southwest of China. The project is a national key infrastructure for scientific and technological research. It was proposed by the Chinese astronomer Nan Rendong in 1994. It was completed in 22 years and was opened on September 25, 2016. Tianyan was built by the National Astronomical Observatory of the Chinese Academy of Sciences. It has China's independent intellectual property rights, the world's largest single-caliber, and the most sensitive radio telescope. The overall performance is ten times that of the famous radio telescope Arecibo.

天眼工程帮助人类看到了新的星体。截至 2018 年 9 月，天眼已经在宇宙中发现了 59 颗优质的脉冲星候选体，其中有 44 颗已被确认为新发现的脉冲星。天眼工程能够把中国空间测控能力由地球同步轨道延伸至太阳系外缘，将深空通信数据下行速率提高 100 倍。脉冲星的到达时间测量精度由 120 纳秒提高至 30 纳秒，成为国际上最精确的脉冲星计时阵。

Tianyan project helps humans see new stars. By September 2018, Tianyan has found 59 high-quality pulsar candidates in the universe, of which 44 have been identified as newly discovered pulsars. Tianyan project can extend China's space measurement and control capability from the geosynchronous orbit to the outer edge of the solar system, and increase the downlink data rate by 100 times. The pulsar arrival time measurement accuracy has been increased from 120 nanoseconds to 30 nanoseconds, making it the most accurate pulsar timing array in the world.

天眼还承担着外星生物的搜寻任务。基于天眼的强大功能，如果银河系（直径约为 15 万光年）内存在外星人，他们的信息就很可能被发现。国际科研项目“搜寻外星人计划”（SETI）的首席科学家丹·沃西默向中方提出意愿，希望在 FAST 上加装设备，共同合作搜索外星人信号。

Tianyan also takes mission for the search of alien creatures. Based on the powerful features of the Tianyan, aliens in the Milky Way (about 150,000 light-years in diameter) are likely to be discovered. Dan Wormer, the chief scientist of the international research project "Search for Extraterrestrial Intelligence" (SETI), expressed his willingness to the Chinese colleagues, hoping to install equipment on FAST and work together to search for alien signals.

（三）蛟龙号
Jiaolong (Submersible)

"蛟龙号"载人深潜器是中国首台自主设计、自主集成研制的作业型深海载人潜水器，设计最大下潜深度为 7 000 米级，也是目前世界上下潜能力最深的作业型载人潜水器。蛟龙号为人类开展海洋地质、海洋地球物理、海洋地球化学、海洋地球环境和海洋生物等研究做出了巨大贡献。

中国是继美国、法国、俄罗斯、日本之后第五个掌握大深度载人深潜技术的国家。在全球载人潜水器中，"蛟龙号"属于第一梯队。目前，全世界有 90 艘各种类型的载人潜水器投入使用，其中下潜深度超过 1 000 米的仅有 12 艘，下潜越深的潜水器数量越少，只有上述的五个国家才具有 6 000 米以上深度的载人潜水器。除中国外，其他四国的作业型载人潜水器最大工作深度为日本深潜器的 6 527 米，因此"蛟龙号"载人潜水器在西太平洋马里亚纳海沟海试成功到达 7 020 米海底，创造了作业类载人潜水器新的世界纪录。

Jiaolong, manned submersible, is the first self-designed and self-integrated working deep sea manned submersible in China. The designed dive depth is 7000 meters. It is also the world's most capable maneuvering submersible. Jiaolong has made great contributions to the study of marine geology, marine geophysics, marine geochemistry, marine earth environment and marine life.

China has become the fifth country after the United States, France, Russia, and Japan to master deep-dive technology. Among the global manned submersibles, the Jiaolong belongs to the first class. At present, there are 90 types of manned submersibles in use around the world, of which only 12 have a dive depth of more than 1,000 meters. The larger the depth gets to, the fewer the submersibles there are. Only the five countries mentioned above have manned submersibles which can reach the depth over 6,000 meters. The largest working depth of the other four countries' working manned submersibles is 6,527 meters of Japanese deep submersibles. Therefore, Jiaolong manned submersible successfully reached the seabed of 7020 meters in the Western Pacific Mariana Trench, which sets a new world record for manned submersibles.

（四）嫦娥工程
Chang'e Lunar Exploration Projects

中国的探月工程是中国自主对月球的探索和观察，又叫作嫦娥工程。中国正式启动绕月探测工程后，将第一颗绕月卫星命名为“嫦娥一号”。“嫦娥一号”卫星由中国空间技术研究院承担研制，主要用于获取月球表面三维影像、分析月球表面有关物质元素的分布特点、探测月壤厚度、探测地月空间环境等。月球上具有可供人类开发和利用的各种独特资源，其特有的矿产和能源是对地球资源的重要补充和储备，将对人类社会的可持续发展产生深远影响。

China's lunar exploration projects are the independent exploration and observation of the moon by China, also known as the Chang'e project. After China officially launched the lunar exploration project, the first moon-worn satellite was named “Chang'e No 1”. The satellite “Chang'e No 1” was developed by the China Academy of Space Technology. It is mainly used to obtain three-dimensional images of the lunar surface, analyze the distribution characteristics of related elements on the surface, and detect the thickness of lunar soil and the space environment of the earth and moon. The moon has various unique resources for human development and utilization. Its unique minerals and energy are important supplements and reserves for the earth's resources, which will have a profound impact on the sustainable development of human society.

人类航天活动主要包括三大领域：发射人造地球卫星、载人航天和深空探测。重返月球开发月球资源，并建立月球基地已成为世界航天活动的必然趋势和竞争热点。开展月球探测工作是中国迈出航天深空探测第一步的重大举措，实现了中国航天深空探测零的突破。

Human space activities mainly include three major areas: launching artificial earth satellites, manned spaceflight and deep space exploration. Returning to the moon to develop lunar resources and establish a lunar base has become an inevitable trend and a competitive hotspot for world space activities. The launch of lunar exploration is a major step in China's first step in deep space exploration, and it has achieved a breakthrough in China's deep space exploration.

三、新四大发明

Four New Great Inventions

中国经济社会的发展不仅表现在大型基础设施建设和高端装备的制造上，还体现在贴近普通民众日常生活的方方面面，其中就包括了扫码支付、高铁、共享单车和网购等“新四大发明”。它们极大地方便了人们的日常出行，提升了购物的便捷性和体验。

China's economic and social development is not only reflected in the construction of large-scale infrastructure and manufacturing of high-end equipments, but also in the aspects of daily life of ordinary people, including the "Four New Great Inventions", such as QR code payment, high-speed rail, bicycle sharing and online shopping. These greatly facilitate people's daily travel and enhance the convenience and experience of shopping.

（一）扫码支付 QR Code Payment

扫码支付是一种基于账户体系搭起来的新一代无线支付方案，具有简单、快捷、高效和安全等特点。在扫码支付方案中，商家可以把收款账号、商品价格等交易信息汇编成一个二维码，并发布到网络、报纸、杂志、广告、图书等载体上。用户通过手机客户端扫描二维码，便可实现与商家账户的支付结算。最后，商家根据支付交易信息中的用户收货地址、联系资料，就可以进行商品配送，从而完成交易。

QR code payment is a new generation of wireless payment scheme based on the account system, which is simple, quick, efficient and safe. In the QR code payment scheme, company can compile the transaction information such as the payment account number and the commodity price into a two-dimensional code, and puts it on the network, newspaper, magazine, advertisement, book and other carriers. The user can scan the two-dimensional code through the mobile phone to realize payment settlement with the company account. Finally, according to the user's address and contact information in the payment transaction, company can deliver the goods and complete the deal.

伴随着手机的普遍使用，以及移动互联网等通信技术的快速发展，用户对快捷安全的支付手段具有强烈的需求。携带一部手机出门，即可完成车票购买、餐

馆就餐、超市购物等日常活动，这极大地方便了普通人的交通出行，提升了购物体验，真正实现了无现金生活，得到了中国人的广泛使用和外国来华游客的赞许。

With the widespread of mobile phones and the rapid development of communication technologies such as mobile Internet, users have a strong demand for fast and secure payment methods. Traveling out with a mobile phone, you can complete daily activities such as purchasing tickets, ordering in restaurants, shopping in supermarkets, etc., which greatly facilitates the transportation and shopping experience of ordinary people, truly helps people realize cashless life, and is widely used by Chinese people and enjoyed by foreign tourists in China.

对于商家而言，有了扫码支付手段，商家可以抛弃传统厚重的记账本，轻松地建立电子账务；建立起日常经营中智能化、信息化、模块化的强大数据系统，让商家在营销中更加得心应手；商家可以主动发放电子会员卡，提升顾客数量和消费次数，提升交易业绩。对于用户而言，只需要拥有一部可以上网的互联网手机，绑定个人的银行卡账户，在手机上安装二维码识别软件，随时随地都可以在贴有二维码的地方简单扫描一下完成实时交易，既缩短了支付时间，也避免了携带钱包外出而遗失银行卡或者现金等情况的发生。

On the part of sellers, with the means of QR code payment, they can leave the traditional heavy bookkeeping away and easily establish electronic accounts, establish a powerful data system that is intelligent, informative and modular in daily operations, so that marketing will be more convenient. Sellers can proactively issue electronic membership cards to increase the number of customers and consumption, and improve trading performance. On the part of user, you only need to have a smart phone that can access the Internet in hand, bind your personal bank card account with it, and install the QR code recognition software on your mobile phone. You can scan it anytime and anywhere to finish a deal in seconds. The convenient way of payment not only saves time, but also avoids the loss of bank cards or cash when people carrying a wallet.

虽然扫码支付快捷高效，但是它的安全威胁依然不能忽视，因为它直接关联着用户的银行账户，如果手机遗失扫码账户被人盗用，那手机持有者也将遭受不同程度的损失。由于许多扫码软件并不具有恶意网址识别与拦截的能力，这给手机病毒带来了极大的传播空间。对此，中国颁布了支付机构开展条码业务需要遵循的安全标准，在用户使用支付软件扫码时，支付机构必须有针对在线恶意网址的安全扫描与检测。

Although QR code payment is fast and efficient, its security threat cannot be ignored because it is directly connected with the user's bank account. If the mobile phone is lost and the account is stolen, the mobile phone user will suffer different degrees of loss. Since many scanning software does not have the functions to identify and intercept malicious websites, this has brought great space for the spread of mobile phone viruses. In this regard, China has implemented the security standards that payment institutions need to abide by in their bar code services. When users use payment software to scan codes, payment institutions must have an effective method to detect online malicious websites.

（二）高铁
China Railway High-Speed (Chinese High-Speed Railway)

高速铁路，就是铁路设计速度高、能让火车高速运行的铁路系统。“复兴号”CR400系列动车组是中国目前运行速度最快的高铁，最高速度可达400 km/h及以上，持续运行速度为350 km/h，车次最前面使用字母G，中国全面系统地掌握“复兴号”高铁的核心技术。

A high-speed railway is a railway system that is designed to run at high speed. The Fuxing CR400 series train is the fastest in China with a maximum speed up to 400 km/h and above. The continuous operating speed is 350 km/h. High-speed trains are named with letter G in the beginning. The operation of Fuxing trains symbolized that China has fully and systematically mastered the core technology of high-speed rail.

世界上第一条正式的高速铁路系统是1964年建成通车的日本新干线，设计速度200km/h，后来随着技术进步，火车速度更快。2007年，中国首次开行和谐号CRH1型动车组，将火车速度提升到200km/h，随后中国工程师又研发出CRH2、CRH3、CRH5、CRH6以及更快的CRH380系列动车，动车车次前面使用字母D，2015年底中国高速铁路营业里程达1.8万多千米，位居全球第一。

The world's first official high-speed rail system was the Japanese Shinkansen, which was opened in 1964. The designed speed was 200 km/h. Later, with the advancement of technology, the train ran faster. In 2007, China first launched the Hexie CRH1 train, which improves Chinese train speed to 200 km/h. After that, Chinese engineers developed CRH2, CRH3, CRH5, CRH6 and faster CRH380 series trains. The letter D was used to name the fast trains. Till the end of 2015 China's high-speed railway mileage had reached more than 18,000 kilometers, ranking first in the world.

高铁悄然地改变了中国人的生活。第一，让跨省上班不是问题，居住在成都的市民早上乘坐1小时20分钟的高铁，即可到达300千米外的另一座大城市重庆工作，下午下班后可以再乘坐高铁返回成都。第二，高铁可以让旅客在一天内在中国多个大城市间穿梭。由于发达的高速铁路网和快速运行的列车，旅客可以早上从华南的大城市广州出发，中午到达华中的大城市武汉，晚上则可以到达北京，一天的时间内将体验到不同的地理风情。第三，高铁带动了短线旅游发展，推动了经济发展。不论是在东部地区，还是中西部地区，高铁已经成为人们短途出行的首选，既省时方便，也可以避免自己驾车的劳累或旅途中塞车等情况。

The high-speed rail has quietly changed the lives of Chinese people. First of all, it is not a problem to work across provinces. For example, people living in Chengdu can take a high-speed train for 1 hour and 20 minutes in the morning to Chongqing, a municipality 300 kilometers away. After one day's work in Chongqing, they can return to Chengdu by high-speed train. Second, the high-speed rail allows passengers to shuttle between various major cities in China in one day. Thanks to the developed high-speed railway network and fast-running trains, passengers can depart from Guangzhou, the biggest city in south China in the morning, and arrive in Wuhan, the biggest city in Central China at noon, and finally reach Beijing in the evening. They can enjoy different kinds of landscapes in one day. Third, the high-speed rail has driven the development of short-term tourism and promoted economic development. Whether in the eastern region or the central and western regions, high-speed rail has become the first choice for people to travel in short distances for its timesaving and convenience. Meanwhile, people won't be stuck in heavy traffic on roads.

在中国，还有一种更加快速的轨道线，也就是上海磁悬浮轨道线，列车速度高达 430 km/h。由于它没有接入中国铁路网，所以不计入常规高速铁路的范畴。

In China, there is another faster track line, the Shanghai Maglev track. That train can run up to 430 km/h. Because it does not have access to the Chinese railway network, it does not count in the conventional high-speed railways.

（三）共享单车 Bicycle Sharing

共享单车是指企业在校园、地铁站点、公交站点、居民区、商业区、公共服务区等提供单车共享服务，是一种分时租赁模式。共享单车是一种新型的环保共享经济。

Bicycle sharing refers to the bicycle sharing service provided by enterprises on campus, subway stations, bus stations, residential areas, commercial areas, public service areas, etc. It is a time-sharing lease mode. Sharing bicycles is a new type of environmentally friendly sharing economy.

共享单车可以大幅提高城市效率。通过自行车出行，可以完善社会的交通体系，人们可以通过交通工具到达大型景点，也可以通过共享单车走街串巷，到达其他交通工具不能前往的地方。共享单车也提升了人们生活和工作的效率，不论是在生活还是在工作中都可以大幅缩短在途时间。共享单车是一种更低碳环保的出行方式，可以降低汽车出行带来的二氧化碳排放，鼓励人们多运动，倡导健康的生活方式。

Bicycle sharing can greatly improve city efficiency. Bicycle travel can improve the social transportation system. People can reach large scenic spots by means of transportation, or walk through the streets to reach places where other vehicles aren't available by bicycle sharing. Bicycle sharing also improve the efficiency of people's lives and work, and can greatly reduce the time in transit both in life and at work or not. Bicycle sharing is a lower carbon and environmentally friendly way to reduce carbon dioxide emissions from cars, and it encourages people to exercise more, for a healthier lifestyle.

共享单车可以带动物联网发展，从自行车共享，中国逐渐衍生出共享充电宝、共享雨伞、共享纸巾机，乃至无人商店，这些都创新了商业模式。它还可以完善社会信用体系，将共享物品的使用与个人诚信关联起来，增强守时守信的个人品德。中国的共享单车企业不仅在国内得到了成功发展，也将业务拓展到了美国、英国、日本、澳大利亚等国家。

Bicycle sharing is beneficial to the development of Internet of Things. In China, mobile phone charger sharing, umbrella sharing, tissue machine sharing, and even self-service stores, all have derived from bicycle sharing, all of which have contributed to innovated mode of business. It can also improve the social credit system, link the use of shared goods with personal credits, and enhance the personal punctuality and trustworthiness. China's shared bicycle companies have not only successfully developed inside China, but also expanded their business to such countries as the United States, Britain, Japan, and Australia.

（四）网购
Online Shopping

网购是中国 8 亿多网民最感兴趣的话题，已经成为人们日常生活不可或缺的一部分。顾客可以随时随地在手机上轻松选购，完成支付，即可在数天内收到自己购买的商品，节约了前往商场的时间，减轻了购物的疲惫。同时，网络上的商品品种丰富，价格透明，顾客通常可以以更加低廉的价格购买到心仪的优质商品。

Online shopping is the most popular topic with more than 800 million internet users in China and has become an indispensable part of people's daily lives. Customers can easily make purchase on their mobile phones anytime and anywhere, and complete the payment. They can receive the goods they bought within a few days. This way of shopping saves the time for going to the mall and reduces the fatigue of shopping. At the same time, there are various varieties of products on the network and the price is transparent. Customers can usually buy the best quality products at a relatively lower price.

归功于互联网的普及和网上支付的快速发展，网购在中国的崛起异常突出。网购降低了商品的销售价格，由于商品不需要在传统商业营销中经过多次的转卖，消费者可以以更低的价格购买到与实体店一样的商品。并且，网络商城不会像传统商店一样有固定的开关门时间，顾客可以在任何时间选择消费，也可以购买到当地没有的商品。在支付订单后，快递公司会在几天内将商品送到客户的收货地址，省去了顾客往返商场的时间。

Thanks to the popularization of the internet and the rapid development of online payment, the rise of online shopping in China is extremely prominent. Online shopping reduces the selling price of goods because merchandises do not have multiple intermediaries like that in traditional stores. Consumers can purchase the same goods with the same quality as in real stores at a lower price. Moreover, the online mall does not have a fixed business hour like a traditional store. Customers can choose at any time or they can purchase goods that are not available locally. After paying the order, the express delivery company delivers the goods to the customer's shipping address within a few days, eliminating the need for customers to travel to and back from the mall.

中国最大的网络购物平台阿里巴巴公司从 2009 年 11 月 11 日开始举办双十一购物狂欢节，每年举办一次，交易额逐年增长，到 2018 年该公司全天交易额达到 2100 多亿元人民币。购物的人群中既有发达城市的白领，也有偏远农村的乡村人员，购买的商品不仅来自国内的企业，也有国外进口的化妆品、电器、时装、食品等各式商品，极大地活跃了商业氛围，丰富了普通民众的日常生活选择。

Alibaba, the online shopping giant company in China, has organized the Double Eleven (11.11, November 11th, also known as Single's Day) Shopping Carnival since November 11, 2009. The annual transaction volume has increased year by year. By 2018, the company's full-day volume reached more than 210 billion RMB. Customers include both white-collar workers in developed cities and farmers at rural villages in remote areas. The products purchased are not only from domestic enterprises, but also imported from abroad, such as cosmetics, electrical appliances, fashion, food, etc., which greatly stimulate the commercial atmosphere and enriches the daily choices of ordinary people.

四、"黑科技"

Futuristic Technology

黑科技是一个源自网络的新名词，是由于高科技快速发展而产生的更强大或者更先进的技术以及创新、软硬件等，也包含了基于现有技术的改进升级以及产品的使用体验等。黑科技同时也泛指生活中让大家感到新奇的新硬件、新软件、新技术、新工艺、新材料等，例如常见的民用无人机。

Futuristic technology is a new term derived from the internet. It is a stronger or more advanced technology and innovation, software or hardware generated by the rapid development of high technology. It also includes improvements and upgrades based on existing technologies and products. Futuristic technology also refers to new hardware, new software, new technologies, new processes, new materials, etc., which renew people's lives from tradition, such as the popular civilian drones.

中国无人机是全球市场中的佼佼者，全球一半以上的民用无人机都是中国制造。移动互联网给无人机带来了新机遇，也降低了操作门槛。用户通过手机 App 就可以对无人机进行飞行操作，将原来需由专业飞手操控变得简单、极易上手。无人机被广泛应用于民众的日常生活以及工作领域。

Chinese drones are among the best in the global market, and more than half of the world's civilian drones are created in China. The mobile internet has brought new opportunities to drones and lowered operating barriers. With the mobile phone App, users can fly the drone, not like that it can only be operated by professional persons. Drones are widely used in people's daily lives and different areas.

在航拍摄影中，无人机应用得最广泛。在广告、影视、婚礼视频记录中正越来越多地出现无人机的身影，从天空中的视角可以给人们的感官和好奇心带来意想不到的绝佳效果。在新闻报道中，无人机可以快速地到达记者无法抵达的地方，例如高楼火灾、洪水、山体滑坡等灾害现场。不仅如此，无人机还能利用红外热像仪在空中搜寻受困人员。在工业领域中，无人机可以用作电力巡检，它具有不受高度限制、巡视灵活、拍照方便和角度全面的优点，特别适合于大型的电线高塔。

In aerial photography, drones are the most widely used. UAVs are increasingly appearing in advertising, film and television, wedding video recordings. The perspectives from the sky can bring unexpectedly great effects to people's senses and curiosity. In the news reports, drones can quickly reach places where reporters cannot reach, such as high-rise fires, floods, landslides and other disaster scenes. Not only that, drones can use infrared thermal imager to search for trapped people in the air. In the industrial field, the drone can be used for power inspection. It has the advantages of no height restriction, flexible inspection, convenient photographing and comprehensive angle, and is especially suitable for large wire towers.

无人机还将用在快递送货中。中国最大的网络购物平台阿里巴巴公司已经在北京、上海、广州进行无人机送货服务测试，使用无人机将盒装姜茶快递给客户。这些无人机并不是直接飞到客户门前，而是会飞到物流站点，由最近的快递员负责将商品送到客户手中。这样可以大幅地缩短包裹等待时间，增加新鲜商品的购买选择，提高用户的满意度。

The drone can also be used in package delivery. Alibaba, China's largest online shopping company, has conducted drone service testing in Beijing, Shanghai and Guangzhou, using drones to deliver boxed ginger tea to customers. These drones do not fly directly to the customer's door, but instead fly to the logistics site, where the nearest courier will be responsible for delivering the goods to the customer for the last step. This can greatly shorten the time for customers to wait, increase the options of fresh goods, and improve user satisfaction.

课后练习题
Practice

一、选择题
Multiple-choice

1. 刻在龟甲和兽骨上的文字称为（　　）。
   Text engraved on tortoise shell and animal bone, called (　　).

   A. 甲骨文
   A. oracle

   B. 小篆
   B. the lesser seal character

   C. 大篆
   C. big-seal style character

   D. 金文
   D. Chinese bronze inscriptions

2. 世界上现存最早的印刷物是在（　　）印制的。
   In (　　), the earliest extant was printed.

   A. 公元 868 年
   A. 868 A.D.

   B. 公元 1150 年
   B. 1150 A.D.

   C. 公元 612 年
   C. 612 A.D.

   D. 公元 121 年
   D. 121 A.D.

3. （　　）最早把火药用于军事。
   The (　　) were the first to use gunpowder for military affairs.

   A. 中国人
   A. Chinese

   B. 阿拉伯人
   B. Arabs

   C. 欧洲人
   C. Europeans

   D. 韩国人
   D. Koreans

4. 什么可能会发现外星人？（　　）
   What might discover aliens? (　　)

A. 航母
A. Aircraft carrier

B. 天眼
B. FAST

C. 蛟龙号
C. Jiaolong (submersible)

D. 嫦娥工程
D. Chang'e Lunar Exploration Projects

5. 下潜越深的潜水器（　　）。
Submersibles that dive deeper are (　　).

A. 形状更大
A. larger in shape

B. 形状更小
B. smaller in shape

C. 数量越多
C. greater in quantity

D. 数量越少
D. smaller in quantity

二、填空题
Fill-in-the-blanks

1. 指南针的发明为________________________提供了条件。
The invention of compass provided conditions for ________________________.

2. 雕版印刷术发明于______，在__________开始普遍使用。
Block printing was invented in __________ and began to be widely used in __________.

3. 中国“天眼”工程，由我国天文学家______，在______年提出构想，历时______年建成。
FAST (Five-hundred-meter Aperture Spherical Telescope), Tianyan, was proposed by Chinese astronomer ______ in ______ and was completed in ______ years.

4. 人类航天活动主要包括三大领域：________________________、载人航天和__________________。
Human space activities mainly include three major areas: __________________, manned spaceflight and __________________.

5. 在____________中，无人机应用得最广泛。无人机能利用____________在空中搜寻受困人员。
In _____________________, drones are the most widely used. Drones can use ______________ to search for trapped people in the air.

三、判断题

True or False

1. 在春秋时期中国创造了刻在龟甲和兽骨上的文字，称为甲骨文。
   When the history developed to Spring and Autumn Period, text engraved on tortoise shell and animal bone, called oracle, firstly appeared in China.

2. 中国最早把火药用于军事。
   China firstly used gunpowder for military purposes.

3. 截至 2018 年 9 月，天眼已经在宇宙中发现了 62 颗优质的脉冲星候选体。
   As for September 2018, Tianyan has found 62 high-quality pulsar in the universe.

4. 2015 年底，中国高速铁路营业里程达 1.8 万多千米，位居世界第一。
   Till the end of 2015 China's high-speed railway has reached more than 18,000 kilometers, ranking first in the world.

5. 网购降低了商品的销售价格，是由于商品的价格低。
   Online shopping reduces the selling price of goods because the costs of merchandise are low.

四、简答题

Short-answer Questions

1. 指南针的作用是什么？
   What is the function of the compass?

   ____

   ____

2. 骑共享单车的好处是什么？
   What are the benefits of bicycle sharing?

   ____

   ____

3. 中国的新四大发明是什么?
   What are four new great inventions of China?

   ____

   ____

参考文献

一、参考书目

[1] 蔡宝中，2015. 武术与文化. 太原：山西科学技术出版社.

[2] 陈海萍，1993. 推不倒的长城：中国“麻将热”面面观及其思考. 武汉：长江文艺出版社.

[3] 陈青之，2016. 中国教育史. 北京：中国文史出版社.

[4] 程裕祯，2013. 中国文化要略. 北京：外语教学与研究出版社.

[5] 冯友兰，2011. 中国哲学史. 北京：华东师范大学出版社.

[6] 广元，1978. 中国书法概述. 天津：天津古籍出版社.

[7] 龚维斌，2018. 中国社会体制改革报告. 北京：社会科学文献出版社.

[8] 靳海林，2001. 中国传统节日及传说：中英文对照. 重庆：重庆出版社.

[9] 井上靖，2016. 孔子. 北京：北京十月文艺出版社.

[10] 李永全，2015. 丝路列国志. 北京：社会科学文献出版社.

[11] 李跃龙，2005. 婚嫁习俗. 北京：五洲传播出版社.

[12] 李泽厚，2003. 中国古代思想史论. 天津：天津社会科学出版社.

[13] 老子，1998. 道德经. 北京：外语教学与研究出版社.

[14] 刘涛，2014. 极简中国书法史. 北京：人民美术出版社.

[15] 林语堂，2004. 老子的智慧. 西安：陕西师范大学出版社.

[16] 罗大伦，2017. 中医祖传那点儿东西. 北京：北京联合出版有限公司.

[17] 路远，2010. 碑林语石——西安碑林藏石研究. 西安：三秦出版社.

[18] 马可迅，2017. 零基础学中医. 苏州：江苏科技出版社.

[19] 彭晓玲，张申平，佘敏，2009. 中华传统节日文化. 成都：西南交通大学出版社.

[20] 钱穆，2018. 孔子传. 上海：生活·读书·新知三联书店.

[21] 孙思邈，张景岳，2012. 中医解周易. 北京：九州出版社.

[22] 吴同宾，1995. 京剧知识手册. 天津：天津教育出版社.

[23] 王芷章，2003. 中国京剧编年史：第一卷. 北京：中国戏剧出版社.

[24] 徐城北，2003. 中国京剧. 北京：五洲传播出版社.

［25］徐纬光，杨淑琴，2012. 当代中国政治制度 . 上海：上海交通大学出版社 .
［26］严汝娴，刘宇，1996. 中国少数民族婚丧风俗 . 北京：商务印书馆 .
［27］杨光斌，李月军，2007. 当代中国政治制度导论 . 北京：中国人民大学出版社 .
［28］杨详全，2017. 中国武术思想史 . 太原：山西科学技术出版社 .
［29］杨建新，2005. 中国少数民族通论 . 北京：民族出版社 .
［30］于丹，2001. 庄子心得 . 北京：中国民主法治出版社 .
［31］余水清，2006. 中国武术史概要 . 武汉：湖北科技出版社 .
［32］张诗雨，2016. 海上丝路叙事 . 北京：中国发展观察杂志社 .
［33］张葆全、郭玉贤，2012. 老子今读 . 桂林：广西师范大学出版社 .

二、网络资源

［1］中国婚礼礼仪 . (2016-10-03) [2010-05-06]. http://www.xzwoo.com/liyi/hunqingliyi/794.html.
［2］人口和计划生育工作的发展历程 . (2007-07-09) [2020-05-06]. http://www.gov.cn/ztzl/rkr/content_677985.html.
［3］国际汉语资源中心 . [2020-05-06]. http://www.blcup.com/Res/ResList/index/30?pid=1&lx=0.
［4］全国彩礼图示 . (2019-02-15) [2020-05-06]. https://finance.sina.com.cn/roll/2019-02-15/doc-ihrfqzka5992634.shtml.
［5］中国网 . [2020-05-06]. http://www.china.com.cn/ch-shaoshu/.
［6］民族网 . [2020-05-06]. http://www.minzu56.net/.
［7］中国旅游研究院 . [2020-05-06]. http://www.ctaweb.org/index.html.
［8］可可英语网 . http://m.kekenet.com/read/201510/397348.shtml.

中国人民大学出版社读者信息反馈表

尊敬的读者：

感谢您购买和使用中国人民大学出版社的 ________________________ 一书，我们希望通过这张小小的反馈表来获得您更多的建议和意见，以改进我们的工作，加强我们双方的沟通和联系。我们期待着能为更多的读者提供更多的好书。

请您填妥下表后，寄回或传真回复我们，对您的支持我们不胜感激！

1. 您是从何种途径得知本书的：

□书店 □网上 □报纸杂志 □朋友推荐

2. 您为什么决定购买本书：

□工作需要 □学习参考 □对本书主题感兴趣 □随便翻翻

3. 您对本书内容的评价是：

□很好 □好 □一般 □差 □很差

4. 您在阅读本书的过程中有没有发现明显的专业及编校错误，如果有，它们是：

____

____

____

5. 您对哪些专业的图书信息比较感兴趣：

____

____

____

6. 如果方便，请提供您的个人信息，以便于我们和您联系（您的个人资料我们将严格保密）：

您供职的单位：______________________________

您教授的课程（教师填写）：______________________________

您的通信地址：______________________________

您的电子邮箱：______________________________

请联系我们：黄婷 程子殊 王新文 王琼 鞠方安

电话：010-62512737，62513265，62515580，62515573，62515576

传真：010-62514961

E-mail：huangt@crup.com.cn chengzsh@crup.com.cn wangxw@crup.com.cn
crup_wy@163.com jufa@crup.com.cn

通信地址：北京市海淀区中关村大街甲59号文化大厦15层 邮编：100872

中国人民大学出版社